Östen Ohlsson & Björn Rombach

The Tyranny of Metaphors

Pathways to Freedom

Santérus
Academic Press
Sweden

www.santerus.se

© 2014 The authors and Santérus Academic Press Sweden
ISBN 978-91-7335-041-9
Cover art: Robert Delauney, *Window*, 1912
Cover profile: Sven Bylander
Santérus Academic Press is an imprint of
Santérus Förlag, Stockholm, Sweden
academicpress@santerus.se
Printed by BOD, Germany 2014

Contents

1. The Power of Metaphor

Not understanding is a form of insight. This being the case, we have a great many deep insights into the question of how organisations are constructed and how they work. The question of management, in other words. We have a good grasp, and yet there is much that we do not understand. We do not believe that this is because we are stupid or ignorant, rather that it is due to the deficiencies of the explanations offered.

This book is emancipatory in its purpose. The aim is to provide release from the repression of inadequate explanations. The idea is that we should get a better picture of how organisations work by trying out various methods for reading them better. Our attempt to reveal or render intelligible[1] what happens is based on the fact that what happens within organisations, as in their construction, is so often expressed using suggestive descriptions or images. In short, metaphors.

Metaphors make description more comprehensible and easier to sell. But when it comes to organisations, metaphors also suppress our reasoning and our feelings. They control what we are able to see, and how we interpret what we see. It is from this tyranny of metaphors that we will try to liberate ourselves. Often, metaphors themselves will be the tools we will use for revelation. Our liberation will therefore be only partial.

Originally this book was written in Swedish for a Scandinavian readership. It should not have mattered too much, because even if metaphors change somewhat between languages they are often quite similar. Hazy ideas and rock-solid convictions are hazy and rock-solid in both Swedish and English. What is more, we are against hazy ideas and sceptical towards rock-solid convictions, which does not prevent us, of course, from being encumbered with such defects ourselves. Be that as it may, we have made only slight adjustments to the original text for our English readership. We believe that the differences are so small that anything odd our readers find in the text will not spoil their reading. On the contrary, these might add a bit – just a little bit – of exoticism to the reading experience. For example, the text still retains a number of quotations by classic Swedish poets – in translation of course!

For a time we were concerned that the organisational pyramid is a metaphor which is much more widely mentioned in Swedish and Scandinavian literature than in English, but we still came to the conclusion that the argument works well anyway. Pyramidal hierarchies are fairly well known everywhere.

This book is aimed at all those active professionals who are not yet able to vote through solutions without first knowing what the problem might be. Those who have grown tired of simply relying on their gut feeling and who want to understand before saying 'No, I don't agree with that' or 'OK, I'll go along with that'. These members of organisations who are more critical in their thinking cannot be few in number.

At the same time, we also address colleagues carrying out research and higher education students. We believe that the time has come to throw out much of what has been written about organisation and the process of organising. The field is bogged down by a great many theories and models that have lost the explanatory power they once held or may have held. This book aims to be one of the new voices after the clean-up.

Our approach fluctuates between two methodological extremes. We sometimes employ intellectual tricks such as semiotics and critical theory to unpick these metaphors. But equally often we try more brutal methods instead. Examples of the latter include simply saying the opposite. This approach is experimental, and we give no guarantees that we will always achieve our goals. But where we fail to make sufficient progress, we hope that the reader will be encouraged to continue turning the matter over in his own mind.

The important thing to point out is that our aim is not pedagogical. It's not a matter of disseminating a text in which we announce to the reader what we have long known. Writing is largely about our own liberation. The text is new to us, too. We regard the reader as our travel companion rather than our student.

The language of management: A problematisation

We all allow ourselves to be misled by the words and expressions we encounter. When we are not confused, we are convinced. But that's hardly any better. Many books we have read – and much of what our colleagues and acquaintances say – are based on a certain word or a certain designation having a specific ability to explain things to us. Some time ago, we presented a study of how information technology affects the work and organisation of schools.[2] When talking or writing about information technology, we all know that we call it 'IT'. Yet once we had finished the presentation, someone in the audience said that we should use the correct expression, 'ICT', meaning 'information and communication technology'. We were not unfamiliar with the expression, and indeed had chosen not to use it, but for a moment we had been caught with our trousers down. Surely ICT means much more than old familiar IT? On closer analysis, it turns out to be hard to find anything signified by ICT that is not also signified by IT. It is not particularly clear what exactly IT is, and the added 'C' emphasises rather than reduces the lack of clarity.

Language and words are assumed to describe and explain reality to us, but we often wonder which reality the words represent. We don't want to appear naïve. We do not believe that words should represent reality in any absolute sense. Words create reality while at the same time representing it. This is a book about management and organisation, not a book about linguistic philosophy, but it is still a curious state of affairs having all these words and concepts relating to organisation and management. We believe that there's something fishy[3] about the language of management, and that it prevents us from becoming wiser.

In principle, organisational concepts are always borrowed from fields or areas close to concrete experience. We have structures and pyramids. There is management, and there are strategies. Not to mention forces of change and inertia. Many people want learning organisations that contain dynamic mechanisms. In extreme cases, people want start-up companies and cutting-edge expertise. Head-hunting continues unabated without anyone sniggering, although we've stopped taking seriously those who talk about organisational machineries or bleeding.

The fact that these loanwords should be interpreted as some-thing other than what the words originally meant can hardly have escaped anyone's notice. Nevertheless, it sometimes seems as if people have forgotten that there ever was an original meaning. A glass ceiling can often be something that benefits us. A glass ceil-ing above a shopping arcade improves conditions for those of us at street level, and means that we can enjoy a latte at a street café, whatever the weather. And for those who grow cucumbers, the glass ceiling of a greenhouse is indispensable. In an organisation, however, a glass ceiling is incompatible with a culture of growth.[4] Despite being strongly in favour of glass ceilings in our own garden, we vigorously condemn them in the workplace.

We are not alone in maintaining that metaphors control our understanding of organisations. According to Gareth Morgan's book *Images of Organization*, this is obvious to those who have read up on how organisations should be understood.[5] If we can find a new ingenious simile – 'the organisation is a fishing rod' – we have also contributed a new understanding of how organisations work. The language of love appears to be full of strained metaphors, and organisational theory is not far behind.

For our part, we have been unable to refrain completely from writing the odd piece of poetry, but here we will focus instead on a critical approach. We will discuss how we can gain a better understanding of organisational phenomena where we have got the wrong end of the stick. (Ah, the wrong end of the stick – a classic among metaphors!) We wrote 'phenomena' in an attempt to illustrate the fact that metaphors are hard to differentiate from what they represent. Metaphors tyrannise us in various ways. Consequently, there will be times when we avoid metaphors and times when we use them.

Take leadership, for example. This is something that many people want more of in companies and administrative bodies. In any case, the word 'leadership' meets with strong approval in large groups. The question is simply what exactly it is. We will contend in a later chapter that the word 'leadership' as used in organisations must be understood as a metaphor. The metaphors that are used as if they are primary designations rather than expressive images are interesting. 'Leadership', as mentioned, or 'change' are far more deceptive and treacherous than 'smoke screens' or 'cemented structures'. Organisational cement is obviously not real. We see that this is an analogy. The fact that there could be a problem with the word 'leadership' is far less obvious, but it does resolve a number of issues when we realise that 'leadership' – just like 'organisational cement' – is a metaphor. Leadership as a metaphor has at best certain qualities that can be compared to the mythical 'leadership' from which the metaphor has obtained its descriptive power.

Other metaphors are more obvious, but still exercise power over our thoughts. The pyramids that have needed to be torn down for so long are one example. In order to shrug off the compulsion to demolish them, we introduce two metaphors which we can use to place these pyramids on a scale. This trick enables us to see organisational pyramids of different heights as more or less reasonable compromises between two extremes that have – or lack – height and breadth.

What is a metaphor?

Some readers may worry that this book will place undue emphasis on what we call 'metaphors'. What is necessary and unnecessary is hard to tell, but we will now devote a couple of pages to the actual concept. It won't be any worse than that.

According to *Collins Cobuild English Language Dictionary*, 'a metaphor is an imaginative way of describing something by referring to something else which has the qualities that you are trying to express'.[6] It is a figurative means of expression. The degree of figurativeness is all about how much of the original meaning is activated[7] when we use the metaphor. There may be significant differences in terms of figurativeness between linguistically related metaphors. Jan Svanlund addresses the two abstract concepts of 'balance of payments' and 'striking a balance' (between different interests). 'Balance of payments' has a low degree of figurativeness, while 'the metaphorical use of striking a balance ... shows a strong degree of figurativeness'.[8] Someone who strikes a balance between different interests is achieving a balance in a completely different way to ensuring a balance of payments.

Such subtleties do not prevent any of us from using a large number of metaphors when speaking or writing. Referring to Aristotle, Anna Miller maintains that '... all thought is metaphor'.[9] But if everything is metaphor, metaphor becomes an useless concept. Still, we would like to believe that the classical philosophers had something particularly radical to say on the subject, but when we try to find a more original source we end up with scientific essays which all assert that Aristotle regarded metaphors as comparisons. With reference to *Metaphor and Thought*, edited by Andrew Ortony,[10] we can dismiss an otherwise fairly appealing quotation. If Aristotle ever made such a statement, it was a mistake. Whatever the case, that point of view is unreasonable. We take the view that not even language consists solely of metaphors.

If we are still to follow in the footsteps of Aristotle for a while, as presented by Paul Ricoeur, he does contribute some clarifications. A metaphor is the use of a concept which differs from the normal. When Gerlinde Baumann writes about marriage as a metaphor for the relationship between God and Israel, she is thinking of a more normal use of the concept of marriage.[11] The metaphor is borrowed from another domain in which the concept is normally used, and replaces a concept that could have been used in its place.[12] To further complicate the concept of metaphor, you are not supposed to be too explicit about it. According to *Encyclopaedia Britannica*, metaphor is a 'figure of speech that implies comparison between two unlike entities, as distinguished from simile, an explicit comparison signalled by the words 'like' or 'as''.[13] It is not cool to inform your audience that you have introduced a metaphor. Perhaps it is not even a metaphor anymore if you do.

Language can also be used 'literally'[14], which in turn is a metaphor and a label. We all understand that the figurative expression 'the sun is a jewel' is different to the literal 'the sun is a star'.[15] However, the question of whether the figurative expression, or in our case the metaphor, differs in any fundamental way from 'normal language' is of no relevance to our argument. But it is tempting to quote Albert Katz, a researcher into figurative language, who makes two references to Ortony to raise the possibility that the metaphor occupies a unique position.[16] It should be said that Ortony is a professor of education and psychology, and that metaphors are perhaps his most prominent field of research.

> ...metaphors may not only be nice, they may in fact be necessary in many situations. That is, metaphor might be intrinsically related to the human ability to invent new – and meaningful – concepts that might not be explicable by recourse to some more basic literal description (*e.g.*, "black holes" or "transformer toys"). So one might argue that metaphor might play a central role in translating thought, especially novel thought, into language (see Ortony, 1975). If this position is correct, then metaphor is serving a function that cannot be served by literal language.[17]

Andrew Goatly's point of view is, perhaps, more reasonable when he notes that '...the distinction [between literal language use and metaphorical language use] is often a matter of degree'.[18] In our case, the pyramid is a metaphor. When we talk about the organisational pyramid, few people would think that we mean an 'Ancient Egyptian royal tomb with a quadratic ground plan (with the corners oriented towards the four points of the compass), ascending in a step-like formation (42–57 degrees), so that the walls meet at the top',[19] even though this is what the dictionary definition suggests.

The concept 'label' belongs to a group of concepts which surround – and sometimes merge with – metaphors. The pyramid may be a well-established way of using a metaphor to describe an organisational structure, but it can also be a label for an Ancient Egyptian royal tomb.

Metaphors create myths about how organisations are and work. The myth about the boss as a hero[20] presupposes, for example, that one has a working metaphor for 'hero'. Over the years there has been widespread interest in myths to do with management language[21], while we for our part are curious to know how two Swedish organisational theorists[22] from the past, Sven-Erik Sjöstrand and Gunnar Westerlund, used the term. Their myths are concepts and constructs.[23] The authors discuss myths that affect activities in organisations in an undesirable way. They introduce anti-myths and alternative myths to disarm overly strong organisational myths. Let us illustrate this with an example from the 'list of myths and legends' given by way of conclusion in their book:

- myth: the myth of management as mediator in the organization
- anti-myth: the myth of management as creator of conflicts of interests
- alternative myth: the myth of management as one interested party[24]

Myths can be both good and evil. Sten Jönsson and Rolf Lundin demonstrated in an article about myths and wishful thinking as tools for corporate management[25] that it can be hard to manage a business without myths. There is a duplicity in concepts such as myth and metaphor. They maintain that on the one hand myths should be exposed and metaphors explained, while on the other hand exposure and explanations involve the use of new myths and metaphors. Without myths, the world would be both dreary and hard to understand.

We could over-complicate the definition of metaphors, presenting even more related concepts. In an otherwise interesting book, we find a definition that may be well justified in its context, but which illustrates in this case our point about complexity.

A metaphor occurs when a unit of discourse$_{4.2.1}$ is used to refer$_{4.2.2}$ to an object, concept, process, quality, relationship or world$_{4.5.5}$ to which it does not conventionally refer$_{4.2.3}$, or colligates with a unit(s) with which it does not conventionally colligate$_{4.2.4}$; and when this unconventional act of reference or colligation is understood$_{4.5.2}$ on the basis of similarity or analogy$_{4.4}$ involving at least two of the following: the unit's conventional referent; the unit's actual unconventional referent; the actual referent(s) of the unit's actual colligate(s); the conventional referent of the unit's conventional colligate(s)$_{4.2.5}$. [The numerical references refer to sections in the book.][26]

In this quotation we missed the point – if there actually was a point. We could also make light of metaphors ad infinitum. We should exercise a degree of moderation when it comes to both taking pleasure in definition and making distancing wisecracks about the actual text. For the sake of our argument, it is sufficient to rely on the everyday meaning of metaphor as 'figurative expression'.[27] There is a great deal to suggest that a usable and strict definition cannot be found.[28] Svanlund notes the following in the introduction to his thesis *Metaforen som konvention* ('Metaphor as Convention'):

> The vast breadth of metaphor literature shows a striking difference of opinion when it comes to what constitutes the actual object of study. Nor is there an accepted definition of the concept.[29]

'Linguistic artefacts', or words and expressions as they should properly be called, affect life within organisations and the change processes within them, just as they affect life in general. A good metaphor helps us to understand something through references to something completely different.[30] Metaphors simplify not only explanation but also argumentation. They also affect our way of thinking and our way of acting.[31] Metaphors create attitudes and reactions.[32]

Moreover, metaphors also help us to misunderstand things. George Lakoff and Mark Johnson discuss this in terms of 'highlighting' and 'hiding'.[33] Goatly observes the same phenomenon when he deals with 'highlighting' and 'suppression'.[34] Metaphors can be used by politicians to convince us,[35] by leaders to control or even change us,[36] and by salesmen to persuade us[37]. Of course, there is manipulative use of metaphors[38] but there are also instances when we entirely unintentionally use metaphors to render the world incomprehensible[39] or are guided by them in a direction in which we do not actually want to go.

Hyperreality

Let us now move on to what metaphors mean. If we say that the organisation is a hill or a house in a social landscape,[40] this leads us to think about what a landscape might look like and what sorts of structures might fill it. This can be an entertaining exercise in which we find rewarding and surprising analogies.

However, once we have established that the organisational social landscape exists, the slightly awkward question arises of what phenomena such as the organisational bush represent. We assume that for every word there is an equivalent in reality. The words mean something. The French postmodernist Jean Baudrillard claims that our existence is increasingly filled with concepts – ideally attractive concepts – which are completely devoid of actual content.[41] We use all these concepts to create a hyperreality for ourselves, which increasingly involves addressing the same empty words and concepts to a world containing simulated experiences. A world in which it is important to talk about ICT – not IT.

In this hyperreality, the organisational bush can give rise to a new professional practice. More and more people in society are engaged in developing hyperreality from inside. And it is not only within language that hyperreality is created. The media and the experience industry are key co-creators. A decade ago, we were able to marvel at the widespread public interest in films such as 'The Matrix'[42], which portray a future where everyone lives inside an illusion. These days it is instead Facebook and video games such as 'the World of Warcraft'[43], a phenomenon that makes us wonder whether people actually need or want that which those of us who are older and wiser would call reality. The question of what all these metaphors mean is crucial, and we cannot be certain that even our own favourite metaphors are anything other than an attractive facade.

Sufficiently metaphorical

Within the field of management, metaphors are often clearly visible. Jacques Jimenez and Timothy Johnson identify six main metaphors in the (American) business world. In this male-dominated world, they found male metaphors: 'the gambler', 'the warrior', 'the athlete', 'the farmer', 'the craftsman' and 'the engineer'.[44] It could be argued that the degree of masculinity varies between these. Writing a dictionary of metaphors around a group of metaphors does not actually sound entirely hopeless. The book *Metaphors at Work* also has a certain entertainment value at times. For example, 'lowball' is a slang expression used when someone intentionally tries to underestimate costs. The intention may be to trick a customer or an investor.[45] However, lowball can also be a kind of poker or an alcoholic drink with ice in a short and wide glass. We just don't know which of these is the metaphor.

We often imagine that metaphors are a harmless way of expressing ourselves. Jimenez and Johnson make their *Metaphors at Work* appear sexist, stupid and trite. Perhaps the idea behind the dictionary is a poor one or has been poorly executed. Or perhaps it reflects a reality where most of the metaphors used so frequently in the workplace really are sexist, stupid and trite. In any case, the authors succeed in showing that figurative metaphors are not necessarily a dignified way of expressing ourselves. Peter Dobers and Stefan Tengblad point in the same direction when reaching the conclusion that 'metaphorical control does not make the management of organisations more human'.[46] Veronika Koller goes into greater depth about what the masculine metaphors of business mean for women. It is clear that these metaphors assign qualities which in the case of men are often considered the norm, while they exclude women from what they have turned into a male arena.[47] She advocates the use of gender-neutral metaphors, and believes that business journalists should take on this responsibility instead of imitating and flattering their readers with masculine metaphors.

Farid Muna's book *Seven Metaphors on Management* presents metaphors which, in the opinion of the author, are of use to 'managers in the Arab World'.[48] The book is not sexist, but this broth of platitudes (relating to 'the candle', 'the iceberg', 'the tripod', 'the transit lounge', 'the mosaic', 'the helicopter' and 'the bridge') can, if anything, be seen as a kind of racism.

In purely general terms, metaphors are '… a risky communicative strategy, not always easily interpretable'.[49] If someone does not know what a jab is, or cannot link the difference between a jab and a hook to different marketing strategies, a metaphor based on this will be entirely worthless. The same applies when we note that 'our competitors clearly want to return to the London rules, when the Queensberry rules are bad enough'. The degree of reach makes the metaphor risky.

Sometimes, the metaphor chosen can be downright misleading. For example, we should not use jazz as a metaphor for freedom. The metaphor might have been more effective in the 1920s. It may also be bound to a culture to which we do not belong.[50] Or it could be that we need to know more about jazz than we actually do in order to see the connection with freedom. To us, swing – as discussed in Mike Zwerin's book subtitled *Jazz as a Metaphor for Freedom* – appears to be an unfree and strictly regulated practice in which the musician who improvises freely is deemed to be playing something completely different.[51]

If we allow ourselves to digress further on the same theme, there is a feast of culinary metaphors. These include both strong images and others that do not work at all. In their book *Appetite*, Phyllis Stowell and Jeanne Foster have brought together female poets who use food as a metaphor for all sorts of things. It makes for terrifying reading for those of us who are otherwise poetic omnivores. And nor do the editors do equality any favours when they allege that: 'Sooner or later each woman finds her sense of herself and her perception of the world around her clarified by her relationship to food'.[52]

Even more technical – or, rather, linguistic – factors affect the reach of metaphors. For example, Goatly argues that speech has a role to play.[53] He maintains that nouns are easier to visualise and give rise to richer interpretations, while adverbs and prepositions are limited in their reach.[54] Verbs and adjectives occupy an inter-mediate position.

In another relevant book, Raymond Gibbs presents a little test of researchers' interest in figurative language, including meta-phors, that he worked on for a considerable amount of time. The test, which is presented in *The Fight Over Metaphor in Thought and Language* should not be overinterpreted, but should instead be seen as an illustration. Around 1990, Gibbs used to go to the university library's periodicals room and choose a publication at random. His hypothesis was that at least half the selected publications contained an article on some aspect of figurative linguistic usage. On the whole, his hypothesis was confirmed.[55]

The percentage would certainly have been lower if he had cho-sen from among the journals on management. However, linguists and organisational researchers have spent a great deal of time in each other's company ever since the prefix 'post' came to signify that the Modern Project no longer held any new answers. With organisational theory, the usual thing has happened. We have included and incorporated that which has seemed useful, leaving the rest to fate. This text follows the same pattern.

How thought and language are connected is part of what we leave to fate. Albert Katz has undertaken research which points to a functional disconnection and also research which points to language controlling thought.[56] These are two extreme points of view. Not unsurprisingly, Katz takes a middle approach. We concur, and believe that it matters how the world is presented.

> I argue that an alternative version deserves serious consideration. In this variant the suggestion is that language, rather than merely serving a communication role, is a form of representation of the world.[57]

Living and dead metaphors

Metaphors do not have eternal life. The metaphor works and survives as long as the image is sufficiently expressive and has desirable associations. This means that the metaphor might indeed be unsuccessful as a description yet still work as an image.[58] But if a man says to his girlfriend that she is a flower, or says to his research colleagues that organisations are machines, the metaphor becomes trite. These metaphors are inactive, and do not work. We can call more or less inactive metaphors tired, dormant, rigid, fossilised, frozen, dead and buried.[59] Dead metaphors can be resurrected.[60] Tired and dormant are therefore the best metaphors for weak metaphors. Resurrecting the dead is a tricky metaphor, especially if the dead are already buried.

There are many reasons why metaphors can lose their power. One reason is that they are figurative expressions which become worn down or increasingly faded with overuse. One clear example from our research tradition is the message that yet another thing is a social construction.

> The metaphor of social construction once had excellent shock value, but now it has become tired. It can still be liberating suddenly to realize that something is constructed and is not part of the nature of things, of people, or human society. But construction analyses run on apace.[61]

It is not self-evident that we all see the tiredness of metaphors in the same way. If we were to choose a figurative expression for freedom or yearning, a sailor's suit would not be our first choice. But for others, that metaphor lives.

> The image of the sailor with three stripes on his collar, his short jersey, his bell-bottomed trousers, his rolling gait, his narrow hips and his fluttering hatband have retained their charge and are universal. The seaman in uniform is a metaphor for both the sea and freedom, and well as a yearning for adventure and home.[62]

Some images never become a successful metaphor. If we say to our boyfriend that he looks like a beetroot sprout or tell our colleague that the organisation is a ham pie or a seesaw, this would hardly result in great rejoicing. Such metaphors are tired as soon as they are created. The seesaw is taken from Bo Hedberg *et al.*,[63] and according to Barbara Czarniawska 'is not really illuminating'.[64] We agree, even if her own metaphor has seen better days ...

We would call a metaphor that has lost its vitality a platitude. There is no criterion or test which shows whether or not a metaphor works. So Donald Davidson wrote back in the 1980s.[65] According to him, we have to trust our taste. But we're not so sure. Why can't that ham pie be tested?

Is this science?

In social science, the question of method seems to be much more debated than in natural science – or proper science if you wish. There are many convictions held, but we prefer a more sceptical attitude. And yet we still think it's science – sort of. Someone – we've forgotten who – once said that scientific knowledge is systematic knowledge that has been created using a formal method. That sounds reassuring – the scholar produces knowledge that is better and more certain than other knowledge by following a set of established rules for how scientific work should be carried out. And if you just follow the rules to the letter, scientific knowledge is assured. As you may have already guessed, we do not agree.

We believe that methods cannot be anything more than a certain amount of help when seeking knowledge. Methods cannot do our job for us. A desire to understand is also needed. Those who lack such a desire risk indulging in mechanical methodology. This approach obviously cannot create knowledge, but it can be used to build an academic career.

Some believe that formal methods create a kind of mental prison.[66] We are more cautious. We believe that there is a type of metamethod which should be more widely used. We can call this metamethod critical analysis. However, there is no established rule for how to apply this method. Instead, critical analysis is a tool for breaking up old fossilised methods in a rational manner. And within this critical analysis, the use of every imaginable idea or piece of information is permitted, provided that this lays itself open to argument. In this way, we now have a definition of what critical analysis is. It is the production and delivery of good arguments. Admittedly, what exactly constitutes a good argument varies in different situations, which Thomas Kuhn, for example, was able to demonstrate in his description of the development of scientific study,[67] but it is not entirely arbitrary.

We subscribe to Richard Rorty's idea that the quest for knowledge should be understood as a resource in the endeavour towards human happiness – not as a goal in itself.[68] We can perhaps thereby avoid futile brooding over the outer reaches of knowledge and good arguments. However, if we were to seek a rational explanation which legitimises critical analysis, Karl-Otto Apel makes the valid point that the desire for communication in itself assumes that we have a common set of values against which arguments can be assessed.[69] This set of values is all about confidence in rational argument.

This is as far as we intend to go for now. Confidence in human reason already exists by the very fact that we are writing a text and you are reading it. Without having such confidence, we never would have been able to devote ourselves to critical analysis. And without such critical analysis, all scientific study would be in vain. Scientific work begins and ends with critical analysis. At least, we believe that this should be the case.

It is up to the reader to judge whether our arguments are good ones. However, we are convinced that the arguments are good enough if the reader understands them. If the reader simply agrees completely with everything we say, the point has been in part lost. The aim of critical analysis is to encourage the reader to reflect for himself, rather than to convince.

Our text can be likened in its form to an outpouring of discussion in which arguments will occasionally interlock and one build upon the other. However, we will also allow ourselves unnecessary digressions, retakes and fresh starts. Ideas that amuse us will sometimes be followed along the way, while things that we find boring will certainly be abandoned early on at some point. It should also be pointed out that the methodology and tools of critical analysis lead not infrequently to making points that can be entertaining – we hope. Any such entertainment value does not diminish the stringency of the analysis or any claim of truth. On the contrary.

About notes and sources

At the end of this book there is a list of notes, which is preceded by references. These pages are aimed at two types of reader. Firstly, they are aimed at those who want to understand how we know something that we assert. We have looked things up and we explain where we found them. Where we have borrowed something or think we have found an interesting comparison, we specify the source.

Secondly, the notes and sources are also aimed at those who want to know more. One alternative would have been a list of those books that we believe are more intelligent and a list of those containing disinformation. If a food magazine[70] can sample all the wines for sale at the Swedish state-run off-licence chain, then we ought to be able to sample all the management books:

Burns & Stalker 1961: Interesting and well-documented study, with a few roughly drawn conclusions. Suitable for basic strategy seminars.

Maslow 1952: Sickly-sweet and falsely ingratiating motivational model with unreasonable consequences. The best before date has long since passed. Possibly suitable for use as a deterrent.

However, such a list would be long and would need to be supplemented with an extensive text explaining how the sampling process had been carried out. Otherwise, why trust our taste? Besides, the list would soon become outdated. New books come out all the time, views of previous knowledge evolve, and we would never manage to carry out an annual sampling. Instead, the text is our centrepiece and the sources a complement to it.

The rest of the book

In this chapter, we have tried to sell the structure of the book, say a few words about our approach, and take a detour around metaphors. There now follows a number of chapters in which methods for reading or gaining a better understanding of organisations are tested. This is done in different contexts and particularly in different ways. The book concludes with a chapter in which we round off and give the only advice we are actually willing to endorse: think for yourself!

In *Chapter Two*, we begin our review of methods that enable us to gain a better understanding of organisations and organisational methods. Here we attempt to create alternative images by placing the normal image of organisational practice alongside its counterimage. We ask the stubborn question: Why not the opposite? By examining the state of things and goals and metaphors, it is easier to question them.

In *Chapter Three*, we try replacing metaphors and making full use of the new metaphors. In this way, we can question some of what we know about organisations. The healthy organisation is compared with its sick counterpart.

In *Chapter Four*, we investigate what happens if leadership is seen as the metaphor it is. We also apply a simple model for facilitating the process of critical discussion: the two-by-two matrix.

In *Chapter Five*, we compare different ways of reacting to change. One means of testing these is to change foot and see which one others are standing on. We also present three Ancient Greeks who provide a few useful starting points.

In *Chapter Six*, we go into more depth by using a specific technique for questioning a change of direction. We try to add to metaphors and place a metaphor at the end points of a scale of change. If flatter pyramids are desired, we should be able to identify complete flatness and the height of the peaks. More knowledge about the end points of the scale gives a better basis for deciding on a change of direction.

In *Chapter Seven*, we relate the labelled to the label. Here, we compare the metaphor with the reality, in other words, another metaphor. Market-rate pay is a metaphor that is now used in many contexts as if it reflected reality. But does the metaphorical assertion that the market sets salaries really increase our knowledge? It is confusing when a metaphor is mistaken for reality, particularly when it is ill-chosen.

Again in *Chapter Eight*, we can be said to change metaphors in order to gain a better understanding. But here we use a well-known replacement where sound knowledge is also to be found. We try to see a school's management organisation as a bilingual environment. With new metaphors comes knowledge that can be introduced and tested in new contexts.

In *Chapter Nine*, we should perhaps present a manifesto which, if followed, would liberate us all. However, we do not offer any complete liberation from the tyranny of metaphors. Our hope is to lay a foundation for those who want to greater freedom. Besides, in this context freedom is nothing more than a metaphor for something, that being perhaps the destination that makes the journey worth the taking.

2. The Art of Complaining Constructively

If our concept for understanding and dealing with organisations could be misleading, we must ask ourselves which concept might put us back on the right track. We do not have an answer to this question. What we can offer is something more modest, but also more complicated.

Instead of correct concepts which could give an accurate picture of how organisations work, we offer instruments for creating alternative images, supplementary images and sometimes even better images. But images and metaphors are not true or false in a way that permits them to be proven or disproven. Rather, they are more or less usable as tools for thinking. Anyone who only has one image has a woefully inadequate toolbox.

In this chapter, we will discuss the simplest method for creating alternative images.[71] We contradict. It isn't hard, and we readily acknowledge that it's great fun to tell others that they are quite simply wrong. For example, we maintain that flat organisations are characterised by a concentration of power, not by decentralisation. Once we have said this, we can take a step backwards and add a cautious: 'sometimes'. This is often the way when presenting counterimages.

When we contradict and say that the matter is the opposite to what others say, we test the critical approach. However, it is not reasonable to believe that everything is exactly the opposite. It is only hooligans, dogmatists, teenagers, political extremists and various confused organisation members who believe that. The actual question of whether things really are the opposite is, nevertheless, productive since it places things on their head and thereby brings to our mind a counterimage.

We start by dealing with the image of the present time. We often hear wise people saying that things are starting to go downhill. Consequently, we maintain that everything is great and things are only getting better. Thinking about how satisfied or dissatisfied we have reason to be is a useful exercise. This leads to discussion of what constitutes a good argument. We then examine the extent to which one can be against standardisation.

The conclusion is that the method of saying the opposite works, but that it only takes us part of the way. If we want to get any further, less blunt methods are needed.

Things are great ...

There's a great deal to suggest that things aren't as bad as people say they are. The affluent Western world in which we live works well on the whole. From a practical point of view, most of us have the essentials such as food, housing, healthcare and culture. But in order to be entitled to all this, you need to be young, old, sick, employed or unemployed. Out of these alternatives, employment appears to be the most attractive – but also the most problematic. We can determine how old people are without too much difficulty, and assign rights, like pensions, according to their age. But what people do at work to justify a salary is, these days, often a mystery.

Our world also works in such a way that we think we understand it sufficiently well. Science has supplied us with explanations. Of course, we don't understand everything; we understand to varying degrees and in different ways. We can very well imagine that the order of things has been simplified or that the mechanisms of order have been analysed and disseminated more broadly. Our scientifically based world view seems stable enough.[72] No dramatic changes have been demanded here. There are no scientific disputes or thrilling debates in sight. When researchers get excited these days, it is at the prospect of being published in prestigious contexts, not for having radical ideas they want to assert, such as that mankind has evolved from a woodland mushroom. And then there's much ado about nothing.

Another indication about how good things are is that we are surrounded by a self-evident functionality. Certainly, the practical reality that surrounds us features plenty of temporary friction, but revolutionary suggestions for improvements are lacking – or, at least, are lacking in popular support. In this nice, well-functioning world of ours, much of the social research carried out finds it hard to identify significant shortcomings to which to devote its attention. The same seems to be true of practical experience. The absence of serious problems means that we do not see any grand solutions. We are in the midst of a period of time which, when history is written, will be referred to as relatively uninteresting. This is the end of history, as Francis Fukuyama puts it.[73] Here in the rich world, we are living in a time of contented vegetation.

It's all a mess!

When looking for descriptions of true contentment, we have to dig deep. Works of fiction are full of declarations to the effect that we should feel sorry for mankind. August Strindberg's *A Dream Play*[74] is one example of how proper, deep literature should deal with the matter of contentment. It's a case of misery and angst. The depiction of contentment is freely described as superficial and naïve. Satisfaction is not simply assumed to be unthinking. It also lacks entertainment value.

> The Lawyer: I wake up in the morning with a headache; and then the repetitions begin, but so that everything becomes perverted. What the night before was pretty, agreeable, witty, is presented by memory in the morning as ugly, distasteful, stupid. Pleasure seems to decay, and all joy goes to pieces. What men call success serves always as a basis for their next failure. My own successes have brought ruin upon me.[75]

When the tabloid newspapers proclaim in their eye-catching headlines that the wrong team won or that boards of directors are lining their pockets at our expense, we can remain confidently assured that everything is still a complete mess. Even those who consider themselves to be intellectually disposed and who read the editorials and opinion pages in the broadsheets and follow the right persons on the web might get the impression that there is no end to all the problems that have grown so much worse since yesterday. We become increasingly burnt out, and our money doesn't stretch far enough. Our morale drops, and the inequality gap yawns wider. We bully each other in the workplace and at school, and those starting university know nothing about mathematics.

Many people describe life today as dramatic, uncertain and worse than it was yesterday. Most people actually subscribe to this opinion. At least officially. No one wants to appear content and stupid. We know several people who are often wrong, but no one thinks them foolish. However, the fact that they are not aware of any feeling of contentment does not mean it doesn't exist. The images obscure their counterimages.

An even better construction

One benefit of asking the opposing question is that the answer provides a counterimage. The Modern Project that rolls onwards, despite all post-theoretical assertions, is sometimes based on us improving and refining our points of view and theories by exposing them to critical review. However, what is presented as criticism in everyday life is often not criticism at all, but rather support. Those who criticise a phenomenon are often for it, not against it. The critic wants more. If we watch TV programmes offering social criticism or listen to the political opposition when they blame the government, the criticism is often based on wanting more of what those being criticised are already doing. And ideally getting it more quickly.

The images we see are social constructions. They are interpretations rather than precise reproductions. The fact that the construction is social by nature means that it is the opinion of the majority – or possibly the strong – that applies. This is a table! A differing construction that does not permit itself to be corrected by the majority is easily seen as stupidity or lunacy. To say that the earth is flat, for example, is an inferior social construction. The problem is that it is not sufficiently social. There are too many people who disagree.

We would like to exemplify both the technique and the benefit of reconstructing, well aware that everything around us can be reconstructed – and that everyone already knows this. Our reasoning is that the prevailing construction of our time is an inferior one. The flat earth comparison is not entirely ridiculous. We want to get involved in the fight over the prevailing construction by asking the question: Why not the opposite? To shore up our argument further, we will use another, much more in-depth social construction; namely the good argument.

Aren't we contradicting ourselves now? On the one hand, people are generally satisfied because they have every reason to be so. They have no reason to listen to a miscellany of criticism or complaints, because the most common descriptions of misery do not hold true. On the other hand, people believe that social criticism is in short supply and too faint-hearted these days. But we don't want to compete in the business of misery. What exactly do we want?

Well, we don't want to maintain that the rich world is now so well developed that there's no point in criticism. Although that is almost what Herbert Marcuse declared in his introduction to *One-Dimensional Man*.[76] There, he states that social oppression currently (at that time) exists in a supposed, one-dimensional form of rationality which makes criticism impossible. We cannot assert the opposite opinion without appearing foolish. Then, of course, he proceeds to do exactly that anyway. Nowadays we are not entirely convinced that Marcuse was completely right, but the underlying logic of his social criticism does make sense. We need to dare to go beyond the accepted 'rational truth' in order to be able to say anything particularly smart. In contrast to the late Marcuse, we believe that this can be done without the text becoming incomprehensible.

Much needed counterimages

Thinking critically does not involve competing to provide the ultimate description of misery. Pierre-Joseph Proudhon wrote about the philosophy of misery in the mid-19th century. He was immediately countered by Karl Marx who wrote a book about the misery of philosophy, although it turned out that his main aim was to depict Proudhon as miserable. He didn't succeed particularly well, though: 'Marx was an entirely unknown and unread writer in France, whereas Proudhon was widely known and read.'[77]

Without making any comparisons with Marx or Proudhon otherwise, our text does something closely related. Our contribution could have been entitled 'The Misery of Misery'. Quite simply, there is something wrong with the descriptions of misery of our time. And people in general do not seem to attach any great importance to them. So far, our critical review is on safe ground. Contemporary descriptions of misery do not come up to scratch. We see more clearly if we replace them with descriptions of contentment. But once the point has been taken, the question remains of whether there isn't something we should complain about in the present time – other than the descriptions of misery, of course.

While on the subject of Proudhon, we cannot help but highlight his ability to turn things around to give an idea wings. Take for example his argument that 'God is evil' and his thesis, still well known to this day, that 'property is theft'. Neither of these counterimages works today. But in the 1840s, these were two exciting counterimages which derived from the question: Why not the opposite?

Back to misery. We can complain about taxes, public sector cuts, hunger in far-off countries, a lack of effort to repair the ozone layer, the eternal existence of naughty boys, secularisation and religious fundamentalists. All according to our own personal inclination. Many such complaints are repetitions of old ones, often made with claims of being brand new. We can agree that some problems are eternal, and are therefore always worth a litany of complaints. But it becomes a little daft when these eternal problems are ascribed to our particular time. The fact that the young people of today are becoming worse is a good example of a tedious complaint that is only reiterated because it can be furnished with a reference to Socrates.

One complaint that we have complained about in another context is that everything is so fast-moving and so complicated these days.[78] Despite the weak arguments and the lack of evidence, a long line of writers continue to repeat the mantra. We refrain from taking the opportunity to ridicule them by quoting what they have written on the subject. Particularly tempting in this regard are texts in which ideas about the speed and complexity of our time lead to the conclusion that everything is therefore also worse.

People have complained about the increase in speed and complexity since time immemorial,[79] and continue to do so despite the fact that this is a poor choice of timing for such a lament. It is as if the actual complaint would make critical analysis of our time particularly difficult. But at any rate, it is not certain that things were better before. We believe that the method of critical analysis should generate different and more interesting problematisations of our time instead of the more general and eternal whining. In the same way, critical analysis shows good potential within the organisation. An initial step to take in regarding the vision of our future must be to liberate ourselves from false or unfounded descriptions of misery. But that is not enough. When many of the eternal problems have diminished in importance and when much of what once consisted of need, want and suffering is turning into prosperity and affluence, we need to identify new problems and perhaps more noble aims. The need, want and suffering of others are close at hand.

Worthless counterimages

Nor does critical thinking mean that the opposite of commonly held notions is correct and should therefore be disseminated to all. It's not even certain that this would be entertaining. In their bargain-bin book *Orienterarsjukan och andra berättelser* ('Orienteering Disease and Other Stories'), Magnus Bärtås and Fredrik Ekman seek to present subversive theories and discoveries beyond the historical mainstream which 'could overthrow our perception of reality'.[80] But what we actually get is a few anecdotes and strange stories that could all have been found in a tabloid newspaper. Allow us to reproduce a slightly longer quotation as an example of something that is not a usable counterimage.

Pastrana was of American Indian descent, and was born in the 1830s in Mexico. She had an extremely large jaw, and her entire body was covered with black hair. Pastrana was whisked away by an American, who took her to New York in 1854. There, she was examined by a doctor who declared her to be a hybrid between a human and an orang-utan. Pastrana was wheeled around America and Europe, where she was billed as The Baboon Lady and put on show for money. Large crowds came to see her performances, at which she danced and sang for the audience.[81]

Pastrana married her impresario, Theodore Lent, and they had a child who died. A couple of days later, Pastrana also died. Her loathsome husband then sold the bodies of his wife and son to a professor of anatomy in Moscow, who mummified them. ...

After a number of successful tours of Europe, during which Pastrana proved to be just as popular in death as she had been in life, Lent grew tired of his life on the road. He hired out the mummies to an amusement park at the Prater in Vienna, and soon tracked down another bearded lady. He found a bearded girl in Karlsbad, whom he quickly married and gave the stage name Zenora Pastrana. ...

The newly-weds went off on a combined tour and honeymoon, accompanied by the mummies.[82]

Of course, the above discourse is slightly titillating. But including it in their book is no better than travelling around and showing the mummies for money. Moreover, what we ourselves have done is no more honourable – particularly so since a hybrid is hardly a counterimage. Strange phenomena, things we hadn't thought about, and historical misconceptions or mistakes do not constitute usable counterimages.

One type of counterimage that we especially wish to warn against is the idea that the effect of actions with good intentions is always the opposite. For example, that efforts to counter misuse always increases use. This is a common rhetorical illustration in public and political debate. Many theorists have contributed examples, but right now at the beginning of the 21st century Ulrich Beck is particularly in vogue.[83] He seems to believe that the risks engendered by modernity cannot be dealt with using rational (modern) methods. Our focus on those threats that are easily dealt with has heightened the risks and given rise to new and worse ones.

> In the modernization process, more and more destructive
> forces are also being unleashed, forces before which the human
> imagination stands in awe.[84]

We may well wonder why those very threats that we have created
ourselves would be worse or harder to eliminate than other threats.
This is a peculiar thought, which is hardly a usable counterimage.
All attempts to resolve the problem would, then, lead to even worse
problems.

The thought pattern whereby all wise actions are bad inspired a
number of commentators to speak out in connection with a 2004
silly-season story about four escaped criminals – and they weren't
the only ones. They argued that the more securely we lock up our
hooligans, the more determined they become to escape. It may be
true that harsher treatment makes it harder to readjust to society
on the outside. But it is less likely that locking criminals up more
securely would automatically lead to more of them escaping. At
the organisational level, the classic TV series 'Fawlty Towers'[85] is
a good illustrative example. In every episode, poor Basil is struck
by some minor misfortune or other. In his attempts to resolve the
problem, things become more complicated and more serious until
they result in a real catastrophe by the end of the episode.

The reason why 'Fawlty Towers' is so funny is because we are
so enamoured with the underlying concept. Society's policy on
alcohol leads to increased boozing, and all attempts to achieve
equality in the workplace mean only increased oppression. Our
fondness for this line of reasoning may be due to the way in which it
makes us feel clever without having to exert ourselves. Despite the
prevalence of this type of argument, it is unlikely that the theory
of counterproductive good intentions would stand up to scrutiny.
How likely is it that all those industrious professionals who get
into their cars each morning to head for the office actually end up
further away from it? No matter how hard they try to get there,
they only find themselves getting further away.

Another type of counterimage which is not particularly usable
is based on stated and actual intentions being the very opposite of
each other. Our policy on alcohol is designed to increase drinking
and thereby also increase tax revenue. And nothing else. This is
neither likely to be true nor productive as a counterimage.

However, stated intentions, motives and aims often differ from the real intentions, motives and aims, which are more or less hidden or unspoken. Of course, sometimes the facade and the hidden, but real, intentions are indeed in direct opposition to each other as well. But this is not so as a rule. Here, the counterimages do more harm than good, because our ability to understand the course of events is reduced.

A third kind of counterimage that rarely does any good is to take a step back and reintroduce the previous image as a new counterimage. Things were different before – and better. One example which has already passed its best-before date is Carl Hamilton who, in his book *Det infantila samhället. Barndomens slut* ('The Infantile Society: the End of Childhood') has addressed the image of childhood – or, rather, of what a good parent should be like – in psychologising jargon that even he himself dislikes.[86] Of course, the image of a good childhood that many parents try to create for their children may need to be called into question. The degree of uniformity is alarming. But Hamilton descends into tiresome moralising and yearning back to a time with more innocent children and more adult – yet still young – parents.

Nor is the view that 'things will be better then' an appropriate starting point for constructing usable counterimages. It is not unlikely that a great deal will actually be better in the future. But only if we try to improve it. Other things may very well be worse – for example, the things we make worse. One refined approach is debaters latching on to the idea that things were better in the past, and will also be better in the future. Right now, we are at the bottom of a U. Things were better, and things will be better. Many researchers have argued in favour of this U theory in completely different contexts, and argued that we are stuck in the dip at the very time they describe a phenomenon. Classic examples include Robert Blauner, who in the early 1960s studied the relationship between work organisation and the degree of alienation.[87] And quite rightly, he found that the pre-industrial period featured a low degree of alienation among the workforce. The same would apply to the future time of automation, when all the boring jobs would be carried out by machines. But right then, during the boom years of the mass production industry, things were really bad.

A general lack of counterimages does not therefore mean that a certain counterimage in a specific case is of use. Many counterimages are simply worthless and unusable.

The good argument

Many social scientists still labour under the misapprehension that their research is value-neutral and non-political. This is not the case. Good social science answers a 'Why?' question which is of interest to society, providing a 'Because ...' answer, which is not value-neutral. How could an explanation of a social phenomenon ever be so?

Good social science research fill gaps in relevant theories. This is a widespread ideal. The theory gap need not be a total lack of knowledge. It could just be a weakness, an indistinctness or an earlier mistake. Good science could also be debunking previous theories or proving old theories to be wrong, but theories always matter. Relevant theories are theories that are used. They are therefore practical, and have a role to play when they are in use. But nor does science with such ambitions produce value-neutral results. Moreover, it must be possible to discuss that which is not value-neutral and non-political in terms of good and evil. Social science can do harm simply because it is relevant.

In order for the opposing question to work, we must argue for the counterimage that will form the answer. If the new image cannot be defended with our honour intact, we must seek another image. We devoted a joint book to defending counterimages, and have done so at many lectures.[88] A smart jacket and a knack for public speaking are certainly an advantage. After decades at the chalkboard of academia, we can talk our way out of most things. But an alert audience will not be satisfied with rhetorical tricks. A good argument is needed, too.

Arguing is most fun when someone offers resistance. During the time when management by objectives was all the rage, we went on tour with a lecture entitled 'You can't manage by objectives!' It would hardly have been entertaining if no one had disagreed – we would have stood there with the one counterimage that everyone shared. Perhaps this would be an attractive end point. But if we start there, something isn't quite right. The only image that everyone sees as obvious cannot be a counterimage.

A lack of resistance sometimes makes teaching students on basic courses hopelessly dull. Many of them sit there, bolt upright with their eyes wide open, pinching their arms at regular intervals to keep from nodding off. They collect attendance credits which are later converted into course credits. Others note down what is said in order to stay awake, while also having reason to avert their eyes and avoid the risk of being asked any questions. If there has to be any communication, they want it to be one-way. A seminar group that nods in agreement to everything can really destroy any pedagogical ambition. Fortunately, practitioners and students who have progressed a little further make for audiences that are more easily provoked. That said, no one is a hopeless case. It's just a case of using better teaching methods to break the silence.

A usable counterimage cannot be the image shared as a matter of course, and nor can it be just any old preposterous idea. Let us reiterate that the potential for argument is needed in order for the image to be reasonable. You can't manage by objectives for a number of reasons.[89] One is that the abstract end objectives set by management cannot be broken up into concrete intermediate objectives further down in the organisation in such a way that the end objectives are actually achieved. Another reason is that no method is included for dealing with the conflicts of objectives arising lower down in the hierarchy between different parts of the organisation. Good arguments are the foundation on which we can build credible claims to truth, according to the pragmatist and social constructivist Richard Rorty, whom we occasionally believe in.[90]

At this point we should give an explanation of how a good argument works. But if we knew precisely what carries conviction, we would of course have already convinced the reader that we are right. What's more, we would be convinced ourselves.

The bad argument

We have sometimes been surprised at what in practice is seen to be a good argument or reason. If you want to get a particularly pessimistic impression of the great modern enlightenment project, take a close look at what people accept as arguments. Some examples of the various forms that bad – but convincing – arguments take might amuse an audience. The simplest of dirty tricks is to make reference to some authority. Depending on the context and the target group, you can say that it says so in the Bible, that Weber[91] has reached a conclusion, or that the health authorities have recommended it. The reference should ideally be correct. In any case, it's not hard to find something that supports pretty much any view. The Bible invites various interpretations, and the health authorities have given out all manner of advice, directions and explanations. Otherwise, you can tell an outright lie if the worst comes to the worst. After all, who can be bothered to take on the thorny task of checking such sources?

Another good trick is to say something incomprehensible. This works a treat in many situations. We allow ourselves to be seduced by that which we do not understand. But this is not really as practicable as referring to authorities. Admittedly, you don't need any knowledge in order to be able to say something incomprehensible, but you do need to be believable. In other words, this isn't a trick that just anyone can pull off. But with, say, a suitable title, the backing of an authority or the support of a big corporation, you can say strange things and still – or, perhaps, for that very reason – be met with rapturous applause.

A third technique, and one that we often use with our children, is to maintain that they do not understand things that we ourselves know for certain because we are better qualified: 'You're too young to understand' and 'Being a woman, I just know' are replies that often gain the upper hand in a discussion. The idea of so-called female intuition monopolises claims to knowledge in a way that excludes half of humanity. As good feminists, we are against that kind of thing. The same dubious strategy is also used by certain men, Pentecostalists, economists and middle managers, among others.

What convinces people differs in different places. Our good friend Bo Westerlund once told us about a visit to Italy, where he found himself sitting on a bus. It might have been in Naples. The bus stopped to pick up another passenger – a man, who was puffing earnestly on a cigarette. 'You can't smoke on the bus!' exclaimed the driver angrily, pointing at a non-smoking sign. 'But I've just had a coffee,' protested the would-be passenger. 'Well, OK then,' replied the driver kindly and let the smoker on the bus. Not only was drinking coffee an adequate argument, it was also quite obviously valid there and then.

When we enquired about the incident much later on, Bo referred us to the source, which was the book *Also sprach Bellavista* by Luciano De Crescenzo.[92] The anecdote thereby raises the question of whether an event has to be experienced by oneself in order to qualify as one's own memory. We know that other people's memories consist of much that would not stand up to close comparison with other sources or other witnesses. When it comes to our own memory, we can be more stubborn when the veracity of our recollections is called into question. But to make our own memory a public one is to invent something ourselves.[93] That would mean that the read conversation on the bus might very well become a memory.

The bad argument is the argument which does not convince. What convinces would seem to shift according to the historical or cultural stance. Anyone who wants to have a better argument must not allow themselves to be convinced too easily. Perhaps a good argument is all about having a critical listener. If you, dear reader, follow everything we say, there will be no need for any good argument. You will be convinced anyway.

The causes of contentment

One benefit of the counterimage, other than that it can be more reasonable, is that it in turn prompts new questions. In a differently constructed world, there are other problems to resolve and other phenomena to explain. If the earth was flat, we would have to explain why we do not fall over the edge ... Only if we see contented people is it meaningful to discuss the causes.

We believe it can be argued that contentment stems from a lack of aptitude for, and an unfamiliarity with, critical thinking. Given obvious circumstances, such as having to fit in taking our car to the garage when it's open, we often have difficulty asking the question: why not the opposite? We could just be happy that it's there and indeed that it's open at all. Moreover, we're happy that we can usually afford to pay for assistance it offers. The opposite would not be good. Yet there are other reasons to be dissatisfied. Shouldn't the opportunity to get the car repaired be fitted in with our lives? With the aid of electronics we might soon be able to forget about fitting in with the garage. Surely the time is ripe for self-repairing cars? Although we are satisfied, such a change would make us even more satisfied.

When we look for plausible explanations for why people are so satisfied with their existence, it is easy to miss the obvious. Among all the more or less preposterous theories that we are duped, misled, manipulated and downright stupid, the obvious answer is right in front of our eyes. We are satisfied because we have good reason to be satisfied. If we were to make a comparison with how satisfied people seem to have been previously with the reasons that existed then, we would actually be even more satisfied than we currently are.

It is appropriate at this point to quote the introductory lines of the epic poem *The Elk Hunters* by Johan Ludvig Runeberg, who would have been celebrating his two hundred and tenth birthday on 5 February 2014.

The evening meal had just ended in the croft. The remains
still lay on the spacious table; around the pail of beer
were pieces of bread and potatoes and vendace served in bowls.
The stove was lit and the cottage was warm; the glowing embers
spread the heat from the hearth and filled
the eaves with a haze of smoke, so that the torches and the sleds
left to dry on the rafters, could hardly be seen.
The smoke hung high in the air, and beneath its darkness
blazed many torches and illuminated the country folks'
evening chores: the hostess, the industrious Anna,
making up the bed for herself and her beloved husband,
their daughter, contentedly cleaning the sooty pot
by the wall while humming gently, and their energetic son, diligently
scooping chopped straw mixed with flour into the sturdy trough
for the pair of steeds standing and stomping their feet at the door.[94]

Undoubtedly it seems like a wonderful existence there in the cottage, despite the fact that the food would have been a hard sell even at our local diner. Perhaps it would have drawn the tourists, although they wouldn't have put up with the smoke. The industrious Anna, her contented daughter and energetic son all contribute towards the genial atmosphere. Nothing is said of the fact that the very next day they plan to leave, tear the bandages from their eyes and the shackles from their wrists, and start a rebellion.

If you didn't complain before, you can't come here and kick up a fuss. Today, the fields are full of crops. The cows bellowing in the cowshed are filled to bursting with milk. The children are fat (in the extreme) and well-fed. And a thin stream of milk flows out from almost every mother's breast, even before the baby opens its mouth.

We are satisfied because we are fortunate, and also because we are satisfied with so little. In actual fact, these two statements are two sides of the same coin. On the flip side, we find the explanation that we are satisfied because we do not know how to question our situation. Questioning requires critical thought – a skill that ought to come into fashion some time.

If we are to be slightly critical of Runeberg's depiction, we should bear in mind that he was a romantic poet. He himself was hardly one of the contented country folk he describes. If anything, he allowed himself to be persuaded by Jean-Jacques Rousseau's notion that people are happier if they live closer to nature. A more natural life would thus be a happier life. Incidentally, 'back to nature' was number two on a slightly dubious list of the most misunderstood quotations of our time which we found on the internet.[95] The introduction to the treatise *Émile, or On Education* begins as follows:

> God makes all things good; man meddles with them and they become evil. He forces one soil to yield the products of another, one tree to bear another's fruit. He confuses and confounds time, place, and natural conditions. He mutilates his dog, his horse, and his slave. He destroys and defaces all things; he loves all that is deformed and monstrous; he will have nothing as nature made it, not even man himself, who must learn his paces like a saddle-horse, and be shaped to his master's taste like the trees in his garden.[96]

Perhaps Rousseau meant that which was better and more authentic in its origin than that which man has sullied with his dirty hands.

But we're not actually interested in what Rousseau may have meant. If we decided to dig deeper into the matter, we soon end up with questions that we still cannot answer. The point is that certain romantics bought an idea that Rousseau is often accused of having come up with.

In this context, we would like to state for the record that we postmodernists have certain difficulties with the distinction between natural and unnatural. We think it is natural to head off to a nearby coffee shop and have a sandwich and a café cortado. And we also think water closets are natural. We're less convinced about horses in the living room.

Perhaps here we should make a distinction between being fortunate and being satisfied. We are fortunate. The same can hardly be said for Runeberg's elk hunters. But according to Runeberg, they were satisfied. And what about us? We look for an opportunity to be satisfied with being fortunate, while still questioning things as if we were dissatisfied.

Standardisation as an example

Let us once again change the object of our discussion on the benefit of counterimages. We have lingered for a while on a description of the general state of our time. Either misery prevails and weighs us down, or we stand satisfied atop the peak of our curve of luxury. We could also throw in a reference here to Oswald Spengler's *The Decline of the West* in which he claimed that we were at the height of our culture and development.[97] The fact that his work attracted so much discussion is probably due to his fitting so well into the negativistic middle ground. In other words, even our western culture is headed towards its destruction ...

If we move on from the whole to the part, we find organisations. We often say that cities are home to as many rats as people. It is doubtful whether this is true, since the rat population is controlled by access to food.[98] A more likely assertion is that cities are home to as many organisations as inhabitants. Misery often prevails in organisations. They feature problems that normally become both more numerous and serious according to the forecasts that management cannot resist producing. But even if these problems exist, the focus is on the solutions. Organisations are characterised by people working within them to resolve the problems. These days, the disparities between organisations are one of the problems we are trying to resolve.

In the debate about health care in Sweden and probably elsewhere, there is a paradox. There is a quest for freedom of choice on the one hand and a demand for comparability on the other. Or, rather: freedom of choice calls for comparability and comparability calls for standardisation.

Representatives from healthcare professional associations are in favour of standardisation. No one seems to be against. The auditors are vocal in their agreement. Everyone seems to agree as well that the process is running too slowly. And that's the government's fault. No one seems concerned that when hospitals all do things in exactly the same way, freedom of choice will be a bit pointless. Competition results in no one wanting to risk being worse than their fellow competitors. And no better, either, for that matter. The latter is more of a problem than the former. But that's often the case with criticism. Quite simply, it's not particularly critical; instead, it tends to be opinionated. That's not the same thing.

Standardisation is a good example in quite general terms. (Almost) everyone is in favour of it. The arguments are presented as being bombproof, and are often repeated. Freedom of choice, equal treatment, transparency and demands for the application of best practice are things we can't just wave aside. But there's certainly a nagging worry that standardisation might also lead to regimentation and stagnation. Could there be a dangerous confusion between best practice and same practice? And what is the value of freedom of choice if it only allows us to choose between very similar alternatives? Other choices are forbidden by removing the differing alternatives from the selection available.

We see standardisation almost everywhere, and it's hard to be against it. Language is a form of standardisation, if you like. Many people think it practical when words mean precise things. The Swedish Academy is often seen as the standardisation commission for the Swedish language. Not least by the majority of Swedish Scrabble players. But since people have abandoned the lettered tiles of the real world for those of Wordfeud, the Swedish Academy is no longer in control of which words really are Swedish. That said, most linguistic standardisation has been neither initiated nor scrutinised by the Swedish Academy. It seems practical that language should be allowed to evolve 'by itself' without anyone having – or assuming – the power to make a formal decision on how things should be. But we still have the feeling that language is increasingly subject to formal endeavours towards standardisation. For example, the Swedish language has long been subject to strict orthography, as disseminated in the form of the Swedish Academy Glossary. The Gods may know why. Those who understand Swedish can still read what was written before everything became so incredibly prescriptive.

Without knowing for sure, it seems to us that readers of English have even less problem with reading age-old texts. As far as we can tell, the spelling has simply been allowed to remain as it is. In this way, of course, age-old texts remain legible. The problems arising instead are in part that many English speakers cannot write correct English without using a spell checker, and in part that those of us from other countries quite often fail to pronounce correctly the English we read and understand.

Other things are standardised on the basis of custom or imitation. Many organisations strive to create formal standards that are then introduced via mandatory rules or certification, or simply by many others following the standard. Such standards are often entirely indispensable, such as people knowing what we mean when we inform them that we weigh eighty-two kilos or that the light bulb we bought at the convenience store fits the standard lamp by the sofa. We can, at a pinch, accept a couple of different types of screw-threads – but things become impractical when each screw only has one nut that fits.

There are also standards that only apply in everyday life. For example, who determined how much red wine there should be in a red wine glass, or the diameter of a digestive biscuit? And yet these standards also contribute towards our general well-being. If we risk being given a litre jug of cheap plonk with our steak, we can't just order a glass of the house red. And in the same way, a packet of biscuits would be cumbersome if it were a metre long. Yes, we know that there's an ISO glass now for standardising drinks. ISO is named after the Greek for 'equal', and also happens to work as an acronym for International Standards Organisation, but that's not to say that they have standardised the size of wine glass to be used. Biscuits are also standardised, in that no one would accept them being the same format as a loaf of bread at the breakfast table. This despite the fact that as far as we know there is no set standard for digestive biscuits. When it comes to biscuits, we have noticed in recent years a differentiation in the standard. The biscuits at coffee mornings are smaller these days than at many take-away coffee shops. Perhaps the latter have adopted a king-size North American standard while others have stuck to the more Lutheran.

No, there is no limit to the number and variety of measures that can be designated as requiring standardisation. As Bengt Jacobsson and Nils Brunsson point out, there is a standard for what now constitutes a standard, but no one pays any attention to that particular standard.[99] Now that standardisation represents so many different things, it is clearly impossible to be either for or against it. Nor are we entirely certain that standardisation necessarily means uniformity at all times. A standard for clothing sizes doesn't mean that everyone walks around wearing identical trousers. It just means that most people (not everyone, regrettably) wear trousers that fit. We would simply like to point out on the quiet that when comparisons are introduced within healthcare which require comparability, we force through new standards. And we should then think about whether this is a good thing, instead of just throwing our caps in the air and cheering.

A pedagogical example

Our teaching work sometimes involves acting as examiners, merrily reading our way through student essays of various lengths. It isn't always the case, but every so often we are amazed at how gifted and diligent these students are. And much of what turns out to be not particularly good is more our fault than theirs.

But suddenly one day, every written submission we received included a section entitled 'Source Criticism'. Time after time we were forced to read through pointless, superficial and irrelevant nonsense which called itself source criticism. When we asked the students about this, they looked at us in surprise. 'If we don't follow the standard essay template, we get points deducted and we might fail.' True enough. Some development group had drawn up a standard for 'essays that meet the standard for Pass with Distinction', and the template included source criticism. Such a standard is a prerequisite for high quality, isn't it? The fact that the students knew all about this and we didn't may be because it is hard to reach a consensus on such a template among teaching faculty.

We took it upon ourselves to give a lecture on scientific methodology, in which we maintained that the structure of a paper should be based on content rather than form. If the writer has something significant to impart about the various sources used, this can be done under the heading 'Source Criticism', for example. However, a skilled social scientist does not of course limit himself to source criticism under the designated heading.

To be on the safe side, we consulted some other examiners about the issue. They were not inclined either to deduct any marks for an essay not following the standardised template. And they were all against headings which the writer was unable to fill with content. When we put these views to the students, several of them subsequently maintained that we were clearly radicals, and were generally insubordinate to authority. This was intended sometimes as praise and sometimes as censure.

So how important is source criticism deemed to be? It would appear to be extremely important if all students are always required to write about the issue, but not important enough for us to be given any training on the subject. We have positive opinions of historians, and are therefore convinced of the benefit of students in the history department having to practise source criticism analyses from day one of their courses. Can we really rely on the details of Gustav Vasa's exploits in Dalarna? And so on. But on management courses no one seems to think that the issue is sufficiently important to be paid any attention.

Such a state of affairs could drive anyone to despair. On the one hand we have a standard, and on the other hand no one thinks the issue is important enough. When students follow the standard, they do so because they believe they must. Every time a student complies with the standard, he is given a lesson in choosing form over content, standards over quality, and ultimately prioritising irrelevant matters over important matters. If one encounters many such instances during one's education, one might well wonder whether the aim is to blunt the student's judgement instead of sharpen it.

The point of our example is to show that criticism can be fundamental. Its very foundation is open to criticism. Perhaps healthcare would benefit from less standardisation and more variation when it comes to control measures and administrative procedures, instead of the recommended standardisation. Standardisation often means our behaviour becoming more uniform and predictable. Often this is good and useful – but often it is not.

Criticism need not involve taking part in a misery contest. Continued standardisation of healthcare, for example, will certainly lead to a great deal of good being done. But it will also lead to more administration, less freedom of choice and perhaps even stagnation, and of course students' essays may need to be standardised. But only if this produces good results. It's a conundrum. And nor does criticism need to be opinionated. There is still no risk that everyone will agree.

Time to stop

We thought about stopping here. We hope that those who have read the chapter this far have got the point. We have tried to investigate the causes of practical and theoretical contentment. We have also tried to sell a technique for questioning and thereby thinking critically. This chapter has been all about influencing the accepted construction of our everyday lives by simply saying the opposite. It worked in this context, and we maintain that it works in others. We have not claimed it is easy. But it's worth going to the trouble, since questioning means that we can understand certain things in a new way. We will return in the final chapter to the fact that this method leads to other problems by not indicating an end point at which the questioning should be discontinued.

The method we examined in this chapter made it somewhat easier to understand organisational phenomena. However, it was clear that the method is not quite good enough to give us a full understanding. And that's why this book doesn't end here and now.

3. Draining the Metaphor

Mona Lisa, Mona Lisa, men have named you
You're so like the lady with the mystic smile
Is it only 'cause you're lonely they have blamed you
For that Mona Lisa strangeness in your smile?[100]

An organisational metaphor is certainly a picture of an organisation. But it is no photograph, and no da Vinci (1452–1564). If anything, metaphors are sketches or caricatures which highlight certain features and hide others – just like photographs or paintings by Leonardo da Vinci. The method for gaining a better understanding of organisations that we will be examining in this chapter is to push the metaphor further, to stretch it or even to drain it entirely. We take as our example the sick organisation. We infer that an organisation can be sick or ill from the remedies that are offered by management experts of different kinds. As we will find, remedies are the most common indications of illness in the world of management. Because English is a foreign language to us, we have some difficulties with making the distinction between being ill and being sick. We use those two words synonymously, even though we are aware that a sick organisation might be a morally deficient one whereas if an organisation is ill it deserves our pity and care rather than reprobation. That said, if you are sick to your stomach you are ill and in need of a remedy.

At a theoretical level, this chapter should be regarded as an examination of the consequences if one chooses to view organisations as carriers of sickness and as being curable.[101] Similar examinations relating to other images of organisations can also be found elsewhere in the literature of metaphor.[102] We can regard our text as being ultimately an analysis of the typical discussions held regarding the organisation or an examination of a generally applicable narrative about organising.[103] The practice of offering cures for real or imagined illness calls for external and critical disclosure. However, it should be acknowledged that we have found it hard to refrain from the pleasure of arguing within the framework of the concept of sickness and remedy.

Quality deficiency, as an example

Organisations are usually sick, the exception being those organisations that have just undergone surgery or received strong medication. But these temporarily healthy organisations will very soon fall sick again. Deficiency diseases seem particularly amenable to treatment. When treatment stops, the same deficiency crops up again. Vitamin deficiency and anaemia might well be treated with pills. Insulin deficiency requires injections and constant checks. In the world of organisations we find management deficiency, competence deficiency and creativity deficiency. And pills do exist, of course; a fair number of pills are on offer in order to treat quality deficiency. That disease has been widespread in recent decades, and all kinds of organisations appear to have been affected.

Quality deficiency is reminiscent of an impaired immune defence system. It is not dangerous in itself, and might not even be regarded as a disease. Suffering from quality deficiency need not mean that the patient feels ill. However, the costs incurred by quality deficiency can ultimately lead to the death of the organisation.

Just like sickness in general, quality deficiency is normally regarded as being self-inflicted.[104] This does not mean that people within the organisation affected have consciously and actively endeavoured to achieve quality levels that are too low. Nor does it mean that no exceptions exist whereby the responsibility for this clearly lies outside the organisation as a result of, say, identifiable individuals acting negligently, or – to take a more indeterminate example –, the development of the industry. However, 'every preventive ideology must include the idea that human actions, whether individual or collective, direct or indirect, can prevent the onset of sickness'.[105] If we believe in prevention that focuses on organisations and the actions of its members, there is sickness which is self-inflicted just as there is a responsibility for returning to good health.

The risk of being stricken by quality deficiency disease is not in any way connected to how good that quality is. Good or bad, that quality needs to be improved. We ask whether organisations have quality deficiencies (does the diagnosis agree?) and whether the common treatments available actually have the effects described. This means that, for a while at least, we will go along with the assumption that organisations can be sick and that they can be treated and cured – despite certain weaknesses in this line of reasoning.

Who is the patient?

And so we go back to sick organisations. In our attempt to address more in-depth or turn around the sickness metaphor, we will first determine who the patient is. One common way of approaching this question is to take the doctor's relationship to the party being treated or cured as the starting point. This has been done since the time Hippocrates (circa 460–370 BC), during his time on the island of Kos, formulated (or rather was ascribed) the Hippocratic Oath.[106]

1. In all his actions, the physician shall have the patient's health as his primary goal, and shall if possible cure, often alleviate and always comfort, following the dictates of humanity and honour.

2. The physician shall act in accordance with scientific and proven experience, constantly seek to expand his own knowledge, and contribute to the best of his ability to both scientific advancement and the public's knowledge thereof. To the best of his ability, the physician shall always make his knowledge available to others.[107]

The highly ethical physician who can easily stick to the Hippocratic Oath may well exist in reality. In the best-selling, much scorned literature as written by the likes of Frank Slaughter, he plays the leading role. The introduction provided by one example of back-cover blurb to such a work reads as follows:

> Bruce Graham is a young American surgeon who takes up the position of a u.s. Army medic during the Second World War. His path constantly crosses that of a former schoolmate, a man who is now a successful career-driven politician. The focus of both their interests is Janet, a famous film star and the daughter of a well-known Congressman.
>
> The medic is a man whose life is guided by integrity and honesty. In his fight for these ideals, he often encounters resistance, making himself unpopular, both with his colleagues and with officers and politicians. His former schoolmate, however, is a man who understands the importance of maintaining his popularity.[108]

On one level, the answer to the question of who is the patient is simple and actually quite obvious. The organisation is the patient. But an organisation is an evasive concept. One might wonder whether organisations actually exist, although it would be more productive to wonder in which respects they exist.

We are easily led into regarding companies, associations and public-sector organisations as almost physical objects with a clearly discernible form and substance. This kind of world view creates unreasonable expectations of the consequences of organising. Organisations are not things. They are, rather, our notions of how people act together. When we talk about them as pyramids, machines, channels or food chains, this is therefore in a figurative – metaphorical – sense. But even that which we assign to metaphor is a metaphor.

The patient in this metaphor-stretching description is the notion held by the members of the organisation and those around them of how a group of people that can be demarcated from those around them operates. The University of Gothenburg, for example, is the name of a patient we know well. With this, we leave the discussion of organisations as physical objects until another time.

The concept of sickness

In our everyday language, sickness is the opposite of health. And health is seen as a condition of complete functionality. All other conditions are equated with sickness. Health then becomes an exception, and we must then be seen to be sick most of the time. We are sick if we have any of the possible diagnoses offered by medical science. It is also the case that 'health is regarded as something positive, while sickness is something negative, in that health is a desired condition and sickness is undesired'.[109] The concept of health and the concept of sickness can both be problematised.

One aspect of sickness as a metaphor that we soon leave unresolved is that even bodily illnesses are 'encumbered by the trappings of metaphor'.[110] It is not surprising that things we sometimes find it hard to speak about – and are afraid of – are written about using metaphors.[111] Yet it does not follow, as Susan Sontag also notes, that illness is not a metaphor.[112] The notion that metaphors conceal, distort and hinder our understanding of relationships, which characterises Sontag's 1978 essay *Illness as Metaphor*, appears primitive even though there are plenty of examples of metaphors having been used in precisely this way. Metaphors can of course also open up, clarify and contribute towards the understanding of phenomena. We believe that the key to knowledge does not lie in calling phenomena by their 'correct names', but in making the effort to see their correct meaning.

Viewed philosophically, the concept of sickness is a shaky one. It often means a lack of something, a deficiency. In other contexts, sickness is a combination of various things. The distinction between sickness and symptoms is like Plato's cave. The one assumes the existence of the other, in the same way that the shadow of the tree in the cave must, in Plato's view, be caused by a tree outside. This line of reasoning assumes that we only believe in shadows with known explanations. The shadow cannot then be, for example, a forest's shadow-like spirit. But if we introduce the concept of remedy, we can coin a definition of sickness. Sicknesses are conditions that unambiguously permit themselves to be linked to a treatment plan – a remedy.

Jørgen Jørgensen, one of the sick doctors featured in the book edited by Herman Anker, points out how imprecise the Swedish word *sjukdom* is,[113] encompassing as it does 'sickness', 'illness' and 'disease'. 'Disease' refers to functional failings, while 'illness' refers to 'the patient's experience of being sick, his reactions to the sickness, such as pain, anxiety and worry, and its spreading to the family'.[114] Both the functional failings of the sick organisation and its members' experiences in a broad sense are therefore also included in the concept.

It appears that the diagnoses of diseases are based on completely different types of observations.[115] Sometimes it is the external symptoms that give the disease its name and identity, and sometimes it is the pathogenic microbe or the biological process. And here we would like to add that sicknesses in both humans and organisations can be identified based on their remedies.

Both medicine and social science harbour the dream of identifying the underlying causes and mechanisms behind the state of things. Once we have identified what happens behind that seen in the body or the organisation, we believe that we can influence the course of events ...

Sicknesses and medicines

One way of making further progress with the concept of sickness is via the available treatment methods and medicines. We want to believe that medicines are the solutions to sickness-related problems, but sometimes it seems more like sickness is the solution to the problem of a surfeit of remedies. Particularly when it comes to organisations. The picture is, however, complex. Those who appear to be healthy may simply be too exhausted to withstand any more treatment for a while. It's hardly surprising that the rich and relatively healthy do the most to cure their ailments.

To the layman, it seems that groups of diseases might lend themselves to classification. We will not concern ourselves here with the fact that medical experts have at hand what they believe are better classifications. We will start by illustrating how the more widespread knowledge of diseases is often driven forward by the development of remedies. We do not want to go so far as to maintain that diseases are defined on the basis of the available remedies, but there is certainly a reciprocity that is hard to address. If the remedy did not exist, we would not see the ailment.

The same is true of the sicknesses from which organisations suffer.

We will identify here a number of different relationships that diseases may have to treatment, in the case of both individuals and organisations.

Sicknesses whose causes should be eliminated

The most common deadly diseases of our time are due to poverty and its effects, in the form of hunger and lack of water in particular. The diseases that follow in the wake of poverty can be alleviated in most cases, and can often be cured. But in actual fact, it is poverty that should be treated. Healthcare is a humanitarian necessity, but offers entirely the wrong type of medicine.

Illnesses due to stress in the workplace and lifestyle are on the rise. Once they have occurred, many of them can be treated and the effects alleviated, but alarmingly few are cured. It is unfortunate that more energy is not put into preventive work. Cardiovascular diseases are also the result of causes that should be avoided. In this way, many sicknesses are lifestyle-related, and we might ask ourselves whether the possibility of medication leads to them becoming more common.

Repetitive strain injuries of various types are now treated with great success in the rich world. To a certain degree at least, this has led to less exercise of caution by employers and, for example, sportsmen.

Both within and among organisations there are sicknesses that should not be treated; instead, the causes should be eliminated. When owners of small businesses complain about stress, poor profitability, insufficient growth and so on, this may be because the state regulation to which they are subjected is intended for much larger organisations. If it is the environment in the form of external administrative requirements that makes many owners of small businesses ill, it would appear to be more effective to remove the cause instead of treating every patient and every symptom individually.

Incurable diseases

Another large group of sicknesses is that of incurable diseases. Here, a great deal of medication is administered to help curb the progress of the disease and to improve the quality of life of the sufferer. The difference between rich and poor is significant. Age-related diseases can be said to be incurable. Fewer and fewer of us die young and healthy.

'Incurable disease' is an unsatisfactory term, since the boundary of what is curable is constantly shifting. Cancers that were deadly just a few years ago can now be treated with great success.

Everyday ailments that need not be treated

Flu, Norwalk virus and colds that are best left to run their course are, perhaps, some of the most common sicknesses. Traditional household remedies and over-the-counter pills often provide sufficient relief without having to send for the doctor. Besides, he can't prescribe a small glass of Calvados. Everyday ailments also include less serious bouts of aching joints, backache or muscular pain. They tend to pass even before you've reached the operator in the telephone queue.

Examples of incurable sickness within organisations may include the manufacture of products that are no longer needed. Hand-held calculators are a classic example, and CD players are heading in the same direction. In the long term, no medicine in the world can keep a company that makes things no one wants in good health. The same was true of the government bail-outs of the 1980s. Individual shipyards, for example, could not be cured when the structure of the entire shipbuilding industry needed restructuring. Here and there, sterling efforts have been made – and continue to be made – to give employees new job opportunities, but the organisations where they work cannot be cured.

Within organisations, everyday conflicts are examples of ailments that often do not require any outside intervention or advanced treatment. These may be unpleasant, but can often be cured successfully without too much fuss.

Sicknesses that healthy people believe they suffer from

We have recently seen a new type of sickness which has attracted the interest of the mass media. People have suddenly started to suffer from noses that are too small or breasts that are too big. They certainly didn't suffer from these complaints to the same extent before it was possible to cure them with reasonably reliable results. Access to a cure has therefore meant that many more people have become more sick than they would have been otherwise.

Organisations also compare themselves with others. The differences or deviations they then notice can be compared to the sicknesses suffered by healthy people. Before they noticed the difference and knew of the cure, the organisation was deemed to be healthy. Now the healthy organisation might, for example suffer from a hierarchy with too many levels.

Treatable sicknesses

Finally, there are sicknesses that can be cured with a pill. It's as easy as that. The pill makes the sickness disappear for good, and the patient suffers no side effects.

This category includes all those sicknesses that can be treated with major interventions and those that are treated with less success. Medical science feels its way forward and makes constant progress. When it comes to organisations, however, there is less certainty that more sicknesses will become treatable or that the treatments will keep on improving.

The diagnoses: different types of diseases

Without a diagnosis, it is doubtful whether one can call oneself sick. Ingrowing toenails, bubonic plague and scrofula are sicknesses. Someone who feels ill only shows indications that he might be sick. But this must be determined via the deliberative process which, at best, determines the name of a sickness: in other words, provides a diagnosis. You cannot decide for yourself whether you are sick. At least, not if it's up to a doctor:

Those who are not members of the medical fraternity can, of course, use words such as appendicitis and pneumonia, but the words have been borrowed from medical terminology, and have no precise meaning except in the context of scientific medicine.[116]

This really stopped us in our tracks. Is pneumonia a metaphorical expression when we use the word? When we mere mortals use the name of a medical complaint in everyday language, it's a metaphor for not feeling well or something being wrong. Only once the doctor has pronounced that we have pneumonia can we phone our boss and say: 'I've bloody well got pneumonia.'

If we look at the patient's own pathological picture as presented in the popular press and in the perceived pathological pictures we encounter in organisational change literature, we find recurring features: every organisational sickness is unique even if it is reminiscent of well-known sicknesses; the patient is in all significant respects unlike other organisations, and, despite the fact that organisational sicknesses can be severe and even life-threatening, there is always a cure.

As every citizen and more and more people at the social security office and within the medical profession and even one or two politicians know, allowing patients to make their own diagnoses has its risks. It might not only be a case of the patient lacking the necessary knowledge. Patients also include hypochondriacs, malingerers, various kinds of treatment abusers, the generally hypersensitive and those yearning for company all of whom will attribute excessive care needs to themselves. And there are also those with a fear of dentists. In certain cases, the experience of ill health or good health will be taken seriously if we imagine that functionality is key, and in other cases it will not. It is worth pointing out that even when the experience is correctly observed, the self-diagnosis can easily be wrong.

Professionals who assess organisations do not always provide a more correct or even better diagnosis than the patient.[117] Here, commercial interests come into play. Curing organisational sickness is often difficult and the medication prescribed can also be called into question. After a while, the patient may lose the will to pay and switch over to cheaper versions of the medicine offered by other suppliers, or even just make their own medicine. Then a more reliable living might be made from carrying out thorough patient examinations, particularly if the diagnosis reached has a better chance of being one for which a patented medicine can be sold. The question is whether the organisational physicians even dimly recall that there may be diagnoses which suggest sicknesses for which they do not have a cure.

If we look beyond the ambition of organisation representatives to portray their organisation as unique, a number of standard ailments appear. We do not rule out the possibility that there are unique cases, although we have never seen one. That said, ailments vary in prevalence at different points in time. Not all organisations have the same sickness, but at any one time a smaller number of afflictions dominate. These sicknesses spread between continents, countries and sectors of society. Some of the routes of infection are more common than others; for example, the spread of contagion from English-speaking nations to Sweden and from our companies to public-sector organisations are common at the time of writing.

Here, a clear difference can be seen compared with individuals' sickness preferences and the healthcare system's assessment of diseases as they appear in the media. We have not studied the care of human beings, but surely it is preferable to have well-known diseases with a clear connection to the human body rather than the more vaguely defined experiences of pain after having collided with the invisible walls of modern life? For organisations, the opposite is true. An organisation suffering from a sickness that appears to be simple and has been common for some time is interpreted as being old-fashioned and outmoded. A cutting-edge organisation is immune to simple, old-fashioned ailments.

Structural deficiencies

One diagnosis that has become so common in recent years that we can talk about a national disease affecting organisations is structural deficiency. We have previously turned our attention to the height of the organisational pyramid.[118] These pyramids have long been deemed to be too high and have therefore been lowered or even torn down. Our analysis showed that lowering the pyramid was often a kind of misdirected cosmetic surgery. The problems that were supposed to be solved didn't normally exist, and the effects that were supposed to be achieved did not materialise if the flattening itself was not the effect intended. In several respects, the effect was the opposite to the declared intention. For example, it turned out that the flat organisations became more pyramidal than the pyramids that had been torn down. Even in the most written-about example – Jan Carlzon's SAS – the flat organisation meant that power became more concentrated at the top of the hierarchy than had ever been the case before. Whether or not this was actually an unintended effect is a matter for discussion.

Ineffective distribution of power is an example of another common and more general structural deficiency. In this case the diagnosis has changed over time. It is sometimes alleged that too much power lies with the middle managers, and sometimes that they do not have enough power. The power should be either decentralised down to the middle managers or centralised up from them. The pendulum swings and fashions change. There is also a long tradition among left-leaning working life researchers of attempting to cure organisations by making the organisation non-hierarchical in the hope that power will thereby shift to the base of the organisation. But we are not convinced that anyone takes these people seriously.

Excess weight is also a common structure-related sickness. Organisations find it hard to control their intake of staff, premises and raw materials, and binge when the economic cycle is good. Plenty ends up being wasted. This surplus intake leads to bulging, not least around the middle of the pyramid. One common dieting technique during times of recession is embarking on savings programmes which lead to anorexic profiles at the mid-level. The base of the organisation also shrinks as a result of dieting, while the top remains the same size but rarely replaces its staff. One feature of organisations is that all types of adversity have a tendency to be explained by management actions. So after every rainy summer, the campsite manager is replaced. And this brings us almost over to the question of management.

However, we will first look at a method which has been used in recent years in very many contexts to achieve weight loss: outsourcing. The various operational elements are sorted according to whether they belong to the core that must be protected[119] or whether they can be bought in from unknown other parties. What counts as the core often appears to be entirely arbitrary to an outsider, but is seen as obvious within the organisation in question. And obviousness is probably the biggest obstacle to wise actions. Dealing with outsourcing can take dramatically different manifestations such as organ donation, self-mutilation and surgical removal, such as an appendectomy, depending on what the ailment was, who had it and what was amputated.

Bad management

Bad management is, in a way, an age-related repetitive strain injury. If the organisation's management survives long enough, it is sure to turn bad. Such is the way of nature. The present is always preceded by the past. Almost every form of management has been preceded by a management that was worse. (Where other assertions are made, members of the current management are probably related to the previous management.)

Although all managers become worn out, this can happen at different rates. For example, members of management become worn out more quickly in companies where anticipated profits have failed to materialise for a number of quarters, and in parts of the public sector which are unable to stick to their budgets. Despite the fact that new cases of bad management increase during poor financial periods, the problems encountered seem to be at their worst when there is plenty of money. This is when medication is at is most widespread. One sign of this is providing managers with further academic education, which as we know very well is much more widespread during good times. That's not to say that bad managers are actually cured by this treatment. Perhaps one symptom of bad management is a refusal to be cured?

Incidentally, management training need not always be a medicine. What we see here is possibly doping rather than sickness-related medication. It may also be a matter of providing a vitamin cure which is taken in order to stave off the increasingly common affliction of bad management. Or it may be a case of a visit to a spa retreat in the countryside for those who have earned it. The organisation is not sick, and no one expects it to become any healthier, but a little organisational seaweed wrap during the day and a spot of wine tasting in the evening is a popular reward. And perhaps management development becomes an even more common benefit as the media monitors backscratching ever more closely.

Management can of course be bad in different ways. One deficiency is a failure to control the organisation and then be dissatisfied with this fact. But the latter is not a necessary consequence of the former. The fact that management is not exercising control may be appreciated by subordinates and perhaps even by management itself. But if something is to be done about it, it's the instrument of control that needs to be rectified. In this case, extensive and expensive investment is common. Reforming zeal in large organisations focuses more often on control systems and instruments of control than on the formal structure.

Lack of adaptability

A lack of adaptability is often put forward as an ailment suffered by organisations with mixed symptoms. One imagines that the sick organisation is standing still amid the flow of change which surrounds the organisation. Once everything else has changed, the organisation no longer fits in with its surroundings, and this explains why it feels ill. The idea is that organisations which change in line with their surroundings feel so much better. However, this diagnosis is often based on a misapprehension.

Organisations do not feature stability; instead, they are constantly undergoing change. This can be hard to see when it comes to those organisations that we encounter on a daily basis. It's just the same with the height of a child. If we watch them growing day by day, it can be hard to see the difference. But if we've been looking at other things for a while, we see that something has changed when our family comes back into our field of vision.

The main task of an organisation's management is to keep the rate of change in check. Few would put up with an organisation in which there is constant rapid change. An organisation undergoing such a rate of natural change would be unable to maintain stable relationships either internally or externally, in the latter case because the rapid changes made would not be in line with the changes in the organisation's surroundings. In order for development to be in sync, an organisation and its surroundings must be as one, thereby resulting in new surroundings.

Change is often a sign that the organisational management has failed. Those failures dealt with in the media, and in the scant literature with scientific ambitions within the field, often relate to events that are mainly outside the management's control. Analyses of the work of management fail to identify the stabilising function of organisational management. But how else can we understand the incredible interest in planning and developing so many formal and slow-moving instruments?

It is worth noting that the ambition to achieve stability in certain situations increases instability. If management is to succeed in disabling undesired processes and stopping ongoing processes, a degree of speed and flexibility is required. In purely general terms, management literature is pretty dismal.[120] What we see is either advice to managers that has been plucked out of thin air or superficial descriptions of what they apparently do. In amongst this mass of grey is some sensible reading on leadership and its terms – why not start with Sven-Erik Sjöstrand's book *The Two Faces of Management?*[121]

Lack of perception

Being hard of seeing and hearing are not often counted as sicknesses. But these are deficiencies that require curing, or otherwise, you risk walking into lampposts and missing airport announcements. Plenty of examples are recounted in management education about the dangers of a lack of perception. These tales include one about Facit, which made the world's best mechanical adding machines but sent their salesmen out with pocket calculators – since they were more practical to carry around. The story might not be entirely true, but it's illustrative and amusing.

Today, there are actuarial reasons why certain parts of the body such as the teeth and functions such as sight do not really count as belonging to the body. One such demarcation can be disregarded when we expand the metaphor beyond the hospital. Organisations with a lack of perception do nothing about any problems, since they are unable to detect them. 'Insight inertia' is the slightly restrictive name given to the ailment in organisational literature.[122]

Quality deficiency – symptoms and remedies

Over recent decades, the concept of quality has at times come to dominate the consultancy market's offers of achieving a healthier organisation. It may be that quality deficiency and the number of acronyms denoting cures – such as TQM – are terms which will become outmoded, but so far remedies such as quality measurements and the satisfied consumer index are in plentiful supply in the medicine cabinet. Other sicknesses, such as obesity, may be about to replace these in terms of dominance, but there are still many organisations taking high doses of quality medicine. The term 'quality deficiency' is worth thinking about for a moment. 'Deficiency' appears to be the simpler part. It is present with a similar meaning in the well-known expression 'vitamin deficiency'. We understand it as being at the end of the food chain.

A deficiency is often implied. When we browse through the restaurant menu and all the tempting dishes it contains, we rarely see reference to any deficiency. The very reason for going to a restaurant is to rectify a state of deficiency. The menu often describes the food as delicate, but rarely as satisfying. Nevertheless, hunger should be the primary seasoning. There was a restaurant which went by the name of Proppmätt, meaning 'Stuffed to Bursting', and it has now closed down. It was no doubt an excellent choice for hungry diners, but the name was a little too explicit. (We never went there.)

A wealth of quality improvement measures are directed at organisations, but the marketing is rarely so insensitive that it implies that its potential clients suffer from a quality deficiency. That would be tasteless. And we never hear anyone talking about their own organisation's quality deficiencies, despite the fact that they might be midway through a costly quality improvement project.

Quality is a more elusive concept than is deficiency. This is not because there is any great uncertainty about what it means, but because so many people are quite sure what it means. Let us expand on this.

A great deal has happened within the field of quality. Twenty or thirty years ago, the concept of quality was unproblematic. Quite simply, good quality applied to companies that offered good products. Professionals and operational managers safeguarded quality.

Of course, there were conflicts between those who wanted to cut costs and those who designed and produced the products, but there was enough money to ensure high quality.

Then came a boom in interest in quality, which could be seen mostly in the widespread use of quality measurements. This interest was aimed at specifying how good the quality was, rather than improving it. In particular, so-called satisfaction measurements – which themselves were of dubious quality – became widespread in their use.[123]

In the meantime, more and more quality concepts have been developed. For a long time, technical or physical quality applied only to goods. Then service quality was promoted in the private sector. This had previously been included in the concept of service itself. The public sector also saw the launch of service quality and the complex phenomenon of governance quality.

Unravelling the concept of quality requires a firm grasp and significant simplification. Quality can be said to be a set of properties of goods and services that affect how satisfied someone is with them. Those making such an assessment could be customers, consumers and users, or they could also be production staff, officials and managers. This could involve purely physical properties which can be measured easily or properties which should clearly be experienced. However, all these classifications are a chimera. It is very common for service quality to be linked to products included in a service, and vice versa. It is also hard to imagine a purely technical product or service that can be assessed only through measurement, or a case where we have to rely one hundred percent on experience.

How satisfied we are depends on our expectations. We normally have a complex array of expectations. We want to get many different things out of a product or a service at the same time, and the right quality is perhaps just a case of meeting these complex expectations. The link between quality and expectations should be taken seriously, since it has interesting consequences. If expectations are heightened and everything else remains equal, there is a reduction in quality. This means that addressing the issue of quality through carrying out quality measurement, for example, normally leads to a reduction in quality because expectations rise.

Paths towards cure

It follows from this discussion of what quality is that quality deficiency is an ailment which can be treated in three main ways. One
way is to change the goods or the service, a second way is to change
the image of the goods or the service, and a third way is to change
the expectations of the goods or the service when used.

The choice between these paths is complicated by the fact that
the status of both sicknesses and treatments varies significantly
depending on who the patient is. This is true of both organisations
and people. If you can show a major surgery scar which ended a
sports career and then point to a chart of antidepressants for dealing
with never winning a gold medal, the matter becomes quite clear.

The differences in status when it comes to treating quality deficiency are not as obvious as for normal consumer products, such
as mid-range laundry detergents, in terms of quality. In the case of
laundry detergents, which ultimately need to get our clothes reasonably clean without standing out as being particularly harmful
to the environment, we willingly accept quite absurd attempts to
influence the image of the product's quality in TV adverts.

More objectionable are the attempts at quality improvement
which are based on changing the image of those laundry detergents
failing to get our clothes clean at all. In those cases, the manufacturer can expect to have the consumer agencies and the media on
its back. And the same is true of products and services that are seen
to be important to us. Why not take dental care as an example? Just
as with laundry detergents, advertising is the most effective way
of improving the quality of dental care. Nevertheless, it is hard to
win the same acceptance for the prescribed medication in this field.

The costs of improving quality vary considerably depending on
the type of treatment we choose. It is normally far more expensive
to change the product or the service than it is to change their image.
And the results are the same. The advice we could give to those
who want to improve the quality of products and services is to let
the product itself be what it is, and instead change the image of the
product – how good it is seen to be.

Changing expectations is a more uncertain medicine – here we
have both unknown and undesired effects, not to mention all the
expectations we have of the expectations the products should create:

> Quality is all about expectations. A service is of good quality when we find that the service meets – or ideally exceeds – our expectations. In the future, it will be a matter of competing with high quality when it comes to staff, service and environmental awareness in order to create profitability.
>
> We also believe that those who buy our services will require some form of documented quality assurance in the future. This is one of the reasons why Hotel Småland is investing in quality assurance.
>
> It's also rewarding to provide a high quality service, and this is true for both our managers and our employees.[124]

Trying to lower people's expectations as a way of dealing with quality deficiencies may seem like a good idea. We all recognise the trick, because the majority of after-dinner speakers start by informing us: 'Unaccustomed as I am to public speaking, I would nevertheless like to try to express in my clumsy manner ...' We normally go along with this and laugh politely at all the tired old jokes.

When you charge a lot of money for something, you can't lower the customer's expectations in the same way. When people have paid a small fortune for Metallica tickets, the band can hardly start the concert by apologising for playing so badly, or that the guitar is new and unfamiliar. They must pretend that what they are doing is great, even though the guitar sounds new and unfamiliar. And the concert-goers won't complain about anything other than perhaps a touch of tinnitus. Metallica are good, and that's just how it is. Full stop.

The phenomenon of certain things being good even if they are of low quality reminds us of an old acquaintance we had when the yuppie era was at its worst. He had got a well-paid job as some kind of IT consultant. It may have been 1988. He had just picked up a red Alfa Romeo and offered to take a friend for a spin. When he opened the driver's side door, the door handle came away in his hand. 'That doesn't matter!' he said. 'It's an Alfa Romeo!' It may be an urban myth,[125] just like the rat's tooth in the pizza that we heard about and swallowed. But it doesn't matter – the point is still clear.

The remarkable thing isn't that the concert-goer or the IT consultant had unrealistically low expectations. In both cases, the expectations were very high. What was actually unreasonable was the customers' realism. Nothing about the concert or the car could have failed to meet their high expectations. If it had somehow been possible to lower their expectations in advance, the concert and the car would have only been worse.

If we return to the example of dental care, we would not accept excessively far-reaching attempts to lower our expectations. If the marketing makes it clear that the dentist is incompetent, we would not go there even if a visit did exceed our expectations. When it comes to public or publicly controlled services, high expectations of quality are also important in terms of how successful political management is considered to be. We vote out those who do not make bold promises.

We can't therefore trick people with quality by affecting the image of the product and our expectations of it. Or at least, we like to believe that we can't. We want punishment to be meted out to the companies that sell laundry detergent which leaves our clothes dirtier and dentists who make our teeth fall out.

Different types of pills

Whether or not quality medicines are different is a tricky question, as is the question of whether or not they are of good quality. The labels often feature the same description, but once you open the containers it can turn out that one contains red pills and the other contains blue pills. The various quality concepts are also transformed into all manner of things once they reach the patient. Despite the confusion, it is not hard to distinguish three main types of medicine in the literature on quality.

In this context, we would like to apologise for using pills as our chosen metaphor for all kinds of treatment. A hand surgeon we know well believes that the very use of pills is the root of all evil, and that we should use surgery far more often. In his world, people are like bicycles. And what good is pill-popping to a broken bike? But back to the pills ...

Bureaucracy pills

Quality involves creating a safe and well-documented system of procedures and rules for dealing with quality. We have seen this kind of pill before, but then it went by the name of bureaucracy. Max Weber calls organisations that rely on rules and procedures to ensure good efficacy bureaucracies.[126] He believes (or, rather, believed – he died in 1920) that bureaucracy is an expression of western civilisation's aspirations to objective rationality. And things are more rational if we ensure that we have carefully considered rules for resolving the problems we encounter within operations.

This type of pill also has a strong institutional basis in all the different types of certification that can be obtained if we have conducted ourselves properly. ISO, SIQ and other bodies will give you a certificate if you can demonstrate that your organisation has a highly developed set of rules and procedures, and of course rules and procedures for monitoring these rules and procedures.

Consumer satisfaction index pills

Quality involves having satisfied consumers. And we get satisfied consumers by meeting consumers' expectations. This is not necessarily in opposition to the idea of well regulated quality control, but it gives the concept of quality a slightly different character. At least when it comes to the actual pill.

Consumer satisfaction indices are the active ingredient in this second type of pill. These indices are created by collating survey responses from consumers. These days, virtually every organisation does this. New public management (NPM) means we can tie ourselves up in knots trying to define who is the customer so that we know to whom we send the survey. Much of the remainder of this chapter deals with quality pills, but we also have plenty of scope to discuss other matters.

We are reminded of an episode which illustrates the fact that satisfied consumers are a problematic index, even without surveys. A long time ago, we took part in a management training session for trainee dental clinic managers. One of these trainee managers had a very definite opinion of the quality of one of the employees at her clinic. It was substandard. Actually, the disciplinary board should have been brought in, but we all know how hard it is to get through to people that way, so she didn't do that. The thing that our would-be clinic manager was really upset about was that the patients were on the side of the under-performing dentist. When he messed up, he always managed to explain things away by saying that the patient in question was a very special case. His eloquent excuses made the patient (who was, of course, called a customer in this case) feel exceptional and remarkable. The patient felt acknowledged. So not only was the dentist incompetent, he was also popular with his patients.

A while back, we read in the paper that Lidl was given the lowest rating of all supermarkets in the consumer satisfaction index produced by the Swedish Quality Index.[127] ICA, which is the biggest food retail chain in Sweden, came out on top. We have nothing against ICA, but Lidl's low score is an interesting phenomenon. It does not seem to stop customers from streaming through their doors, or from new stores opening as soon as they have been granted a building permit. And it's not even certain that the low-scoring result means consumers are dissatisfied. Our friend Bosse, for example, was delighted when Lidl finally opened a branch near where he lives. Now he buys everything he can from Lidl for his large family, and he's certainly satisfied!

The newspaper offered the explanation that Lidl can survive on the margins because the market is so big. Only a small proportion of all shoppers need to frequent their stores. But we're not convinced. Lidl is growing at an incredible rate. The argument about existing on the margins hardly explains why the consumer satisfaction index is of no significance or tells us anything other than which box people ticked on a form.

We tried to find out more about the index from the Swedish Quality Index's website, but in our opinion it was of such poor quality (the website, that is) that we ended up none the wiser.

And nor are we satisfied with Lidl, in case the reader is led to believe otherwise. Just recently, Bosse came to visit, bringing a gift he had bought from Lidl. This was a pair of secateurs on a long pole, with a cord to pull when cutting off a branch high up in a tree. Green-fingered readers will know what we mean. The secateurs only cost about a tenth of what they would have cost in a hardware shop, Bosse told us cheerfully. And sure enough, they broke the first time they were used. The pole sheared right off when Bosse gave a firm tug on the string to demonstrate what a brilliant purchase he had made. And so we remain sceptical about Lidl. We're also sceptical about ICA, but for other reasons. The fact that Lidl sells useless secateurs doesn't give the ticks in the boxes on the quality survey any greater worth.

The example of Lidl and the Swedish Quality Index is significant, since it goes right to the very core of quality measurement. When we discuss consumer satisfaction indices, we tend to assume that their origin and their clearest relevance lie in commercial service. It is the private service sector that benefits most from finding out about customer experience via surveys. And if we manage to ask the right questions about the right things, and if people are able and willing to answer truthfully, they ought to work. But there are too many 'ifs' involved.

An episode involving our ejection from a large service company (as it calls itself) may serve at this point to illustrate that information on quality deficiencies is not always wanted, even though it may at first seem that it is. Our task was to participate in a change process, and we ended up in a group charged with drawing up a new customer survey. It was clear that we could ask the customers about pretty much anything. We wondered, slightly foolishly, what would be done with the results from the surveys, since knowing about their use would help us to formulate constructive questions. That's when we found out that the results from previous surveys hadn't actually been used for anything. But if those results weren't being used, what was the point of producing new surveys? Surely they, too, would not be used. Would it not be better to try to use the information that already existed, instead of generating new information? Or so we thought, in our youthful ignorance. We will spare the reader the details of how this influenced our own consumer satisfaction index. Suffice it to say that we will not be welcomed back.

Measurement pills

There is a third type of pill which might not have much to say for itself, but which we would like to mention anyway: measurement. This involves quality control measuring the product with as great a degree of engineering precision as possible. Perhaps that was what was meant by quality in industry before TQM arrived on the scene. The nut had to fit the screw in order to be of good quality.

Medicines and their status

If a quality deficiency is to be cured, many different medicines are on offer. Not all medicines are intended to cure the sickness. Some only aim to stop its spread or the consequences, thereby extending life or improving quality of life during the course of the sickness. Such medicines are used when sicknesses are deemed to be incurable or not worth curing for various reasons. These medicines can be sorted into categories such as quality assurance and quality control. The field is certainly not regulated in the same way as a pharmacist's product range. Here, it is much harder to draw the distinction between traditional medicine and the modern medical science.

The remedies to counter quality deficiency include medicines with differing degrees of suitability. Much of what is offered to organisations is in direct – and apparently obvious – contrast to science and proven knowledge. There are no best-before dates here. Instead, once you find a buyer you can sell any old ointment, or for that matter any new one that will have been cobbled together yesterday and will have never been tried before.

The lack of regulation can be frightening, and to a certain extent the filthy lucre has pushed the salesmen too far. Within the consulting industry, which accounts for much of the research, medicine development and prescription-writing that goes on, there are some who ought to be ashamed. Despite a growing number of studies, knowledge about the consulting industry remains limited.[128] It would be interesting to find out what happens when the physician himself falls ill[129] – whether he dares to take the treatment that is sold to others.

But the responsibility for the choice of medicine lies not only with whoever makes the diagnosis and writes the prescription, but also with the patient. If both the sickness and the patient are entirely unique, proven knowledge alone is not enough. Something unproven is also needed, and it may be a case of kill or cure.

Incidentally, an interesting similarity can be noted between successful treatment based on knowledge and that which is based on nonsense. It is often said that faith can contribute towards cure:

> Those of us who take a more scientific view towards the causes and cure of disease may sneer at the superstition of all the quacks and their clients, and may often shudder at the thought of the tragedies that a 'cure' like theirs must surely lead to in many cases, but one thing is certain: few doctors have understood the importance of creating such faith in the infallibility of their abilities and their cures as these quacks.[130]

Is quality deficiency a single sickness?

Before we address the effects of medication and treatment, it may be worth examining the diagnosis in a little more depth. We cut the discussion about the concept of deficiency short in order to move onwards. Quality deficiency has thus far been interpreted as a lack of quality. This means that the quality is not optimal – but the question is whether it could be too high and thus imperfect. The answer seems obvious. Of course quality can be too high. Here we can differentiate between a small range of deficiencies:

- The quality is not worth the price. A hotel room may be better than a large suite with its own butler if you are paying out of your own pocket.

- We cannot afford really high quality. Here, perhaps, medical care is the clearest example. Today, medical care is capable of much more than we are willing to pay for – particularly when it comes to paying for the care of anonymous others. Continued research can be assumed to result in an increase in the gap between willingness to pay via tax or insurance premiums and the price of the best possible care.

- The quality is unnecessarily heterogeneous. Stainless steel bodywork is unnecessarily good for a car in which the engine is completely wrecked after the end of the guarantee period, particularly if this weakness is generally known.

- We are unable to appreciate high quality. The expensive vintage wine tastes sour and musty. Fortunately, we know of a semi-sweet rosé in a curvaceous bottle with a seductive label. What's more, it only costs a fraction of the price. And that book by a Nobel Laureate will remain unread in favour of a more accessible spy novel. Not everyone wants the kind of headache that Burgundy and Jelinek can produce.

Once we have noted that quality deficiency can also exist in the case of quality that is too high, we see that the medicine falls into the same main groups as the medicine to counter quality that is too low. It's a matter of changing the product or service, changing the image of the product or service, and changing expectations. If costs are to be kept constant or reduced, changes to the product or service are the only option available. When it comes to important goods or services produced within or in connection with the public sector, however, excessive quality is an ailment which is completely taboo.

A moral tale from our early lecturing days illustrates the taboo of quality reduction. It all took place at a conference retreat during the heady days of the 1980s. Chief physicians were to have a full day on the subject of organisation. Several of them arrived in Porsches, and they all had their pagers turned on during the lecture. At least one of them dashed out to save the life of a cardiac patient. As an inexperienced lecturer among all these self-assured participants, the prospect of a full day was nerve-racking. So why not launch into a workshop session where the doctors could have their say before meeting back up again as a group? The task was to discuss in groups how to put an end to the continuous rise in quality within medical care. The justification for this was that ever better medical care also becomes increasingly expensive. And the spark ignited a rebellion. The groups refused to leave the room to discuss something so stupid and generally unethical. They then spent half the morning in a heated group discussion, which turned out to be an unexpected but fortunate solution.

The ailment is taboo, and so is the medication. The need to halt the improvement in quality or to reduce the quality in order to address the quality deficiency is denied, and so no medicine is required.

This detour around the diagnosis can be concluded by noting that its role should not be overstated. In both medical care and organisations, it is primarily a tool for communicating with the patient. Organisational scientist William Starbuck recounts a conversation with a doctor who is entirely correct when he argues that good doctors treat combinations of symptoms and not diagnoses.[131] The reason is that there are far more symptoms than diagnoses. There are also more treatments than diagnoses. Let us leave Starbuck just before he loses his way in a line of argument to the effect that it is not symptoms that are important; only the way in which the patient reacts to specific treatments. Only an organisational consultant would be delighted to see positive reactions from the customer while the symptoms remain unchanged.

The treatment plan

We have now discussed the matter of what sickness the organisation had. This is the rational medical approach. But all along we have allowed the reader to imagine that perhaps it is not so much about which sickness a possible – or perhaps, rather, virtual – patient is suffering from. Instead, it is a case of which remedy could be marketed under the name of quality assurance. So now let us see what the market has to offer in terms of treatment plans, and which pills the pill bottles contain.

We will start at the University of Gothenburg's School of Business and Economics Library, where we amassed a pile of books which claimed to point the way towards quality. The selection was both random and systematic. We took books which happened to sit on the shelf and which made this promise without raising our expectations. Out of nine publications, seven were focused solely on certification in accordance with some standardisation concept.[132] Normally ISO 9000. Two books were a little more comprehensive.[133] These included subjects such as processes and benchmarking. All nine books advocated bureaucratisation.

In the first instance, the books we borrowed from the library described how to arrive at a set of rules and procedures which might mean that guaranteed quality is delivered, and which will most certainly guarantee certification. Consumer satisfaction indices come in by way of the back door, as a necessary procedure or something similar. For those with ISO aspirations, Eva Söderstedt states: 'Quality is getting that which one expects'.[134]

But a visit to the Library is not a reliable route to knowledge of how quality deficiencies should be dealt with. Some years ago we carried out a supplementary search for the term 'quality assurance' in the University Library's database, GUNDA. This gave somewhat more than 130 hits. Healthcare was by far the dominant field for these books. About eighty publications dealt with healthcare of some description. Next came the environment and education, with about twenty hits respectively. We're talking about the public sector! Where quality projects are carried out, and where one writes about one's own experiences so that others can find out about them. The titles on the internet gave a completely different impression to the quality literature we found in the library. But here, as in many other contexts, the public sector borrows accessories from industry in order to acquaint itself with the radiance of beauty.[135]

One impression that we got from both our literature searches was that the concept of quality is headed downhill. If we look at the years of publication, few works appeared after 2004. The top years were 1998 and 1993, with twelve publications each. Before 1990 there was almost nothing. Searching directly on the shelves gives a more exact indication of time.

Still not satisfied, we tried to broaden our approach by heading to Gothenburg's biggest book shop to investigate the situation in the field of quality. The general management shelf had nothing on quality. When we asked the lady at the information desk, it turned out that there were no books available on quality work or quality assurance in the entire shop. The helpful lady wondered whether perhaps we would like to order a booklet about quality assurance in medical care. But we had already found out what we needed to know.

In order to complete our investigation, we wanted more information about how the concept of quality is used in practice. We googled the term 'quality assurance', which gave around 15,000,000 hits. Not surprisingly, it turned out that there were plenty of consultants trying to peddle their pills. Yet there were even more organisations who were keen to tell us which pills they had taken. It appears that the term 'quality assurance' is a sales pitch for both those who sell pills and those who buy them.

When we tried the library again in 2013, the circumstances were different. The Library contains many new literary works which are at least in part on the subject of quality. However, they are mostly about how specific organisations have introduced some form of quality measurement. Out of the first ten hits on the library's database, eight addressed the way quality measurement has been introduced in healthcare. The public sector's welfare-providing organisations would appear to be the ones calling for it. At least in Sweden. A number of more general books have been published in a new and revised edition, but these too appear to be aimed primarily at the public sector. The long-term view has changed. There is more talk about what has been done rather than what should be done in the future.

Which pills the consultants prescribed and which pills the patients swallowed is a tricky question. Sometimes these are the standardised procedures that the literature usually recommends. But equally often it's a matter of whatever seems sensible in a given situation. The Swedish Customs draws up agreements with trusted companies to make the process of customs clearance easier. Some offer classic – and, according to more recent research, slightly suspect – project management methods which have been around since the days of Henry Gantt (he with the Gantt chart, 1861–1919).[136] Others offer methods of measurement, and the Police report on their statutory obligations.

But when our search led us to pages which offered reviews of websites in relation to their accessibility for the disabled, we started to wonder whether some heading other than quality assurance was available. For example: 'We do the best we can', or: 'We hope our customers will be satisfied'. Sometimes the term 'quality assurance' took a back seat in favour of more specific technical information: 'We have measured our boards with tape measures and set squares' or: 'A litre measure has been used to ensure that the customer gets a precise quantity of milk every time'. Four websites are quoted below.

A large number of tourism companies (hotels, holiday camps, restaurants, museums, activity providers, etc.) have now undergone or are currently undergoing training through the quality assurance programme, and have been able to document their quality work in such a way that they have been awarded ETOUR's quality diploma and seal.[137]

Policy statement: Defective quality can have devastating consequences for a company. Dissatisfied customers change suppliers, and the company's reputation can be jeopardised. More and more companies therefore see the importance of establishing testing and quality assurance processes in order to improve the quality of their products.[138]

During the implementation of the commission, Metamatrix applies a development process which borrows many thoughts and ideas from the Rational Unified Process (RUP). The process also covers project management methodology and configuration management principles.

Monitoring is carried out on an ongoing basis in accordance with established procedures and against set intermediate objectives, *e.g.* through regular project and control group meetings. After completing the commission, a follow-up is carried out against set targets in the project specification and the training plan.[139]

We review and test the accessibility of websites for users with disabilities. This review results in a report which illustrates the current status of the website and what is required in terms of technical adaptations in order to comply with international guidelines.[140]

The concept of quality was applied to many types of use and meaning during its golden age. Whenever anyone produced anything half sensible they had to give it a name associated with quality because the concept of quality signified rationality itself. In this way the concept was the name given to any manner of pills in the organisational medicine cabinet. The word 'quality' now seems to grace ever fewer labels on bottles. Other labels have been pasted over the old ones, so to speak. Writing Viagra on a jar of stomach ulcer medicine isn't viable, but changing the name of one's consultancy offer from TQM to Lean won't result in any accusations of maltreatment.

Effects and side-effects

Before we finish stretching the sickness metaphor, we will round off the discussion with a few words on the effects and side-effects of quality assurance. Much of what is written and said about quality assurance consists of meaningless mumbo jumbo. If all this empty rhetoric about the consumer at the centre and management by objectives has any effect, it must be down to the placebo effect. Employees hear the word 'quality' and understand that it's full steam ahead. And the consumer can have faith that now the product has been quality assured, it is therefore also good. If he doesn't like the taste, it's his own fault. Much like with the music of Metallica. It's dreary, but it received glowing reviews so we give it polite applause. Booing would be unthinkable unless we want to disgrace ourselves completely.

If there was enough space and the audience had more energy, we could reflect for a while on whether pill dependency is a problem of the organisations of our time. They never used to send for the doctor just because they were feeling a little out of sorts. But organisations have become sicklier and are now accustomed to such frequent doctor's visits and treatments that they could perhaps be described as addicts. It might be a matter of price. But it is by no means certain that being at a distance from the doctor keeps organisations healthy in the same way as it does people who live in rural areas. If the doctor has to make a journey of 'a total of 350 kilometres by sledge on poorly cleared and non-existent winter roads in Lapland',[141] he will also expect to be paid more. But when organisations need to be treated, there is a correlation between the price and the perception of quality. The more expensive the medicine, the more effective it is.

The risk of unnecessary medication and dangerous overdosing is almost tantamount to abuse. If we treat healthy organisations, they become either more sick or even more healthy. No one ever manages to be entirely healthy.

When medicines become something else

In conclusion, we intend to argue that quality assurance has ceased to be a medicine that must be prescribed by a doctor, and it can now be sold from any old outlet. In the best case, quality means that something is good. In a not quite so good case, it is conventional. Quality assurance contributes towards something being good or else towards a levelling. The latter is dealt with in a thought-provoking way by Marten Toonder, in a story in which Bumble of the Levelling Committee is appointed official standardiser for the whole of Bumblestone.[142] 'Expiria jocus est,'[143] as Brother Just would say. Since we are not Latin scholars, we don't really know what that means. But at the same time as the hero of the series Tom Puss is saving Bumblestone from all the problems that complete conformity have created, the driving force that is Brother Just does not leave empty-handed.

A parallel may be drawn with most of the Swedish pharmacy chains' policies on product range. We do not wish to pretend to know anything about their product range. However, a visit to the website of one of these chains[144] has confirmed that many products available are not medicines. Lots of them aren't even health-related. Nor does everything which, according to the Swedish National Pharmaceutical Benefits Board, is covered by high-cost protection measures count as medicine in the sense of pills used to treat sickness. Quality assurance would therefore fit in well with this product range, and could simply be sold on prescription.

Instead, we must wriggle our way out of the grasp of the reviewed metaphor and draw a comparison with a precursor in the field of organisational improvement: scientific management or – as it was labelled in Sweden – rationalisation. For a long time, this was a measure that organisational consultants could propose and on which to base systems for ushering in improvement. That would never work today. The work of rationalisation now comes under the concept of work. Everyone does it without regarding it as a specific task that requires the help of a consultant. Nor does the concept of rationalisation have the same ring to it that it once had many years ago. We have a book on our shelf entitled *Hushållets rationalisering*[145] ('Household Rationalisation'). This is a nice book about cleaning, bookkeeping, winemaking and many other useful things. In the early 1940s, the word 'rationalisation' had come to mean everything that was useful and good, in the same way that 'quality assurance' does now. We now look forward to a book entitled 'The Quality-Assessed Home'. Organisations will definitely be ripe then to pick up another disease. If we were to hazard a guess, the problem would be related to rapid growth and size: a luxurious ailment at organisational level. Obesity would be a good guess.

A fully-stretched metaphor

The line of reasoning has not been entirely ineffective, if we may say so ourselves. If we push the metaphor further than we normally would, we discover its shortcomings. Who is the patient actually? And what is sickness? If there are sick organisations, there should also be healthy ones. How reliable is the organisational diagnosis? Not all pills can contain the same thing. If there are medicines, there should also be side effects. Where does the organisation report malpractice?

But as the discussion showed, the questions also result in us finding a whole host of new answers. If we had not seen the organisation as being sick, we never would have ended up here. Essentially, therefore, there is nothing wrong with the metaphor. It can be used to understand the organisation better, simply by stretching it a little. But why not have a little more fun and drain it entirely?

4. The Leader on the Heels of the Led

Leaders are the ones the rest of us follow. They stand at the head of their flock.[146] 'Follow me!' calls Prince Valiant[147], as did Jesus before him. The latter was followed by Levi.[148] Whether or not it is wise to follow Jesus have been questioned by Richard Dawkins.[149] In his day, everyone followed Prince Valiant without worrying about the wisdom of doing so. If there is a true leader, we cannot resist the call and simply follow wherever he leads us. The problem with this idea is that there are not so many situations these days in which we follow someone who leads us. It's mostly only when we try to learn about unfamiliar cities. There we join a small flock of people who obligingly traipse around after a young person with a megaphone who stops occasionally to explain what we are looking at. We follow and listen politely, or perhaps even with interest, but it hardly corresponds to our picture of real leadership.

This chapter begins with a couple of pages that illustrate how little we actually know about leadership. Neither we nor anyone else can say anything universally applicable and still interesting about leadership. Well, apart from the universally applicable but not particularly interesting declaration that it is hard to understand what leadership is. We then turn to leaders. Knowledge about leaders is also pretty scant. However, in this case the situation is not confusing; on the contrary, everyone seems to know exactly what's what. It's worrying. It almost seems impossible to be serious about it, so in this chapter we refrain from being serious. It seems to be the only way of being serious. Anyhow we would like to launch a simple model for breaking up the leader metaphor and conclude with a guiding example. In short. We take the lead. Any followers?

Different types of leadership

The people we regard as leaders today are prime ministers, company directors, section managers and perhaps generals. It is hard to see how we follow them, unless we are forced or tricked into doing so. No modern individual in full possession of their faculties tends to follow the umbrella held aloft. And now we're back there again. It's easy to forget that the word 'leader' is a metaphor.[150] Leader and leadership have borrowed their meaning from a practice which existed in the past.

Managers do not stand at the head of a flock, other than in a figurative and metaphorical sense. They rarely call out: 'Follow me!' – if they did, they would risk being confused for a tour guide. Nor do they march off anywhere unaccompanied. Emperors are careful about the clothes they wear. Company directors talk about earnings or growth, and we are expected to follow in a figurative, metaphorical sense. They tend not to give any orders. Without knowing for certain, we would venture to assert that not even generals give orders in the same way as before. Instead, they make decisions. But perhaps these are still a kind of order – 'same shit, different name', as we would have said not so long ago.

Every now and then, people are divided up into leaders and the rest, as if a leader were a specific type of person. The tabloids often talk about leaders and the led. But all talk about leadership has a ring of incantation to it. We want things to allow themselves to be led. And leadership development is a profitable industry, in which many want to learn universal remedies but few ask about boring things like demonstrable effects.

The question is whether leadership is a quality or a certain type of behaviour in those we call leaders. It would seem sensible to differentiate between the concepts. The designation 'leader' brings together a whole category of people around the same table. The extent to which leaders are similar to each other in any respect other than that they have been assigned the label of 'leader' is uncertain. The same could be said of everyone called Ivan. They don't have much in common other than that they are called Ivan. Perhaps one other example is that the vast majority of them are men. We will attempt in a moment to find out whether there are any common features that are often attributed to leaders.

'Leadership' is a concept that has its roots in the same metaphorical mycorrhiza as 'leader'. Both concepts derive from the same ideas. Leadership is not just about what leaders do, even though it might sound like this is the case. The sheer volume of literature in this field is almost crushing. We only had to turn our head to look over at the shelf full of American textbooks. Almost every textbook on management or organisational behaviour has at least one chapter on leadership.[151] There are great similarities in content between these sections.

One classic is Robert Blake and Jane Mouton's *The Managerial Grid*, published in 1964.[152] According to their model, leaders (or managers) can be involved in the task at hand and with their employees to varying degrees. The brackets are due to a minimal difference between the concepts of 'leader' and 'manager'. Leadership training often makes the point that those who have not undergone such training often mix up the two. This is the same as when auditors become indignant that the rest of us pay no heed to the distinction between expenditure, costs and payments. According to leadership trainers, a manager is the holder of an office and a leader is someone who leads. We can go along with the assertion that a manager is the holder of an office. We intend to discuss what leaders are in this chapter.

Most of our readers have probably come across the managerial grid model, even if they've forgotten about it. The idea was not new when Blake and Mouton wrote their best-seller. It can be traced back to what are known as the Ohio studies in the late 1940s.[153] According to the managerial grid model, the manager's behaviour and commitment can be divided up into two dimensions. He can be task-oriented to varying degrees, and he can be relationship or employee-oriented to varying degrees. Both dimensions are graded from one to nine. One signifies slightly or perhaps not at all, while nine is the maximum. According to the model, the ideal is to be a democratic leader. A democratic leader scores the highest value on both scales, and is designated 9:9. And then there are leaders whose commitment is focused entirely on their task and thus designated 1:9, and those who are committed solely to their employees, meaning a 9:1. And then, as you can imagine, there are all kinds of combinations. Someone has said that 5:5 would be average, but we wouldn't discount 6:3 as being just as good. The very worst would be a 1:1 leader, who according to Blake and Mouton has no commitment to either the one or the other. A 9:9 leader would be best in both the respects that are important according to the model. But we might wonder whether perhaps there could be a third or fourth dimension.

After Blake and Mouton came a number of individuals who used the managerial grid to present their own models. Paul Hersey and Kenneth Blanchard[154] are perhaps the best known. But for those of us who do not have as much patience for the basic model, it is simply tedious to find out that 1:1 leadership with weak commitment in both dimensions might be good if everyone knows their role.

The idea that a manager could be strongly committed to his work tasks without having the slightest interest in those who carry out the work is, however, a strange thought. The most extreme examples can be found in the trenches of the First World War. General x sends forth ten thousand men to take hill Y. All the soldiers get their heads blown off, and no hill is captured. You could say that he was only interested in his task, and not at all in his men. Far from it – his entire focus must have been on his men dying as men. The hill made no difference to him.

It can be hard to find any 9:9 or 1:9 leaders in reality. And even if we were to find people who unequivocally matched the definition, we would have a hard time demonstrating that one is better than the other. However, we can believe that there are people who don't care about most things (1:1), and this is more worrying. And anyway, we should be wary of generalisations.

The managerial grid model does have a kind of superficial credibility, and so it survives in textbooks and consultancy. But for those seeking usable theories, it appears worn out. It is too difficult to establish whether a person belongs to one category or the other. It is even more difficult to ascertain whether their leadership has been successful or not.

Everyday leadership

A number of amusing studies have been carried out into what leaders do during the day.[155] Their everyday life is not as grand as we might imagine. Most of their time is spent dealing with minor urgent issues, and they do not have any uninterrupted time for long-term strategy work. Nevertheless, it is likely that leaders' behaviour is of some importance to what happens in and with an organisation.

When we evaluate leadership, we usually look at what those who have been led have achieved. This is interesting when we want to find out whether an organisation fulfils its function. For those outside the organisation, the question of leadership is usually an internal affair of no interest to them. If leadership is evaluated on the basis of the performance of those who are led, this becomes an attribute of those who follow, not those who lead.

Someone once recounted the following tale about Maximilien de Robespierre. The truthfulness of it is a minor concern. One sunny afternoon in 1792, he sat as usual at a café, hatching his plans. After all, what else would one do with plans?[156] Suddenly, a noisy mob came rushing by in the street outside. The crowd was on its way to a dungeon where an aristocrat awaiting the guillotine was being held. Robespierre hurried to his feet and cried out: 'Those are my people. I must follow them, for I am their leader.'

It is not at all unreasonable to assume that Robespierre (1758–1794) was a leader. The simple point we are trying to make is that this doesn't say very much at all. Even those who have spent a long time studying the subject in great depth would doubt whether any rational and systematic knowledge about leadership exists at all.[157] We believe that this is going too far. However, commonly held notions lack evidence to determine, for example, which character traits or behaviours singled out by management literature are sufficiently typical to have any significance. The fact that so much advice and training is available for would-be leaders may be because it is lucrative. There is a demand, and there is now an entire leadership training industry willing to deliver. But it could also be because there is still something to teach. The world is not white, but nor is it entirely pitch black.

We agree with the contemporary organisational researchers who think that the concept of leadership should be less about people and more about relationships.[158] If we want to understand leaders better, the concept of leadership is problematic. One of our colleagues just stuck his head around the door. He was frustrated after a meeting. That's only natural. At the meeting, other colleagues had been calling for clear leadership. It was obvious, he believed, that they only wanted clear leadership so they could avoid taking responsibility for themselves. But they still wanted to keep their power.

We're always hearing amusing ideas and stories about leaders. Most of them are probably untrue – and it's a long time since we social scientists heard the truth. Let us see what we can find if we scratch away at the picture of the leader.

We recount stories about our own managers and other people's managers on a daily basis, and we always listen to such stories. If we are to call these stories fairy tales, then they are fairy tales for adults only.[159] Talking about other people is a fundamental human behaviour which is almost a fundamental need. Claes Gustafsson calls us 'homo garrulus', or chit-chatting man.[160] Those fellow men about whom we most like to talk to each other would appear to be our leaders. Perhaps the amount of gossip is an operative measure of the manager's status, although the content of what is said should perhaps also have some significance.

Theories have been formulated about leaders in the wake of the Modern Project. Most of these theories are a kind of refined small talk – stories about managers or leaders which are based on handed-down, archetypal basic narratives. We are fascinated by these theories because they connect to the archetypal basic narratives, not because they have any high explanatory value.[161]

A few words about human nature

Every kind of social science which enjoys any self-respect should be based on some kind of psychology. For the subject of psychology, this is a troublesome problem because essence and existence precede each other, or however Jean-Paul Sartre put it.[162] Some psychologists write as if their own psyche had nothing to do with their psychology.[163] Anyone who likes the idea of a grisly string of old classic psychological experiments should read Lauren Slater's book *Opening Skinner's Box*.[164] In other social sciences, the psychology of psychology is not easy to use in order to explain why, for example, the European Song Contest is such a big event or why the efficiency of the automotive industry varies from continent to continent. Psychologists' theories about people's attributes and the differences between them are too complex. So the rest of us normally take a more home-spun kind of psychology as our starting point.

If psychologists on the one hand have made the matter unnecessarily complicated, then economists on the other hand have based their theories on an overly primitive psychology. The latter assume, quite simply, that man makes rational decisions which benefit his own interests. When we look for the source of the idea of the economic man, we soon stumble across Adam Smith.[165] It is uncertain whether he was the first to have the idea of an economic player who maximises utility, but in 1784 he was an early proponent of this particular view of human nature.[166] When we were keen young students of the subject, we were initially flattered to be included in the wider community of clear-thinking, intelligent utility maximisers. But once the first wave of euphoria had evaporated, we reflected a little on some of the consumer decisions that vexed us. There were clothes that were uncomfortable and impossible to wash, and food that we didn't like but had bought anyway. More important decisions such as our choice of education (just think: economics ...) and housing were even worse. But sometimes they turned out all right. The question is simply whether it was our innate abilities that decided the outcome.

One possible explanation was that the blame lay with us. Mankind consists of all those clever utility maximisers, and then ourselves as the exception. But several of our acquaintances also didn't seem to be particularly clever, so that swelled the ranks a little. A division arose between the clever people on the one hand and our friends and ourselves on the other. Well, there are economists who maintain that mankind is bounded in his rationality, and there are plenty of highly tedious books about this.[167] Still, this limitation doesn't make it any easier to understand human choices. The crux of the matter is that even these theories are based on people being similar. Every theory that includes people must be based on them being different.

We would now like to put forward a differentiated psychology which explains why people are the way they are. One of the starting points for our simple model is that people are either intelligent or stupid. Psychologists have made the same observation, but have then argued over the matter to the degree that they maintain that this intelligence is scattered across the population according to a normal distribution function. This is the sort of scattering around the target that occurred when, in the olden days, people tried to hit a bull's eye with a cannon – or when we try to do the same with a modern pea-shooter.[168] The outcome is that psychologists assume that most of us are a bit semi-intelligent and a bit semi-stupid at the same time.

Some human qualities vary in accordance with normal distribution. Our height is normally distributed around the average value. We might then imagine that there is an ideal height for men and one for women, and that deviations from this ideal height can be regarded as flawed. If we replace ideal with most practical, the flaw lies not with the body. With intelligence, however, things are different. It is quite absurd to regard average intelligence as ideal or most practical. It would also be absurd to assume that the distribution is random.

Psychologists have also come to the conclusion that those who are most intelligent often do better in life than those who are stupidest. That sounds reasonable. If we assume that there is a fair covariance between intelligence and educational level, the matter can simply be considered as settled. Throughout the ages, things have turned out better for those who know their stuff.[169]

Let's play a little with the concept. The theory that people are usually somewhere in between does not correspond at all with what we see in everyday life. It is reasonable to assume here that people are either intelligent or stupid in roughly the same way that people are either under the age of forty or not. Many classifications into two categories come unstuck because there is something lying in between (for example, young and old) or because social constructions are mixed together with physical constructions (for example, men and women). Our classification could have been carried out on a scale, but for our purposes a division into two is more suitable.

Of course, there are qualities other than whether one is intelligent or stupid that may be important if we want to understand how people tick. What appears to be most important of all in everyday life is whether one is nice or nasty. In order to manage in life, we must constantly determine whether those fellow human beings with whom we transact or cooperate could conceivably have evil intentions. In the eyes of science, this question might almost represent a blind spot.

Although psychologists have developed advanced methods for testing the degree of semi-intelligence in all these aspects of human thinking, they are noticeably reticent regarding the moral dimension. There are now theories about empathy, and we can test the degree to which it is felt. The question is simply whether those people with a great deal of empathy are also nice. Those who empathise with others can easily exploit this feeling for evil purposes. The protagonist in Michael Winterbottom's film 'Code 46' contracted an empathy virus in order to use mind-reading to unmask the enemies of the state.[170] That wasn't a very nice thing to do. The opposite applies to violent criminals, who are usually portrayed by the media as lacking in empathy. When violence is part of everyday life, it is not necessarily true that lack of empathy is any greater than in, say, farmers. And if acts of violence are committed for the sake of entertainment, empathy would be a precondition. Only those who are afraid get anything out of horror films.

Political scientists have all manner of ideas about different political parties and ideologies, but have nothing to say about which of them are nice. Nevertheless, that is exactly what we want to know before we vote. Who is nice or nasty is a question of opinion and taste, replies the objective social scientist. But that's where he's wrong; clear objective criteria can be put forward for who is nasty. Here is a suggestion:

> – A nasty person is someone who prefers the misfortune of others to his own pleasure.

The vast majority of people have a certain degree of *Schadenfreude* in them. We howl with laughter when Stan Laurel falls over and hurts himself, and if our neighbour's new Ford gets a scratch, that's pretty funny too. For most of us, this Schadenfreude isn't so great that we wouldn't forgo the neighbour's car getting scratched if we could tuck into a cream cake instead. But then there are those who would far rather see blood than eat cake. Those are the ones we call nasty.

Whether those who choose the cake should really be called nice is, of course, uncertain. There's quite a difference between not caring about the neighbour's Ford and inviting him round to share our cream cake over a cup of coffee. But so as not to lose our momentum, let us agree for the time being that we can imagine dividing people up into those who are nice and those who aren't.

The situation is probably the same when it comes to nastiness. There's everything from the rotten types that most of us have in our circle of acquaintances to generals who are not satisfied with anything short of a total massacre. They are unpleasant in different ways, but they all come under the model of nastiness. In this way, the demarcation line is just as clear between intelligent and stupid as it is between nice and nasty:

> – Those who understand what is
> going on are intelligent.

At first glance, this criterion for intelligence might seem a little inadequate. We might assume that almost everyone understands what's going on. But for most people, life's changes come as a total surprise – after watching a detective show on TV, we might have to go back over it to work out what happened: 'So that's why he had an axe in the fridge ...' or: 'But I thought she was married to him – the one with the nose ...'. Sense-making is retrospective, according to a thinker we have read, and that works for us at least, but hindsight doesn't count if we're hoping for a place in the 'intelligent' category.[171]

Filling a two-by-two matrix with content

We now have two clear pairs of opposites: nasty and nice, and clever and stupid. That's all we need to put together a social scientific model. The two-by-two matrix is one of the most commonly used model types within social science, and it is ideal for our purposes. One classic two-by-two matrix is Nobel Prize Laureate Harry Martinson's analysis of the middle class. 'There are four kinds of middle class: 1) those with education and a piano, 2) those with education but no piano, 3) those with no education but with a piano, and 4) and those with neither education nor a piano.'[172]

Martinson placed his own parents in the latter (fourth) category. Harry Martinson (1904–1978) had a tragic childhood. He was orphaned at the age of six and grew up in the miserable circumstances offered by the rural poor relief of the time. After living a number of years as a vagabond and sailor, he achieved huge success both as a poet and as the author of a heartbreaking account of his childhood.[173] In later life he wrote an epic poem on the future of mankind; a pessimistic yet dazzling reconciliation with modernity.[174] He shared the 1974 Nobel Prize with Eyvind Jonsson.

Now, there are those who maintain that someone who is intelligent is also nasty. Being nice would, as it were, simply be another expression for being stupid or foolish. 'Why is the good man stupid? Why is the clever one evil? Why is everything in tatters?'[175] writes the downhearted poet. If we describe our fellow man as nice, he is then regarded with compassionate disdain as a feeble-minded being, unable to take care of himself. If instead we represent him as a nasty rogue, he is looked upon with a mixture of fear and admiration. But this is wrong.

According to our definitions, morality and intelligence are dimensions that are entirely independent of each other. It can no doubt also be empirically proven that all combinations exist. In this way, we represent – as you have probably already realised – a comparatively light and optimistic view of humanity. If there are people who are both intelligent and nice, then there is also hope for our world.

A two-by-two matrix is a figure – and after all this text, it's high time for an illustration.

The heroes – our ideal

For many of us, those people who are both nice and intelligent represent an ideal that is worth striving for. It therefore seems eminently suitable to call them 'heroes'. It is these people who smooth out all misunderstandings and put things right. 'Blicha, a colourful character and mother of seven who never went to school, is now treasurer of the group that deals with the villagers' loan applications,' wrote the Church of Sweden's relief organisation.[176] This in contrast to Måns' mother Anna, who is 'a worn-out mother of seven who once dreamt of a different life, but who, after years of

Intelligent

Conspirators	Heroes
Clientele	Regular folk

Nasty   Nice

Stupid

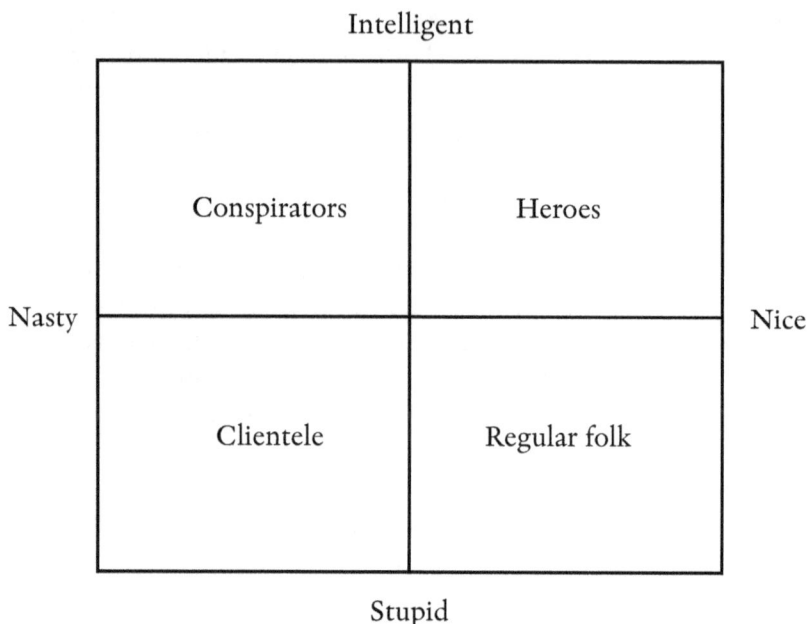

Figure 1: The two-by-two matrix illustrated.

hard work, hunger and childbirth, has grown ever more bitter and sick in spirit.'[177]

Heroes are people who succeed and who deserve our admiration. They achieve social progress from which we can all benefit. Without heroes, no society could function. Superman, Modesty Blaise[178], Marie Curie[179], Mohandas Karamchand Ghandi[180] and Madonna[181] are examples of such heroes – although Superman's intelligence is borderline and Madonna is probably not as nice as Ghandi was. But in both cases, they still qualify for inclusion under heroes.

Heroes need not necessarily be leaders. But they often lead. Stories about heroes feed our dreams about being saved from the dangers that threaten us, or save us simply from general feeling of melancholy about which we ourselves can do nothing.[182] Above all else, however, they make us dream about performing heroic deeds ourselves. Many books in management literature combine elements of poetry and science. Successful leaders are presented with detailed descriptions of what they have achieved and analyses of how they have got so far with niceness and intelligence.[183]

The problem often is that this becomes neither poetry nor science but rather success escapism. This literature serves as a source of inspiration for young careerists, but large doses of escapism do not lead to success. It can certainly be entertaining, but if it is interpreted as providing guidance for action the results will seldom be good.

Two sorts of clientele

If heroes are the ideal, then those who are both stupid and nasty will be their opposite. This is not a group to which one would want to belong. There are two sorts of clientele. One is what we would ordinarily call clientele. These are the types of people that you cross over the road to avoid if you see them when you're out and about. For the most part, this isn't a problem because they're easy to identify. They dress in a uniform-like get-up such as bomber jackets and army boots, which sends out such clear signals that even those who are stupid but nice cannot fail to spot them. Outside the organisational world, it is the clientele who often fall foul of the law. They cheat, steal and harass other people in such a ham-fisted manner that they get caught.

The other type of clientele is harder to recognise from a distance. This is not because these people have succeeded in concealing their nastiness, but simply because they have a different taste in uniforms. We do not see the objectionable qualities of these more affluent clientele until we come closer. The problems they pose do not attract the attention of the legal system. This is not because they cleverly avoid detection, but because they have different habits when it comes to fraud and harassment.

When these clientele commit their nasty deeds, they do so with such clumsiness that not even they themselves get any pleasure out of it. However, they do succeed in making others feel bad. Anyone who has had their home broken into will know what we mean. Typically, one comes back from holiday and finds that one's home has been ransacked. The thieves have taken an old stereo and a little bit of cash that was lying around. Clientele can just as easily ruin that visit to a smart restaurant to which the mother treats her family when she retires. The clientele buy on the black market, take up space, make a racket and sneer at our suburban manners in such a way that we wish we had stayed at home.

Both types of clientele can be compared with rattlesnakes. Venom has taken up some of the space in their heads that should have been used for something else. We can live with them and learn to deal with the risks they present. But if there are too many of them, it's hard to know where to step safely.

A great deal of research has been carried out on the highly visible clientele. Criminologists and sociologists study how they operate, and psychologists and educationalists try to devise methods to reform hooligans. The results are depressing. Prison doesn't make anyone nice, and therapy doesn't seem to help either.

There is no corresponding information about reforming the more affluent clientele. But there's nothing to suggest that making these nasty people nice would be any easier. In purely general terms, we think it should be possible to trick those who are stupid and nasty into being nice. So far, it doesn't seem to have worked. Nevertheless, it seems inconceivable that nastiness should be congenital. There are far too many nice parents with nasty children for us to be convinced by that genetic argument.

Worries about conspirators

Those people who are both intelligent and nasty play a central role in our world view. They are the ones who can practise their wickedness more cunningly. They are able to work out in advance what will happen, and how to achieve the maximum effect from their treacherous plans. We call the people in this category 'conspirators', since it is their capacity for the secret planning of nastiness that worries us.

Evil geniuses such as the Penguin in 'Batman' are commonly portrayed in world literature.[184] We often explain the course of history with reference to such evil geniuses. People can say: 'Hitler was a genius' in everyday conversation, in print[185] and (at least a few years ago) on the internet.[186] It is not likely that he actually was, but in explaining history this seems to be of no importance. Many explanations of the development of society make frequent use of conspiracy theories. For example, there is a kind of vulgar Marxism based on the bourgeoisie taking care of their class interests by organising the society and forming the state apparatus in a way that assists them with oppression and exploitation. The fact that oppression and exploitation occur is misinterpreted as a consummate plot. Nothing suggests that the bourgeoisie are this intelligent.

However, it is not only in the extreme political left that people believe in conspiracy theories. A group of mainly American economists explained in the early 1960s that behind the growth of the public sector lay a conspiracy between officials and politicians to further their own ambitions of power: the bigger the public sector, the more power its leaders would have.[187] The politicians were on board as long as it promoted their own goal: maximising the number of votes. This line of reasoning has a number of catches. Exposing oneself to public scrutiny, which one is forced to do as a politician, suggests shortcomings in terms of self-preservation instinct rather than conspiratorial capacity. Choosing the path of officialdom when the pay is restricted and the power is curtailed suggests that they were conspiring in the wrong sector. If, that is, they were conspiring at all and not operating with entirely different motives. And the suggestion that officials and politicians would form a specific group with common interests does not sound likely. The most important objection to the explanatory value of these conspiracy theories, however, is that the proportion of intelligent politicians and officials was probably no greater than that among those around them. Conspiracies that can be seen through are of no use for anything. Besides, it cannot be ruled out that people who are nice and who would therefore not take part in any conspiracy would be found among the intelligent public sector managers.

Ethnic groups and population groups are sometimes singled out as being particularly intelligent and nasty. Their conspiring explains the problems and frustrations that the rest of us wrestle with. They may be social democrats, freemasons, Jews or Jesuits. Less frequently, they may be Danish aviators.

Conspiracy theories come about in the form of both ideas in general circulation and social scientific theories. These stories can be found on the street and in the media. All conspiracy theories are based on an overestimation of the conspirators' nastiness and intelligence. That's not to say that there aren't conspirators, but there is a limit even to their planning abilities.

It is also likely that there are few of them. If there were many of them, the situation would be worse. But it's hard to know how many of them there are. They're not so stupid that they expose themselves. We can't avoid them like we can the clientele, because they don't advertise their nastiness.

However, the intelligent and nasty people are a problem for all the nice people. We can find examples in the world and in history where they have been particularly problematic. Many of those who are stupid and nasty can be dealt with, But it's a bigger problem if the intelligent and nasty people become more commonplace in society. Then there's a risk of being tricked so often that there's no longer any point in being a decent social citizen. The majority will not understand that the intelligent and nasty people have taken over, and will continue with their reasonably honest behaviour long after it has become unprofitable. The intelligent and nasty people can therefore dominate society for quite some time. One common example is Sicily and its Mafia.[188] If the nasty and intelligent people become particularly numerous, everything will grind to a halt and being nasty will also cease to be profitable. The idea of cultures regressing and declining due to general moral disintegration is not, therefore, entirely ridiculous.

Regular folk

The fourth category of people is those who are nice and stupid. It is among this type of people that we can feel at home and relaxed. When they reach middle age, regular folk often turn into the average man in the street who 'has general interests and enjoys walks in the forest and quiet evenings at home'. We call this category 'regular folk' because we believe that we are regular. The individual project has made many regular folk want to be unique. If they are simply nice and not too intelligent, they fit into the box whatever their age, beliefs and interests.

We regular folk do not appear to be particularly interesting, but there is still plenty of fiction written about us. It can be nice to read about people whose lives are roughly like ours, even though conspirators might offer more entertainment value. Nowadays, it is seen to be both desirable and politically correct to write and read about regular folk. Once upon a time, proper literature was supposed to deal with kings and not with regular folk – although kings too can be nice and stupid.

The problem is that regular folk are fairly invisible within social science. The psychologists have their normal distribution which leads us nowhere, and the economists have their utility maximising which assumes we are intelligent. Some political scientists regard much of the population as ignorant voters, but they don't get anywhere with that view. This is a large unploughed field for social science.

We can imagine exposing regular folk to reforms and attempts at improvement in the same way that we try to reform the violent clientele. Our motivation would be not to make us nice, but to make us intelligent – the knowledge society requires more people to be able to deal with the complex problems that need to be resolved in a postmodern, high-tech society. But the sad truth is that we don't become particularly smart just because we've learnt administrative law and double entry bookkeeping or whatever is included in a long and laborious education these days. It's more likely that a long education will make us nice. Putting up with educating oneself until the age of almost thirty requires divine patience and oceans of goodwill. These qualities develop during one's education. The effect on the more cognitive side of learning double entry bookkeeping would, however, seem to be restricted to being able to actually do double entry bookkeeping.

Ambitions

The two-by-two matrix in Figure 1. has been filled with content, field by field. There is more to be said about the numbers and ambitions of those represented in it. It is not equally desirable to occupy just any position in the matrix. For example, it is reasonable to assume that it is not as desirable to be a clientele as it is to be a hero. For most people, the hero category appears to be the one to which they themselves would like to belong. The heroes do not actually have any reason to pretend that they belong to any category other than that to which they do, although a degree of modesty is becoming.

Regular folk look up to and admire those heroes who are able to carry out their good intentions. It is natural for them to try to imitate their heroes. If at times we also try to appear as heroes to those around us, this can surely be forgiven.

The conspirators can be expected to despise the heroes rather than admiring them. Nevertheless, it is common for them to try to appear as heroes, since being regarded as a conspirator is not helpful. When trying to dupe the rest of the world, the process involves concealing one's intentions, and it is hard to imagine a better disguise than a heroic reputation. Some conspirators try to appear like regular folk but pretending to be nice is easier than acting stupid.

The clientele do not have the same admiration for the heroes as regular folk do, nor do they see the advantages of appearing to be nice. However, it is likely that they admire the conspirators. The conspirators themselves have seen the disadvantages of outwardly appearing to be conspirators, and we shouldn't therefore expect them to brag about their exploits. Those who brag about how they have exploited and tricked their fellow men by cleverly taking advantage of their stupidity and weakness are in fact clientele, and are usually no more intelligent than you are.

In Figure 2, arrows indicate the ambitions we can expect to be held by those in the various categories. To avoid the need for another figure later on, it also anticipates the forthcoming discussion on numbers.

Numbers

We have already hinted that the population's distribution within the matrix would be interesting and possible to estimate. The latter is only partly true. In order to arrive at the numbers, we assume that one can be nasty or nice, regardless of whether one is intelligent or stupid. The question is then how many nasty people there are in society, and how many intelligent people there are.

Using the criteria we set, it is likely that there are many more stupid people than intelligent people. Let us propose the hypothesis that ninety percent of us are stupid, and ten percent are intelligent. This may be an overestimation of the number of intelligent people, but this minority must reasonably contain a significant number otherwise social development would grind to a halt completely.

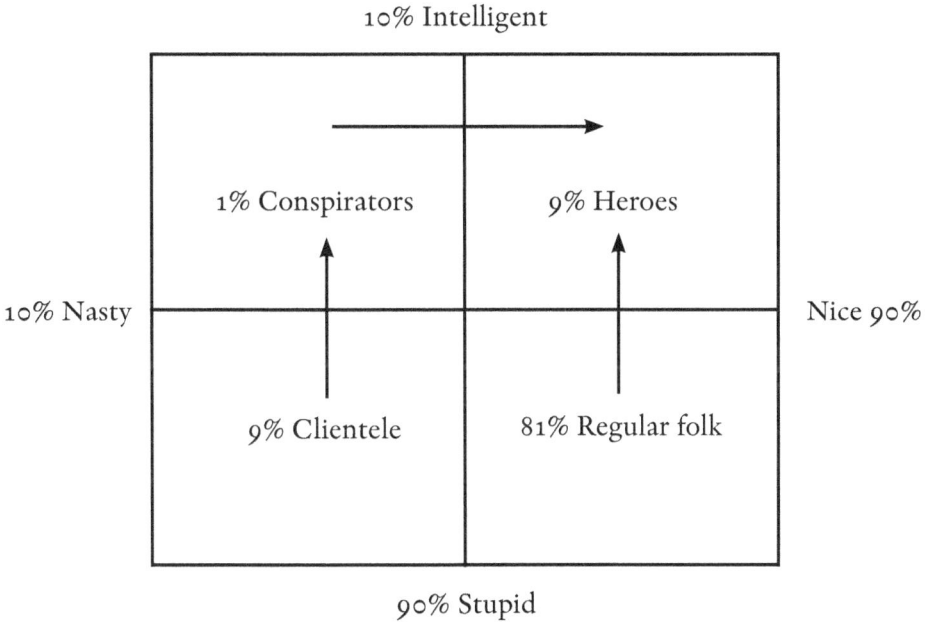

Figure 2: The two-by-two matrix, with estimated population pro-portions and arrows indicating ambitions.

   The group of nasty people cannot be that large, as society is still functioning. Let us therefore propose the corresponding hypothesis that ten percent of the population are nasty, and ninety percent are nice. Assuming that the qualities of nice and nasty do not correlate with the qualities of intelligent and stupid, the proportions of the four categories can then be easily calculated. This gives nine percent heroes and the same number of clientele. As expected, regular folk are by far the most common, making up eighty-one percent of the population, with conspirators accounting for just one percent.

   Although this is based on rash assumptions, the distribution does not appear to be entirely unreasonable. Society has counted the visible clientele. They are easily distinguishable, because they have no desire to hide their nastiness and cannot hide their stupidity. What's more, they are registered in a convenient way when they get caught. Nine to ten percent of the population has fallen foul of the law.[189] Half of these are probably regular folk who have committed transgressions by mistake and without evil intentions.

A few individual conspirators will also end up here. If we assume that the more affluent clientele who are not caught by the police are just as many in number as the visible clientele, our hypothesis of nine percent is given a certain degree of support.

The conspirators must also be few in number. One percent of the population can get up to a great deal of mischief. But if there were many more, we would have given up on social development already. There are probably some grandiose conspiracies, but since the process of developing our society and its institutions continues, one percent may be a reasonable guess.

The leaders take their place in the matrix

The above model has its weaknesses. It may well be that people have other important qualities, and classic humanism probably has a point in that nice and nasty are properties we all possess. And just how we can establish that one particular person falls into a certain corner and someone else into another is unclear – in spite of the demarcation criteria. We have not created any robust theory about human nature, and nor did we intend to do so.

It is not the lack of weaknesses but the strengths that have led us to present this model. It is accurate enough to have an interesting influence on the discussion of leadership theory. Many people have a theory about how something or another works which affects their work and their life in general. Everyone has a theory about leadership. Usually a bad theory. Some show a lack of judgement by publishing their theories about leadership in books and journals. Some call their leadership theories 'leadership theories', while many others give their theories different names. Almost all the leadership theories we know of are based on some simple psychology that can be accommodated within our two-by-two matrix with a little dexterity. One theory which is readily put forward is that leaders should be intelligent and nice, although this is far from certain. Let us now make a few points as the beginning of a systematic review.

Herrings and hooligans

Theories based on the leader being nasty and stupid can be found in critical organisation studies, for example. Mats Alvesson offers a description of how a manager uses primitive scare tactics to push his changes through.[190] Studies of what is deemed to be successful implementation often show leaders who have taken a tough line or got others to do so.[191]

The theory of stupid and nasty leaders is widespread among professional organisations. In connection with field studies within many parts of the public sector, we have often ended up in the break room. Countless conference days have also been punctuated with discussions over salmon and cake. In the everyday conversations we have listened to and taken part in, someone's promotion is often justified by the person in question being so incompetent that his only use is as a pen-pusher. What's more, he's so nasty that he goes along with his being promoted to manager. Overnight, good friends and competent colleagues become despicable swines.

The comic strip character Dilbert[192] is another example of the theory that the stupidest and nastiest people become managers. Dilbert is constantly forced to degrade himself and subject himself to power-wielding which is arbitrary and incomprehensible at best, but is more often cruel and incompetent. The Pointy-Haired Boss can sit in a meeting and say: 'This thankless assignment shall go to whomever asks a question or makes eye contact.'[193]

Until recently, we thought that the above alternatives exhausted the possibilities offered by the box containing nasty and stupid leaders. That was before it became all the rage to see psychopaths as indispensable when bold routes needed to be carved out. The founder of one of the much-hyped IT companies said in an interview that it was mostly by chance that he became a manager instead of a bank robber.[194] He appears not to have been intelligent enough to have come up with this himself. Wasn't it John Lennon who first made this declaration famous?

It's like with herring. You're standing on a rock in an archipelago and catch sight of a large shoal of herring moving with amazing synchronicity. Something flashes deep down, and all the fish change direction. Another flash, and another new direction. It's quite incredible, and is probably due to the strong social instinct of herring. If you catch a herring and remove its social instinct by cutting off part of its cerebrum, the herring loses its social instinct but not necessarily its ability to swim. Any intelligence also seems to be lost. If you then release the herring back among all the others, it swims away without worrying for a moment where the rest of the shoal are headed. And then of course, all the others swim after it. Here, the brainless herring leads the entire shoal. A biologist to whom we told this story doubted that it would be possible to carry out this experiment in practice, and we wouldn't want to try anyway.

The lessons learned from the example of the herring have not come into regular use when it comes to recruiting leaders, and for that we should be thankful. If we put more and more faith in character traits and extreme attributes, recruiting psychopaths as leaders is not far off. Attending a suitable university is currently the preferred qualification for senior positions in industry, rather than committing murder with robbery. But imagine the job adverts of the future: 'Hooligan with motorbike sought for senior position in large municipal geriatric care authority. You should be a dynamic person who is prepared to make unpleasant decisions. Applications should be sent to Mean Recruitment Ltd.'

It's easy to find examples of leaders who were psychopaths: King Charles XII of Sweden (1682–1718), for example, who not only in terms of military leadership but also in terms of judgement and as a human being demonstrated evidence of a combination of stupidity and almost fanatical nastiness. Perhaps that is why it is also easy to find complaints about psychopaths being managers.[195] If truth be told, it is mostly warnings rather than recommendations that we find when it comes to the study of psychopathic leaders in leadership literature.

One snag with the psychopath theory is that the list of common psychopathic traits is insufficient. Psychopaths often give a charming first impression, have delusional self-images and lie to their wives and mistresses. The list is particularly problematic when it comes to examples of psychopathic managers.[196] We are affected by the same kind of hypochondria that Jerome K. Jerome described so well in his book about three men and a dog (Montmorency) in a boat on the Thames, and later on bicycles, in the late 19th century. In *Three Men in a Boat*, J. – the narrator – recalls how he had read a medical book about all manner of diseases. In a moment of dark self-insight, he realised that he was suffering from all the diseases described – except housemaid's knee.[197]

Stories about psychopaths at work tend not to be particularly grisly. Perhaps the people described in leadership literature as psychopathic managers would have been really bloodthirsty given the chance. Common scoundrels are probably often made of the same stuff as mass murderers. We cannot unravel the matter here, but will make the assertion that stories about psychopaths are in fact stories about people who appear to be nasty and perhaps also stupid, but who are usually unpleasant rather than diabolical.

If you want some examples of leaders (or managers) who are psychopaths, history provides some excellent illustrations of how stupidity and nastiness can be combined to create powerful leadership. King Charles XII, whom we mentioned a moment ago, was a real leader. He galloped forward at the head of his ranks, his sword drawn and without any circumspection, and exposed both himself and his men to the most foolhardy dangers. He was convinced that his army would follow him anywhere. King Charles is described by biographers such as Frans G. Bengtsson as being idolised by his men.[198] Bengtsson's biography concludes as follows:

> But the formidable warrior slept on, unmoved by all that came after him; in the calm bronze majesty of his sarcophagus, as if he had been immortalised in a state of exalted indifference and irrevocable serenity. He was one of the last and the greatest to enter the kingdom inhabited by the Lords of God's Grace.[199]

Hero worship indeed! Still, Bengtsson's biography of King Charles XII has been 'extolled as our foremost historical biography'[200] and criticised only for its 'aesthetical bias'.[201] Other much written-about figures in the same genre include Napoleon and General (George Armstrong) Custer. And perhaps that's as it should be. Leaders who stand at the head of their flock and who are not simply tour guides must be both stupid and nasty. What this then says about those who allow themselves to be led is something we will return to on another occasion.

Cesare Borgia

Many entertaining stories are all about people who are nasty and intelligent. The horror movie genre includes such coldly calculating and yet passionate mass murderers as Hannibal Lecter.[202] But we're supposed to be writing about leaders, not villains of the silver screen. Still, is it possible to be both leader and a conspirator? And if so, will one be beloved of others?

King Charles XII earned the epithet of being beloved on account of – not in spite of – being stupid. Niccolò Machiavelli poses the question of the love of the people in *The Prince*,[203] in which he wonders whether it is an advantage for a prince to be loved rather than feared, or whether that prince should be feared rather than loved. He concludes that the love of the people is all well and good, but that it is better to be feared. Just as we thought. The quest for love is futile – for princes, at least.

Machiavelli was a great admirer of Cesare Borgia (1475–1507).[204] The Borgias were a princely family on the Italian peninsula who, during the Renaissance, were closely involved in the power struggles of Italy. Two members of the family became Popes. Cesare was appointed by his father Alexander II to a position of some eminence by which he would lay his hands on a couple of principalities. He inspired Machiavelli's admiration, but was nevertheless forced to flee to Spain. He was imprisoned and died in exile. How intelligent can he have been?

Machiavelli aroused admiration and loathing on the part of his contemporaries, and the kings of Sweden tried to follow his advice as best they could. But wasn't King Eric XIV of Sweden (1533–1577) mad rather than nasty? It's hard to know for sure. He may simply have been a brutal player of power games among other brutal players of power games.[205] Whether he and other kings during the Renaissance succeeded in living up to the ideal of conspirators and evil geniuses is uncertain. They lived in cruel times, and certainly some of them endeavoured to follow Machiavelli's advice and directions.

When Antony Jay writes about management in the style of Machiavelli in our time (well, in 1967), he is not talking about being nasty or conspiratorial.[206] Instead, he points out that Machiavelli based his recommendations on experience. Recommendations for modern managers should also be founded on studies and analyses of one's own experience and that of others. We can only agree, but we now find ourselves stranded with a theory about leadership that does not seem as evil as we had hoped it would. Big deal: we had considered dismissing the conspirators' theory as unreasonable anyway.

Heroes in films

Heroes are, according to our definition of the role, nice and intelligent. When we have come this far and are ready to fill the box with some examples, we are glad we didn't choose 'good'. But it may still be worth thinking about the concept. Goodness feels like an extremely unusual quality. When we think about which sorts of people could be characterised as good and intelligent, and could also be leaders, the good mother is our first choice.

Male figures who have been credited with goodness either have a religious leaning or have helped the needy. The latter has now become a profession that does not require goodness. Those who are too empathic are surely quick to burn out when their resources are unable to match the need and good advice is lacking. When it comes to religious leaders, goodness is now always assessed according to sect affiliation.

We have written about leaders in films in other contexts.[207] We won't be discussing them again here. It can be noted that leaders in films are not particularly common. There are plenty of managers. But those who exercise any leadership are rarer. They're always doing something else when the camera's running. Greeting their colleagues, driving home from work and beating their children.

Heroes, in contrast, are more common in films. However, they are often not leaders. The typical film hero is a lone wolf. He puts things right and hopes to get the girl by the end of the film. En route to a happy ending, he often makes his fair share of mistakes, proving that he's no more intelligent than the audience. As luck would have it, he also has a body that can take a beating.

Intelligent and nice leaders can still be found in films. The football coach played by Al Pacino in 'Any Given Sunday' is neither particularly intelligent nor very nice in private.[208] But what he does at work is both of these things.[209] It's worth noting that one might have to imagine a person of many parts in order to find a leader who can play the role of the hero. The media's hunt for scandals means that fewer and fewer people meet the requirements. Generally speaking, scandals are usually due to a lack of private intelligence. In Sweden, the easiest way to get embroiled in a scandal is to use your employer's funds for your own private purposes and in an improper manner.[210] This often involves relatively small sums of money, making the whole thing seem stupid.

The film 'Elizabeth' throws a different light on niceness.[211] When it comes to the protagonist, there's no doubting her intelligence,[212] but can it be nice to have people executed left, right and centre? No one has done more for England than Queen Elizabeth I (1533–1603). Can we look kindly on the matter, on the organisation or on the majority who permit nastiness against other individuals?

Sometimes the degree of niceness is hard to determine. Martin Beck in the eponymous detective films is certainly reasonably intelligent.[213] After a while, he knows what's going on, and often before we do. But is he actually nice? He's certainly not nasty. Perhaps he is therefore sufficiently nice, but if we had required goodness then Beck wouldn't have had a chance in hell.

The Sun King

The most common leadership theories are those that are based on leaders being regular folk. This is an effect of not only supply but also demand. Desires for leaders who are nice and intelligent are common. You can't look for a stupid and nice manager via job adverts. In practice, however, we normally have to make do with an ordinary person being prepared to shoulder the responsibility. In fact, we may well think that we have just such a manager.

Management training is based on being able to teach people to become leaders. The basic assumption is that it should be possible to train the would-be leaders to lead in the right way through providing the right training. The concept is simple. We bring together a group of people of management material at a remote conference centre and give them a thorough workout. A few days of insulting and unpleasant initiation rites leads to almost a natural selection process. Those who are compliant enough to submit to this treatment and stupid enough to believe that it's doing them good will progress in their careers.

This is perhaps rather a drastic description, even if there are problems with the content of management training courses. In the past (the 1980s), management training courses were too narrow and specialised – if Dag Björkegren is to be believed.[214] Now we tend rather to believe that management training courses have turned into an instrument of delusions of grandeur, which Mats Alvesson believes are a prominent feature of our age.[215]

One example that might raise a few eyebrows is King Louis XIV of France (1638–1715), or the Sun King as he was known.[216] He became king at the age of just four, and assumed administrative power once his guardian – Cardinal Jules Mazarin – had died. His long reign (seventy-two years) coincided with France's glory days. At that time, France was the richest and most powerful nation in Europe. The Sun King was, like the Swedish King Charles XII, a divinely appointed dictator. The actual idea of someone having such mighty royal power may have been French, but he didn't come up with it himself. He may have been an absolute ruler, but he was never alone. He was constantly surrounded by court officials, advisers, women, mistresses, and legitimate and illegitimate children, as well as architects, artists, generals, priests and physicians.[217] His upbringing revolved around the fact that he would become supreme ruler, and Cardinal Mazarin oversaw his education.

In many ways, Louis' life was a dazzling display. France confirmed her position as a great power, and Versailles grew into the biggest and most splendid palace ever imaginable. The wars went reasonably well, albeit not brilliantly. Peter Burke also shares the opinion that Louis' life was a display, describing the Sun King as providing a theatrical performance.[218] The king himself enjoyed performing on stage in his youth, but as he grew old and religious he lost interest even in watching plays.

The Sun King was intentionally portrayed as a mass media product. For example, there are so many magnificent portraits of him that he must have spent a great deal of his life posing. He didn't play the role of king entirely on his own. The theatrical production was in fact a joint effort: he received advice and directions from many sources, and there were officials who were entitled to sign his name. The fact that he did not write all his letters himself is not surprising, although when we learn that even his love letters were ghost-written, we see that Louis the individual was not particularly important. The notion that he was King by Divine Right had been instilled into him, and his contemporaries no doubt regarded him as such. There are also anecdotes about his whims and fancies. And yet he still comes across as relatively modest. He did as Cardinal Mazarin had taught him. When he became religious, he followed the instructions of his second wife, Madame de Maintenon (1635–1719) – at any rate when it came to matters of religion. The abolition of the Edict of Nantes (1685) is, on the whole, the nastiest thing he did, and that was on Madame Maintenon's request! By this act, freedom of religion was no more and the Huguenots fled to America – those that could.

The Sun King did as he had been told. He also followed the advice of contemporary medical science, which hardly suggests that he made decisions for himself, although it may suggest courage. They pulled out his teeth so heavy-handedly that his upper jaw was damaged, as a result of which he had difficulty eating for the rest of his life. He also took a monthly prescribed laxative of such explosive effect that he had to stay in his room for a day or two. And of course, he wasn't alone in there, either. We haven't gone to the trouble of finding out just how many people assisted in what we would imagine to be fairly private business.

King Louis' life is extremely well documented, and if he ever acted or expressed himself in a way that would suggest intelligence, we have not learnt of it. He didn't even come up with: 'L'état, c'est moi' ('I am the state') himself. However, a good education had made him competent and his administration was effective. Whether he really was as stupid and nice as the rest of us we cannot tell for certain, but there is nothing to suggest otherwise. As far as the French are concerned, he may as well have been. He would have been an even better person were it not for all his delusions of grandeur.

What we need is more managers and fewer leaders

'Where will it all end?' ask those who love order. Why not where it all started? Leaders are not the only ones the rest of us follow. By presenting a simple model, leaders have become both greater and fewer in number. The metaphor has been broken up and tested. That's good enough, in our opinion. Our closing remarks will be prescriptive: What does it matter if this is how it is? It's time for an example.

Leaders are popular. We're particularly passionate about leaders who are not formally appointed managers. This involves the idea of natural leadership on the part of informal leaders instead of managers. We have previously argued against this.[219] Informal leaders are often self-appointed, and have power and authority without their also having the accountability that goes with it. Therein lies a problem. Back in the early 1900s, Henri Fayol formulated the simple administrative principle that accountability and authority should go hand-in-hand.[220] Anyone who is entitled to make decisions or wield influence should also be accountable. And anyone who is held accountable should in all reason have the opportunity to influence those things for which responsibility is demanded. Fayol's principle isn't bad. But we breach it from all directions by accepting leaders who cannot be held formally responsible. At the same time, flat organisations have created a proletariat of people responsible for results but lacking authority.[221]

However, the real problem *with* – and in many cases *for* – having informal leaders lies in the fact that they do not have access to managerial tools for maintaining their positions and achieving the desired action. Nor do they have access to leadership training in the same way that most managers do. Informal leaders must find, maintain and construct their repertoire of leadership tools themselves. Here is a significant but relatively overlooked explanation for adult bullying[222] in organisations.[223]

People who have been subjected to bullying are more likely to be affected by exclusion and stress-related absence from work than is the population in general.[224] The fact that people burn themselves out and collapse is a problem associated with the work environment that has attracted considerable attention in recent years. This burnout involves costs for those affected, those around them, their workplaces and society as a whole.

The problem of bullying in the workplace has in Sweden been confirmed by statistics provided by the Swedish Work Environment Authority.[225] Of those work-related illnesses reported to the Authority in some years ago, 1,250 cases – corresponding to around 5 percent of the total number – were caused by bullying or harassment. The average period of reported sickness was around 250 days for men and 210 days for women. A conservative estimate of the annual cost would be at least SEK 250,000,000. Counting the number of people who are bullied is hard. A publication by the Swedish Work Environment Forum dating from 2002 (sorry) put the figure at 340,000.[226] As far as we can see, no one believes they are few in number today.

The costs incurred by bullying are, however, only related to those people who have been directly affected. Other effects include qualified people leaving, productivity falling and a drop in creativity and innovation.[227] Not only do the victims of bullying often feel extremely stressed, so too do those who witness it.[228]

There is cause to believe that there are more reasons for adult bullying to occur than those found by the research on bullying that normally attracts attention. One reason is that this research has mostly studied bullying in schools, among children and young adults. Also, the focus in both research and practice has often been on trying to nip things in the bud, rather than looking for answers to questions about why bullying actually occurs. A long line of legislation, action plans and procedural manuals have been produced, aimed at combating bullying as a phenomenon. The methods have been based on the existing research, which has had two main focuses: the personal qualities of both the bully and the victim, and the distribution and exercise of power and control in social interaction.[229] Björn Eriksson notes that the research carried out includes too few questions and too many statements.[230]

Organisational research has a tradition of looking for explanations of the personal destinies of people in the workplace by using phenomena that are external to the individual. We believe that the lack of managers and the prevalence of leaders who are not managers creates the ideal conditions for workplace bullying. Bullying takes place primarily not for fun but for informal leaders to be able to hold on to power and influence.[231] Bullying is a way of building up and maintaining an informal but supremely reliable powerbase.

There are studies which show that the organisation itself and organisational practice are perceived by employees as bullying.[232] This points in the same direction as our research. It is thin and flat organisations in particular that are perceived in this way.[233] But as Charlotte Rayner *et al.* point out, it is people who bully in organisations, not the organisations themselves.[234]

In an empirical example, Rayner *et al.* showed how bullying increased within a manufacturing company. The system of autonomous teams had been introduced, and at the same time the office of foreman had been abolished. The teams were rewarded according to their performance, and a climate grew up within the teams whereby those who were not deemed to be sufficiently fast were isolated from the rest and excluded from their team's decision-making. Despite the fact that management noticed this trend, the HR department was not allowed to intervene. Since the leaders within the teams did not have access to the company's formal system of control, they used the instruments to which they did have access in their attempts to improve performance. The teams used bullying to get rid of those members who were seen to be having a negative effect on productivity. Other studies also show that bullying is used to flush out colleagues. According to Denise Salin, this explains the relatively high prevalence of bullying she observed within the Finnish public sector following the restructuring of the 1990s.[235]

Clear, formal leadership as exercised by managers therefore appears to result in employees feeling at ease. One unfortunate paradox is that this type of leadership goes hand-in-hand with the dream of having a strong leader. This in turn soon leads to the strong leader crushing whatever entrepreneurial, free and informal spirit exists. And that, if anything, makes us all feel ill at ease.

5. The Ancient Greek Resistance

Change is a concept that has lost some of its power. We have forgotten its basic meaning. Instead, we use the word as a faded metaphor[236] of the kind that Esaias Tegnér reflected on in his 1819 inaugural address to the Swedish Academy:

> ...the image, like the rocket, burns only once: when it returns, it is dead. With every year that passes, a whole family of the airiest forms dies out. Oh behold the languages! What do they impart to us? A gallery of faded metaphors.[237]

Faded or not, change is a word which clearly instils confidence in spades. The current 2014 US President, Barack Obama, succeeded in being elected on the basis of his promise of change, despite his failing to take particular care to reform the healthcare system, and despite delivering his shining promise of a changed and potentially better world without explaining just what would be changed. Change was a fundamental value and was to do with everything and nothing, and change would come about with the aid of modern theories of change.[238] Obama was eloquent and convincing in arguing, for example, in favour of reforming healthcare.[239] The fact that a shining promise of a changed and potentially better world is hard to deliver is something that Obama has hardly been the first to learn.[240]

Many of the experiences gained from holding evaluation workshops give a complicated picture. The reports tend to have titles along the lines of 'Failing to meet expectations'. Many people may have been in favour of change when no change has been achieved.

In this book, we use different strategies to escape from the grasp of metaphors or to make use of metaphors ourselves. Sometimes assistance may be needed in order to move forward. We will see here what the Greeks of antiquity can offer. They ought to be of some use other than just for philosophical mental gymnastics.

To give our critical analysis a little more bite, we will try to argue against what we know many people are in favour of: change. 'Things are fine as they are, thanks' is the heroic reply when a manager wants to introduce change. This resistance to change is seen to be something very serious, and is dealt with at great length in change literature.[241] We want to show solidarity with the powerless victim of the forces of change – in other words, he who is slow to change – and to take part in the popularly rooted resistance against change.

Being in favour of change is often the same as being at the bidding of those in power, and we have no desire to be that if we don't get better pay. Reform comes about from the top, and much of the implementation work involves crushing resistance with massive internal marketing and instruments of force. Follow the white rabbit, or be left alone in the Matrix.[242] Stay a happy sheep.

> The Lord is my shepherd; I shall not want.
> He maketh me to lie down in green pastures:
> he leadeth me beside the still waters.[243]

However, it is not so easy to argue against change if you fail to understand what it is. And the word 'change' is hard to understand. If we are to assume the discomfort of being regarded as old conservative and reactionary, we should at least find out what this concept of change involves. And then, perhaps, we can also do away with the preconception that the old are more conservative than the young.

The word 'change'

The word 'change' is easy to understand in situations such as colour change or even personality change. From these, we can draw conclusions about acids and alkalis or choose our words with care when speaking with a person with an altered personality. Something becomes something else. In these contexts, change can be regarded as something with a literal meaning. Perhaps.

Organisational change, however, is a metaphor, and is usually a pretty vague metaphor. There's nothing strange about that. Management literature uses plenty of other vague and mysterious concepts. Take, for example, the word 'process'. It can mean almost anything. But no one pays particular attention to that. When we hear that we ought to be more process-oriented, the normal reaction is: 'Yes, of course, that would be good.' And what else can we say on learning that:

> When we work with our clients' process development, we cover all the areas included in the change process, from mapping current ways of working to analysing and developing new processes. We guide you by involving every affected part of the company, and also try to extend the processes to include your customers and your suppliers. Broad operational support is essential in order to achieve successful results.[244]

So reads a website trying to sell process improvement. Processes can be absolutely anything and everything. What we do, for example. The term doesn't leave us any the wiser, and nor does that seem to be the intention. And yet – or, perhaps, for that very reason – we are able to see process orientation as the foundation for the organisations of the future,[245] or we maintain that 'focusing on the operational processes ... [was ...] the dominant management method during the 1990s'.[246] It still is it seems.

'Process control' is another common process concept. A management consultant comes home from a study visit within the processing industry and starts dreaming. Perhaps she has returned from a visit to a company in the cellulose industry, a sewage works or a chemical manufacturing company. Perhaps she has seen the application of a mass production technique in the automotive industry, or a specific variant in the construction sector. She has probably seen well-defined chemicals running through the right tube, day after day, according to a predetermined plan. Automatically, and under precise control, the mixture was combined and processed to give a predetermined and entirely standardised end product. Perhaps the consultant had got out of bed on the wrong side, or perhaps she was just having one of those days. She thinks for a while and finds the answer: medical care.[247] It wasn't too long ago that the patient had become customer. Now the customer should become a process. Where will it all end?

Change, on the other hand, is a word that can arouse passion. When we ask our students what work they want to do in the future, many of them reply: 'Change!' without a trace of irony. After having heard such a reply, we can sit for half the afternoon and wonder what on earth they meant. Still, it's certainly true that they could earn a living as a change consultant. No one seems to think that there's anything odd about that. 'But change from what to what?' is a question which shows that the questioner hasn't understood anything. Or he has, as the case may be.

The most typical thing about change is how easy it is to talk at cross-purposes. For example, it is common for people to talk about change in the third person. It's always someone else who should change. When the CEO announces dramatic changes within the company, it's unlikely that he's planning to leave. And this is hardly likely to be because he is so modest that he wouldn't see his own departure as a major change, although there might be a great deal of truth in this insight. No, he actually means that the company will be winding down production in Malmö, outsourcing the IT function and dismissing everyone over the age of 52. The further the remove from head office, the more dramatic the change.

Sometimes the word 'change' means nothing at all, such as when all the virtues listed in a job advert include the stipulation that applicants 'should be well inclined towards change'. What an absurd outlook such an inclination must be based on. As if all change is good? A not insignificant proportion of all the world's changes and opportunities for change go under the name of deterioration. Some changes can mean an improvement. But then one begins to wonder whether life should be based on preventing the former sort of change and possibly trying to promote the latter.

Nor should we forget that there are areas of life where stability has a value in itself. People whose job it is to keep track of rules and follow rules so that consumers and citizens receive equal treatment should, of course, be only moderately inclined towards change. Internal auditors, surveyors and football referees should not simply agree to change their opinions according to the time of day or the situation. We understand that a football referee may be less inclined to penalise the home team when a bloodthirsty mob in the stands is threatening murder and annihilation, but we do not believe that this is due to an inclination towards change; it's more likely to be a self-preservation instinct. And that's something we shouldn't be too inclined to change.

Pessimists and optimists

Change is inevitable. Nothing lasts forever, and things might be getting better and better, day by day. Otherwise, we often hear that things were better before. If we are to map different attitudes towards change, dividing people up into optimists and pessimists might not be a bad idea.

Those who try to describe this kind of mentality at different times in history often point out that, during the Middle Ages, historical developments were often described as being in decline. It was thought that mankind had already had its golden age. Classical antiquity is one period suggested for when this age may have been. The more relics there are from the time in question, the harder it is to be nominated. The theme of the golden age crops up in every possible context. The golden age of music was during the time of Ludwig van Beethoven (i.e. 1770–1827). Or was it when Benny Goodman (1909–1986) was the King of Swing?[248] In any case, nothing of any value has been achieved since the Eurythmics split up at the end of the 1980s.[249] As many of our acquaintances will agree. If we didn't know how progressive they actually are, we would brand them all as hopeless pessimists and reactionaries.

After the Middle Ages came the Modern Age. Or rather the Modern Project, as it is now known. This is when the history of mentality says optimism was on the increase. Mankind's development consisted of advances rather than decline. Everything would be better later on. Then there would be no more soldiers and no more guns.[250] Thomas Moore gave a name to the most unrestrained faith in progress with his book *Utopia*.[251] And even if utopia stands for something unrealistic and naïve, it is still fantastic how many

people have suffered and died for doctrines in which the golden
age of man is yet to come. The most attractive utopia was probably
communism. This would lead to a new type of man arising in a
society free from classes and oppression. Mario Vargas Llosa's tale
of Flora Tristán, who lived from 1803 until 1844, presents a read-
able picture of personal sacrifice for faith in utopian socialism.[252]
Communism was a variation of the Modern Project's optimism in
development. Science and reason would prevail, and no one would
be unhappy. It didn't turn out well.[253] The communist utopia featured a beauty that blinded many. The true greats of world literature include many authors such as Jean-Paul Sartre, Harold Pinter
and Pablo Neruda, who looked the other way when this utopia
proved to be its opposite.

Nowadays the optimism of the Modern (well, not particularly
modern) Age regarding progress is questioned by postmodernists
and like-minded people. They say that history has no direction or
goals. The tale of civilisation's development and progress is certainly entertaining, but there are other tales that are at least as good,
according to Jean-François Lyotard.[254] His book *Postmodern Fables*
includes a number of diverting examples.[255] Georg Henrik von
Wright maintains that the myth of progress is just that – a myth.[256]

Part of our modern-day problematisation of the general faith in
progress which has characterised so much of western civilisation's
thinking during the last few centuries seems reasonable and mod-
erate in comparison with the utopians' promise of a future heaven
on earth. But at the same time, stating that things were better
before can sometimes overstep the mark. And in any case, they
weren't better in every way and everywhere. For those of us alive
now, things are better than they were for those who lived before.
Things are better now than they were before in so many respects
and for so many people that we find it hard to accept any opposite
interpretation.

The division into optimists and pessimists is not very helpful
in our thoughts about change. There are other ways of looking
at things. We thought we might take, for example, three Ancient
Greeks, each of whom had different ideas about what change was
and whether change was even possible. Their opinions still have
their supporters to this day. However, please don't misunderstand
our intention: we leave the history of ideas to the experts and

turn our attention to three possible viewpoints. The three Greeks act as sources of inspiration. Our descriptions of them may verge on the caricature, but let us call this a cultivation of principles instead. Moreover, we will not deal with them in chronological order, for that would have required us to start with Heraclitus, then Parmenides and finally Democritus. Our point will be clearer if we disregard the chronology – although in so doing we will overlook 'the reconciliation between Heraclitus and Parmenides achieved by Democritus'.[257]

Parmenides: there is no change

Parmenides of Elea (born circa 515 BC) was very consistent in this thinking – or, to put it differently, he was an extreme representative of blind faith in the purely logical capacity of thought.[258] Parmenides took an incontrovertible axiom as his starting point, and then derived his conclusions by way of a logical interpretation of this axiom. He can accurately be called a rationalist, although what we know about the chap is a well-filtered broth strained through centuries of interpreters and scientific wisdom. The main sources of our enlightenment are Karl Popper[259] and a number of elementary reference books on the subject.[260] As the references show, we have also read a little more widely than this, but in this chapter we have consistently avoided restricting ourselves to original sources and have referred freely to secondary sources. We social scientists are unused to this, but then the majority of what has been written in our subject field has come about during our own lifetimes.

Consider the following as an example of Parmenides' thinking. That which exists is that which exists. That which does not exist does not exist. Nothing is the only thing – or everything – that does not exist. Therefore, nothing does not exist. This is a nuisance, because we do like to talk about things that don't exist. But we do so because we humans are so stupid. That is what Parmenides would certainly have believed. Well, if nothing doesn't exist, nor then can there be voids in the world. After all, a void is defined as nothing, or the lack of anything.

The assumption of voids is illogical, according to Parmenides. If everything is something, there cannot be voids between the bits and pieces that make up the world. Consequently, the world is joined together in one piece. The world therefore consists of one block – not a mass of parts. If everything is joined together in one block and there are no voids between any of its parts, then there are no opportunities for the parts to move in relation to each other. Movement and change are thus a logical impossibility. It is only we humans who in our imperfection entertain an illusion of change.

Do you recognise your own thinking in this? The company you work for introduces a new financial control system, 'but it won't make any difference'. Everything stays the same. Gösta goes on a diet. He himself appears to have faith in it, but you know how Gösta is: he cannot change.

Some advocates of the idea that change is impossible appear to be pessimists. They believe that democratic reforms are only symbolic gestures, since power still lies where it has always been. According to them, changes in the workplace ultimately lead to the pace of work being speeded up and people being worn out early and burning out. So there is no point in talking about ethics and morals. People are all still swines. They always have been, and always will be. However, one does not have to be a pessimist to believe in stability. True pessimists believe that everything is going to pot. Catastrophe will soon be upon us, and we'll be left high and dry this afternoon or tomorrow morning at the latest. If one believes in stability, things probably aren't much better than before, but they aren't much worse either.

Parmenides and his pupils are said to have advocated a kind of political conservatism, which appears reasonable in this context. If nothing can be changed, it's pointless trying. And what we have is fine as it is.

There is, of course, a theory about organisations that picks up this thread and weaves a tight fabric of explanations about why so many attempts at change end with everything remaining the same as it used to be. The best examples of this genre are those who subscribe to the new institutional organisational analysis that we referred to earlier in this book.[261] Companies and large public organisations protect their operations against harmful attempts at change by pretending to carry out reforms which are called for and politically correct, while actually working in exactly the same way that they did before. They therefore have things like written equality plans, consumer satisfaction indices, IT strategies, ethical boards, environmental policies and a whole lot more that suggests well-meaning motives. Often this is not ill-intentioned, however. Having them in place looks good, and they are easy to tolerate as long as they don't do any major damage. In this way, operations can continue without disruption.

This line of reasoning is very convenient to have to hand when explaining why an agreed major investment or far-reaching change is never carried out. It is absolutely invaluable when, for example, you have been tasked with evaluating the state-funded five-year programme against repetitive strain injuries or IT investment in schools. But there is a real risk of overusing Parmenides. Next thing you know, the schools are full of computers and then you can't report that everything is the same as it always has been. At least not if it turns out that the teachers use the computers to do clever things.[262]

You see, Parmenides was wrong. By following in his footsteps, the proof can easily be revealed. An empirical observation just needs to be added to the starting point.

It is false that motion is impossible, for motion exists.

Thus it is false that the world is full, and that it is one large invisible block. Thus there are many full or corporeal things or small blocks, which are indivisible; that is, many atoms.

Since it is false that only the full exists, the empty, the void, also exists.

Thus the allegedly non-existing void does exist.[263]

But as Popper notes in connection with the text quoted above, Parmenides' ideas proved to be productive precisely when they were disproved. If anyone refutes this, we must tighten up the argument. It can be noted that Parmenides was not a fool, but he was blinded when it came to the conclusion about change being logically impossible.

For a couple of decades, we have been explaining how organisations work using the new institutional theory, and it has often worked brilliantly. It's excellent for describing and analysing stability and similarity. But correct as that may be, something still happens that cannot be called anything other than change: something diverges from the norm, and then you're left standing there with your explanatory model.

Still, we do of course have more strings to our badminton racket. When the new institutional analysis report fails us, we are still able to identify and correctly label real changes – ideally in the form of advance, but setbacks are not despised by a change-hungry organisational researcher. In that case, however, we need another Greek.

Democritus: an early Flash Gordon

As promised, we will continue to make reference to the Ancient Greeks. We use them as a mental clothes hanger on which to hang our reasoning. We find them suitable – although three comic strip characters would work just as well.

Let us take Li'l Abner as an example of the theory of unchangeability. He is an eternally young, muscular and simple-minded hillbilly, although many comic strip characters are eternally young and unchanging. His lack of brains is demonstrated when he falls down a mountain and gratefully notes how fortunate he is to have landed on his head.[264] The backwater of Dogpatch is probably located in Kentucky, but no one knows for certain.[265] It is here that the Yokum family live in an eternal rural slum, and Li'l Abner is satisfied with this, which is wise if one cannot change the situation. However, it's clear that Daisy Mae Scragg certainly contributes to his being so content. She really is a teenage boy's buxom dream. And she doesn't age in the slightest, either.

Flash Gordon is an example of the opposite to Li'l Abner. He flies here and there – entirely according to plan – in his large space rocket, fighting evil and impropriety with excellent results. 'Strap yourselves in! We're in for a rough ride.' But there's never a suggestion of any real action between Flash and Dale. There's no time for such stuff in what is a tightly-packed programme. But we do get to see plenty of fights with fantasy monsters.[266]

The mammoth beast thunders close to the tree ...
Flash grits his teeth and leaps ...
He swings his hatchet at the mighty Gwak's one vulnerable spot
... between the eyes![267]

There is change wherever Flash Gordon goes. And he knows what he's doing. Everything is long-term, well thought-out and well planned. This is true of even the series itself. The basic story stretches over seven years from 1934 until 1941.[268] It's almost as if the cartoonist had been given advice by an organisational development consultant. Every effort leads to a change for the better – but better is never so good that the series can be laid to rest.

And then we have Fritz the Cat, who is often surprised by things not being as he thought. They're often better. In the end, though, things still turn out very badly.[269] Every day and every female encounter are the same. And yet, something new always happens, and there Fritz stands, wide-eyed and astonished. His motto could easily be:

The next step I take is a step into uncertainty.[270]

But back to Flash Gordon. Or, for that matter, to Democritus of Abdera (circa 460–370 BC). As we know, he was the first to formulate atomic theory, unless it was Leucippus...[271] According to Popper, Democritus took the opposite path to Parmenides. Democritus states that there are movement and change, and that the world must consequently be made up of parts. If we divide these parts up into smaller parts, we eventually reach the point when the parts cannot be divided up into even smaller parts: atoms.

These atoms move around and bounce into each other and, when they do so, they trigger new movements which can be traced to or derived from the original movements.[272] This is a mechanical and strictly deterministic world picture. Movement is natural, and change can – at least in principle – be regarded as predictable. The problem remains with the properties of atoms – they are indestructible, unchangeable and have always existed.[273]

We may well be of the opinion that Democritus works better than Parmenides! This entire mechanical world picture fits in very well with the Modern Project and the scientific revolution, and it has provided inspiration for developments in science and technology that can only be regarded as brilliant. However, things can be taken to absurd lengths. The French mathematician and philosopher Pierre Simon de Laplace (1749–1827) provides one example.[274]

There is something called Laplace's demon, or Laplace's Superman. Assume that we have a superhuman intelligence which knows no limits. Also assume that this intelligence has complete information about all matter and all movement occurring at this very moment and that it has knowledge of all natural laws. This intelligence can then calculate and predict everything that will happen, and also describe everything that has ever happened. Determinism right down to the atomic level. A demon. Or perhaps God – except that de Laplace has been attributed the controversial viewpoint of God not being needed as the hypothesis for his history of creation.[275] Naturally, the difficult question is where this demon is assumed to be. If he (and it certainly is a he) is outside the universe, there can't be much to the universe if there is room for such a diabolical demon outside it. If, on the other hand, he is placed in the middle of it all, he should make the effort to explain how his own understanding and interpretation of creation affect everything. Then, as we understand it, he must be twice as intelligent. And if he is twice as intelligent, he will be twice as hard to understand – or in any case, much harder. In that way we can gain a good grasp without getting anywhere.

Oh well, perhaps we went too far with all this quasi-philosophy. The thing is that the mechanical world with all its advantages gives a false impression of providing us with a total understanding. The image of the detached researcher working within certain limits and by way of experiment is one that can be maintained. Even when we evaluate a change project, it may be that some inexperienced client believes we will provide a picture of what we evaluate as if we are standing to one side of the course of events and regarding it without the benefit of our own perspective. But we cannot trick ourselves.

The scientific experiment goes hand in hand with the mechanical view of change. The assumption of 'ceteris paribus' or 'all else being equal' involves keeping all variables constant in an experiment except that which is to be studied. We would ideally like to see this done in organisational change, too, but when we try to bring about change ourselves, the consequences of the change cannot easily be predicted. Once we have carried out our change project, it turns out that the conditions on which we based the project have been changed or even replaced. We may have learnt something new, for example. And now for some more Ancient Greeks.

Heraclitus: on the spring flood

'No man ever steps into the same river twice,' Heraclitus (born during the latter part of the 6th century BC) is said to have declared.[276] And this is usually interpreted as meaning that on the second occasion of doing so, the water that had been flowing on the first occasion has long since passed through and been replaced with new water. The fish may have swum away and new fish taken their place. The sun is in a different position. It is, quite simply, a different flow.

> ...Different and still different waters flow over one who steps into the same river.[277]

That said, we don't think all that talk about different water or even a different river sounds all that disturbing. The crux is rather that one cannot step into the same river twice because one is no longer the same person. Change means that certain things change while others remain constant, except that when time passes nothing stays the same. This happens at different speeds, of course.

Astrophysicists may not need to wonder over the changed position of the Andromeda galaxy in the firmament, but in social science the conditions for those objects for which we want stable measurements are changing all the time. For example, we try to measure the change in the value of money using various indices. These work well for a few years at a time, but over a century they become a little meaningless because the entire circumstances for the use of money have changed. And changing to some other kind of index doesn't help, either. We simply encounter new albeit similar problems.

The Swedish Consumer Price Index is designed to try to measure the cost of living for regular folk. Since new goods and services turn up that no one has ever heard of before while other goods and services disappear completely, we cannot compare the price of the same goods from year to year. When goods drop dramatically in price due to increased efficiency, price comparisons lose their relevance. The composition of goods and services included here therefore changes at times – after thorough investigation, of course.[278] In other cases, a fixed basket of goods is used. None of these methods provides comparability in the long run.

It is fascinating to read about price trends over the centuries, but we need to be aware that the old figures we have represent different things to those represented by the new figures, even though they are found in the same column. If we listen to Heraclitus, we cannot fail to see the problem. For him, fire was the origin of everything, in the sense that it was a typical example of the way in which things are in constant change: 'a symbol of the restless coming into being, which assumes all possible forms'[279], in a world where 'everything is involved in constant change'.[280]

> The question is, instead, how immutability is possible. And he [Heraclitus] has the answer: immutability is an illusion.[281]

Smart thinking on the part of Heraclitus. But we can draw comfort from the fact that he was not always right or even ground-breaking. According to the Swedish tabloid *Aftonbladet*, Heraclitus ended his days buried in a dunghill while trying to cure the ailments (an oedema? a vitamin deficiency?) he had contracted through an unbalanced diet – and which meant, for a while, that he ate only grass.[282] We can also note that Thales' much older stance that 'the origin of everything is water'[283] worked just as well as Heraclitus' fire.

All too often, change literature misses the point about the changeable nature of everything. While we were carrying out our well-managed change project, all the problems we were supposed to resolve with our undergoing change had also changed. Let us present a glimpse from the evaluation workshop.

A development programme, by way of example

Quite some time ago, we were involved in evaluating a development programme entitled 'Measures to Counter Repetitive Strain Injuries'.[284] The programme was run by the now defunct Swedish Work Environment Fund. Somewhere between sixty and seventy (depending on how you count them) different companies and organisations received funding for their own development projects. The whole thing ran for five years, and the aim – at least to begin with – was to find operational organisational methods for reducing repetitive strain injuries (RSI). The Swedish Work Environment Fund also ran several other development programmes during the 1980s and into the 1990s.[285] The best known of these is probably its Leadership, Organisation and Co-determination programme. But the programme we were evaluating was all about RSI. It began in 1988 and ended with a concluding conference in 1994. We will spare you the details of all the hardship that we and others had to endure. Complex organisations suffer from complex problems. Now we wanted to talk about the passing of time.

The issue of RSI became a hot topic during the eighties for a whole host of reasons. During the sixties and seventies, many of the serious occupational injury issues relating to heavy lifting, inadequate safety equipment and toxic chemicals had gradually been dealt with in Sweden. But there certainly remained more to be done. The asbestos scandals of the early eighties showed that even the most obvious health risks in industry were not always given the attention they deserved. Still, the focus gradually shifted towards more insidious health problems in the workplace.

Another contributing factor was that industry had completely modernised manufacturing during the sixties so that everything worked in accordance with Frederick Winslow Taylor's principles of scientific management.[286] Work was divided up into small, basic stages which took a short time to complete and were constantly repeated. These could all be carried out after the operator had had a brief introduction. One obvious consequence was that, after a couple of decades, the repetitive and monotonous work tasks resulted in many people developing repetitive strain injuries. Legislation also provided new scope for the classifying of illnesses and discomfort such as industrial injury in cases that were a little more complicated than accidents and the like.

Anyway, all this and many other things led to the growing opinion that RSI was a problem. The evening newspaper *Aftonbladet* published articles about working conditions in industry, and the documentary film 'Arbetets döttrar' ('The Daughters of Labour') was shown on TV and aroused debate. And then the boom years came, and industry found it hard to recruit people for regular assembly work. The social partners were unanimous: they all thought something should be done about the work environment which resulted in RSI.

Originally, this was defined as the manufacturing industry's problem, but by the time the programme got started the public sector had also been included. Nursing assistants, cleaners and postmen were just as vulnerable. The applications for project funding started to trickle in, and soon a number of projects were underway.

Five years is a long time in an evaluation context. At some point during the programme, there was a recession. The need to present industrial work in a more favourable light for recruitment purposes largely faded away. The legislation was changed once again, resulting in RSI statistics no longer being quite so terrifying. The technical conditions for the manufacturing industry had also changed.

Consumer electronics was one example of an industry in which the conditions had changed. In the eighties, long lines of young women assembled and soldered fiddly little transistors or circuit boards or whatever. Much of this work disappeared during the nineties, since TV sets no longer required as much assembly work. The entire electronics unit came in a ready-made, automatically assembled module. Three screws to mount the unit in the casing, and the job was done. Much of the so-called simpler assembly work had instead been moved overseas, reducing the work environment problem back in Sweden. Other processes had been automated out of the labour market.

The social debate on RSI was less intense in 1993 than it had been in 1985. The problem hadn't disappeared, but it had changed in character. The mass media and opinion-makers also had other things to worry about. So we shouldn't be surprised that the concluding conference didn't include any reference at all to RSI. The programme had changed its name to 'Jobb i förändring' ('Jobs in Transition'). Most of those who had been given money had produced a little presentation on their development project. There were countless brochures, all with the same layout and all with the Jobs in Transition logo. This logo consisted of the project name with a heavily stylised figure of a man captured in an upward motion, as if he were bursting forth from his boundaries or freeing himself from his shackles.

Anyone who wanted to read about RSI could browse in vain through the brochures. However, there were actually a couple of projects that had attempted to measure the number of repetitive strain injuries before and after the project was carried out. This was all well and good, you might think. But the actual concept of repetitive strain injury had been redefined as a result of the change in legislation during the programme, and so this probably wasn't particularly meaningful. Nevertheless, there were plenty of participants who could bear witness to 'successful change work' and the fact that many had been given greater responsibility. This happened at a time when 'lean production'[287] and flat organisations were enjoying their first boom years. Otherwise, we were in a recession. Anyway, everyone seemed to be in favour and no one was against. RSI and all that claptrap was considered far too negative. Instead there was a quest for faith in the future. But we still believe that among all those conference participants there were some who wondered whether all this greater responsibility without authority really was a good thing. And there may have been one or two people in working life who had lost their faith in the future as a result of RSI. Still, in certain situations there's no point in protesting, and so we did not.

Here we had a programme that was supposed to transform working life through a number of model local change projects. And then working life itself was changed so that the programme took a new direction instead. Or whatever the truth of the matter was ...

Just so you don't get the idea that we know all about how everything changes, we would like to point out that Henrik Bäckström carried out a study of all the Swedish Work Environment Fund's programmes.[288] This showed that their agenda was much more stable than the impression given by the individual programmes. All the programmes feature sociotechnical ideas from the sixties.[289] Autonomous groups, more responsibility for the workers and social psychology processes (or 'organisational development') as part of the change projects – that was the formula. And the formula was an excellent fit for the lean production philosophy of the early nineties.

Now we hope we really have turned some heads. Was the change we wrote about actually a form of stability? What should we believe? 'Everything we hear is an opinion, not fact. Everything we see is a perspective, not the truth.' [290] Welcome to the real world!

What should we believe?

Those with low expectations of life might be satisfied with successful change projects. Those with greater ambitions, on the other hand, might not be content with anything less than improvement. The outcome is change, or at least 'change projects'. Or perhaps we don't end up with that much change; it's perfectly possible to maintain that we live in an age of stability rather than change.[291] All this standardisation and quality assurance that we wrote about in Chapters Two and Three are manifestations of this stability. We refine and polish the products and services that we have to offer rather than finding new ones. All the new cars include more and more added features, and the burgers in the hamburger bars boast more and more toppings. Whether or not the cars are actually any better is hard to say,[292] and the same is true of the burgers. Making a choice certainly hasn't become any easier.

There's a catch here. Much of what we describe as change is carried out within change projects. These projects involve people doing the work of change. There's an entire profession devoted to the work of change. When we took a closer look at the change projects funded by the RSI programme, they turned out to be swarming with consultants.[293] The work of change that these consultants delivered was good. There was probably nothing much wrong with the consultants, but what they delivered still consisted of old rehashes. Good quality work of change and successful change projects are not the same thing as change – and plenty of changes were made. People were given more responsibility, and a kind of general modernisation of the organisations affected seems to have taken place. If more of the same is change, then there was change, at least in some places – although in other places we would think not. In one case, no one had heard any mention of a change process when we visited the workplace in question. Parmenides, *douze points*!

What had actually changed were things that no programme in the world could achieve. Technological and socio economic developments had meant that we all ended up in a new situation. We probably could have foreseen that as a general principle. The future will bring changes, albeit not necessarily at the rate which is often alleged. Certain changes will change the way we see the world. But which ones? This would seem to be a walkover for Heraclitus.

So why do we cheer on Democritus? Because we are torn, to say the least. We have based our academic career on Parmenides. In study after study, we have noted how little was achieved with so many good intentions. And our studies aren't seriously flawed. The evidence, analyses and arguments they contain are in good order, although sometimes we worry that these virtues are not part of the natural order. Parmenides plays for the home team, as it were. On the opposing side, Heraclitus is so obviously right that his argument borders on pure banality. Where time goes, the clock follows. And where the clock goes, it ends up falling apart. Still, if we toe the line and make it through to retirement, we might get presented with a new one.

Democritus takes part in this competition without ever actually having signed up for it. The other two Ancient Greeks certainly had change in mind, but Democritus mostly wanted to say something about matter. And we've interpreted what he may have thought about change in as biased a manner as we dare. It seems a shame for him to lose the fight just because we've made him a little stupider than he might really have been.

So in the end we can say that we never act on the basis of the understanding with which Parmenides and Heraclitus can furnish us. 'I'll buy a new bike because nothing really matters.' Or: 'We won't buy two kilos of beef for Sunday dinner, because we can't be sure what our opinion of dinner will be when the day comes. If indeed it ever comes.' If you reason along these lines, you should embark on some form of therapy. Rationality and linear thinking may have their shortcomings, but we can't live without them.

And where have we ended up with the change concept given the help of these Ancient Greeks? It hasn't changed that much, nor become entirely clear; rather, we've ended up with a bit of a spanner in the works. A spanner that calls for reflection. And those old Greeks certainly helped with that.

6. Metaphors at the End Points of the Scale

Metaphors are like mosquitoes in the north of Sweden: if there's a problem, it's not that there aren't enough of them. Nevertheless, this chapter deals with the shortage of metaphors. Not that there's a lack of metaphors in general terms. We discuss the consequences when a discussion in a specific field all too often becomes locked because of a strong metaphor which is actually on a scale with end points. The problem is that the end points are invisible, since they are nameless. Below, we present a method for moving forward by establishing these two end points in the form of metaphors. We have been fascinated by the specific case here, but we believe that the phenomenon – with scales that can benefit from being given end points – is widespread, and that the line of reasoning therefore has considerable universality.

We will start with the question of what we mean by degree of flatness. The basis for our analysis is found in the book *Res pyramiderna* ('Raise the Pyramids').[294] We then present our end points of the scale. What does an entirely flat organisation look like, and what is its opposite?

The chapter concludes with a discussion on the effects of using metaphors to help clarify the end points of the tearing down/raising scale. If both the end points have obvious disadvantages, it is not obvious that continually moving in one direction – towards more tearing down – does all organisations good.

As shown earlier, metaphors are just metaphors to us. In this chapter, we discuss structure-related metaphors. This means that we side with those who believe that the world consists of different sorts of structures within and between organisations.[295] This does not mean that we would say that there are no non-physical structures or that such aspects would be less important.[296] The fact that we discuss one type of metaphor does not mean we are expressing an opinion regarding the reality of practical experience; we are simply considering how metaphors contribute to our understanding or misunderstanding of this practical experience.

Thirty years of tearing down pyramids

For nearly thirty years, pyramids have been torn down in companies, public administration and other organisations. In actual fact, it is surprising that there is no name for an entirely flat organisation in the way that there is for the sort with the highest peak. In the same way, what is surprising that it is almost always the 'flattening' advantages and height-related disadvantages that are addressed. Why does no one want to see the disadvantages of flattening and the advantages of pyramids?

Talking about tearing down pyramids is probably more common than actually tearing them down. That said, a major empirical study shows that thirty percent of companies in Europe were flattened during the period 1992–1996.[297] Tearing down pyramids came into fashion because of the promise of fantastic outcomes. However, whether the tearing down itself was attractive or whether those who had already torn down their pyramid felt any of the effects from that was of minor importance. And we are not particularly interested here in whether those who say they have torn down their pyramids actually ended up with a flatter or a taller pyramid. The flattened organisation stood out as a desirable goal. We have shown elsewhere that describing our current age as one which justifies flattening does not stand up to closer scrutiny, and that the promised effects often do not materialise.[298]

We will not discuss here whether the structures of the organisational pyramids should be torn down or raised. Instead, we will pause here to study the effects of using a metaphor which slides on a scale without end points. We may, of course, wonder whether scales really need to have end points, but in the case of organisational pyramids there is a degree of flatness beyond which further flattening would appear to be impossible. There is also a degree of pyramidal – or hierarchical – height after which further raising cannot be imagined. We will introduce the concept of the peneplain as a metaphor for the flat end point, and the concept of the column for the other extreme. It is worth noting that a pyramid ceases to be a pyramid once it has reached either of the end points of the scale. Neither an entirely flat sheet nor a uniformly narrow column is a pyramid. Immediately before an end point is reached, we still have a pyramid. To push the point, so to speak, we are after the end points for organisational height rather than a pyramid's height.

This discussion concerns not only the end points of the scale and the question of whether metaphors are lacking here and what the effects of this are, but also the reach of the metaphor. Every – or almost every – metaphor can prompt far more thoughts on the matter than that which initially springs to mind. What we see and use by way of a particular metaphor depends on factors such as power of insight and knowledge connected to the individual, the stance taken, etc. Clear examples are gender-related organisational metaphors[299] connected to boxing and warfare.

What does the pyramid metaphor offer?

When describing the structures of companies, public administrations and other organisations, we call them pyramids. The production staff make up the base of this pyramid. A number of the levels above them support supervisors, their managers, and the managers' managers. Only one or a few individuals sit at the top. There are many individuals at the bottom. Experts are placed slightly to one side, although not too far to the side, otherwise the pyramid becomes shapeless and useless. We will discuss here what the pyramid metaphor contains or offers in the way of opportunities. Our intention is to take account of the above discussion on metaphor in order not to be tempted – as is so easily done – to make things out of those metaphors that crop up in general debate.

In this context, the word 'pyramid' does not mean 'an Ancient Egyptian royal tomb'. The pyramid is a metaphor that says something about how organisations are built and operate. The comparison can be taken to great lengths – although not to just any lengths.

Of all the analogies and comparisons that can be made between, say, the pyramids of Egypt and organisational hierarchies, only a few are being used.

The weight and stability of the real pyramids could, for example, be important properties by which to make comparisons, but when describing the sluggishness of an organisation there are other common analogies. The energy required to change the course of a large ship is a common analogy for showing how hard it is to make changes in large organisations. The solid mass of the pyramid is, perhaps, too stable to work as a comparison. Who sees the image of the reconstructed pyramid in front of them? It is not so natural to overturn a pyramid or to place it upside-down. Those who maintain that their own organisation is an inverted pyramid (and these people do exist – we've met them) have made a metaphor out of the metaphor. Their simile is an organisational structure placed on its end.

The most obvious way to change a pyramid is to tear it down. However, this analogy has its drawbacks. Those who tear down real pyramids must break them down piece by piece, and then carry the pieces away so that the pyramid does not rise up again like a conical heap of rubble right alongside. This appears to be both a laborious and time-consuming process. However, an organisational pyramid can be torn down in a flash. If the board decided to wind down manufacturing in one particular location, that pyramid can be deemed to be definitively and thoroughly torn down – no question about it! Yet entirely different types of reorganisation are usually referred to as tearing down pyramids. Management literature has followed in the footsteps of former SAS CEO Jan Carlzon since 1985, and has talked about tearing down pyramids in connection with doing away with a particular type of manager. The metaphor has thus been assigned narrow boundaries.

In this connection, it can be pointed out that the intentions Carlzon now says he had and his current interpretation of his own messages and actions is insignificant. In the same way, his original thinking is of secondary interest. Carlzon is the local icon in the eyes of the movement in favour of tearing down pyramids. But those who come after him are free to make their own interpretation.

Deep inside pyramids are large burial chambers which – so it is said – once contained well-wrapped up mummies and fabulous treasures: gold and precious stones. Today, these burial chambers are mostly empty.[300] Grave robbers dealt with the contents thousands of years ago. As far as we know, neither the gold nor the plunderers fall within the scope of the metaphor. The analogies that can be drawn score only superficial and easy points: The precious core of the pyramid is often empty, we do not know who made off with the value of treasure that the pyramid once held, and it cannot be seen from outside whether or not its burial chambers are empty.

We are usually satisfied with noting the height and the triangular shape as formed by one side. One example of advanced thinking is that provided by Michael Rowlinson, who discusses the question of the division of labour and hierarchy as if the choice were between a flat or less flat organisational structure.[301] If this is the case, the alternatives are simple. If there are many management levels within an organisation, the pyramid will be tall. If there are fewer levels, the pyramid will be lower. The Ancient Egyptians would certainly not have accepted just any old relationship between the quadratic ground plan and the height of the peak. Certain proportions were regarded as sacred. No such sacred proportions seem to feature in the theories about organisational pyramids. The proportions of the Egyptian pyramids, rising prominently above the surrounding landscape, still haunt us when we talk about organisations. Pyramids can be seen to be unnecessarily or uncomfortably tall.

A suitable number of subordinates

There was debate among the first generation of management theorists – Frederick Taylor, Frank and Lillian Gilbreth, William Gantt, Henri Fayol and others – on the suitable number of subordinates for a manager. According to Jay Galbraith, this debate was conducted without the troublesome element of empirical evidence.[302] This was probably a prerequisite. In order to find the ideal pyramid, one has to stick to the world of ideas. The similarities with the Egyptians' mystical interpretation of numbers are otherwise striking. One particular set form of organisational pyramid was to be designated as the standard. The difference between the standard and the sacred is a question of linguistic usage.

When, much later on, they attempted in earnest to investigate how many employees should be included in a department, they reached the conclusion that it must depend on what the work entails. According to Joan Woodward[303], if the work tasks involve a large degree of uncertainty, the span of control[304] must be narrower (with fewer subordinates per manager) than if the work features certainty and predictability.

What may have occurred to some proponents of flat organisations is that the degree of flatness has nothing to do with the number of subordinates per manager. However, a manager with four subordinates should in all reason have a closer relationship with these four than a manager with a hundred subordinates has. The distance between the manager and his subordinates could increase at the same rate as the increase in new employees. In such a case, the distance between the top of the pyramid and its base would only depend on the total number of employees, and would be independent of the number of levels in the pyramid. Just like the Egyptian models, all pyramids would then have the same form and would vary only in size. It is also possible that new forms of communication and democratic dialogue could be used to reduce the distance between manager and employee without changing the number of people on the level in question. However, such a line of reasoning works better if the entire pyramid metaphor is first abandoned and we start to talk about organisations in a different way.

The fact that working relationships change if the number of employees in the group change was illustrated by humourist C. Northcote Parkinson in a short essay about how many members a board of directors should include.[305] Above a certain level, the members begin to hold pre-meetings in smaller groups, and contributions to discussion are made in the form of speeches following a written script. Northcote Parkinson believed that five is a suitable number, and this is probably the clearest instruction on the ideal size of working groups to be found in literature. Although didn't a number of ancient civilisations believe seven to be the sacred number? It may be possible to find support for seven being a suitable number for working groups in social psychology research in the forties and fifties.[306]

Working parties and committees are not the same as a manager's span of control, but there is a connection. Seven appears to be appropriate in many ways. A group of seven people can form a coherent group both at work and socially. A group of seven can keep abreast of their colleagues' work tasks and specialist expertise, and can also remember the names of their immediate family members. The manager can have a good overview of the problems that arise in operational work, while also acting as the group's spokesman – upwardly within the hierarchy and outwardly with other groups or consumers. The manager should then, in turn, be part of a group of seven other managers, each of whom would be relatively familiar with their co-managers and their circumstances. If the manager should also be deemed to be included in the work group of which he is head, the figures become more complicated. In order to complete a pyramid based on the number seven, it should naturally have seven levels. Such a pyramid, in which every span of control consists of seven people who are organised on seven hierarchical levels, would consist of 137,257 employees.

On the subject of divine proportions, we must mention the golden ratio. This consists of proportions which are common in both nature and various types of human construct. The golden ratio is often regarded as being pleasing in purely aesthetic terms. The proportions can be reproduced mathematically, and can certainly be applied to pyramids, which then gives an ideal angle between the base and one side. The Pyramid of Cheops has an angle by which the original size corresponds with the golden ratio to the third decimal place.[307] We have not succeeded in calculating how many subordinates each manager has in a Cheops-style organisational pyramid. The mathematicians we have asked say that it depends on the size of the room and whether each employee would have his own office with a window. It might well be that the calculated result is not as cosmetic as one would have expected. If, for example, the pyramid is divided into storeys of equal height, the volume of the storeys increases in a sequence of one, seven, nineteen, thirty-seven, sixty-one, ninety-one, and so on, giving fewer and fewer subordinates per manager. The thirty-seven heads of department taken together would have only sixty-one heads of section to manage. There's nothing divine or even particularly pleasing about that.

Later discourses on this subject, written by people who were neither mathematically interested philosophers, social psychologists or humourists (but who are not necessarily serious for that), include recommendations to the effect that there should be more than seven employees. And they are not bothered about the gold content of the ratio. A favourite here is, of course, the book by Jan Carlzon published in 1985. Many seem to believe that the number of employees within a department should be greater than is currently the case, and this is true regardless of how many there currently are. The more there are, the flatter the organisation becomes, and flat organisations are the order of the day. The flatter the better. It is unlikely that Egypt's pyramids could be made much flatter. Those who built them had fixed views on the angle at which the sides should be inclined, and even if we subscribe to their views, a stone pyramid ceases to be a pyramid at some point. When it comes to the organisational pyramid, however, we can be more generous. Few would suggest that the organisation has now become too flat, but it is almost always possible to appear wise by maintaining that a touch of flattening is required here and there.

What is flat?

A reasonable definition of the concept of flatness must include the fact that it relates to an organisation with few hierarchical levels. Small organisations are therefore often flat. But the hierarchy quickly shoots up in height when the organisation grows, as demonstrated by Nobel Laureate Herbert Simon back in the 1940s.[308] In a small organisation, the number of workers is so few that they can maintain a joint discussion and can all have a relationship with their manager. If this is an ideal that applies in the event of growth and also applies to the managers and their managers, the pyramid will become taller as the organisation becomes larger – at least it does so if we simply count the number of levels as being the only criterion.

If we say that the number of hierarchical levels in an organisation corresponds to the height of a pyramid, the degree of flatness should be determined by how far the base of the pyramid extends. The pyramid's degree of flatness should be related to the angle at which the sides meet at the peak of the pyramid, rather than to its absolute height. The greater the angle, the flatter the pyramid. In the same way, the organisational hierarchy's degree of flatness should be determined by the ratio between the number of managers and the number of employees. The smaller the quota, the flatter the organisation.

A pyramid can be built according to completely different plans to those used by the Egyptians. For example, it could be a couple of hundred metres high, but could have sides at the base that are several kilometres long. Such a pyramid would be both tall and flat. Henry Mintzberg refers to research carried out by Peter Blau and Richard Schoenherr, and also to Joseph Litterer, the writer of another overview of organisational research, showing that when organisations become bigger, so do the size of the units and thus the width of the span of control increases.[309] The biggest companies should thereby also be the flattest! And the highest, measured in number of levels.

The flattest of pyramids: the peneplain

The very flattest organisation of all will be one with only one department and no manager. Everyone can take responsibility for themselves. The question is to whom they should be accountable. Let us say that in this case that they would be accountable to each other. A football team without a team captain, coach or club manager could operate in this way. It would, however, be forced to act roughly like other teams, otherwise the team would not be allowed to play in any matches or would gradually be moved down and out of the league system. The prerequisite is a situation that is institutionalised through and through. Rules, tactics and training methods are set. The necessary decisions can be made through voting. The members of the team should stand shoulder-to-shoulder on the same flat pitch, not only physically but also organisationally. No one has a coordinating role and no one has greater authority or influence than the others. In order for this to be practically possible, those who stand in this line must presumably be completely independent of each other. It is doubtful whether such a social order (or, rather, disorder) can be called an organisation – and in any case, it is not a hierarchy nor a pyramid.

But even an entirely flat football team risks being affected by a division of labour in which certain tasks can at times be such that someone must take on more work than others. Steven Gerrard and his contemporaries in the sport distribute their passes to those in the team whom they consider suitable for tasks such as kicking the ball into the goal or dribbling it around their opponents. In our small flat team, he generally avoids those who simply rush back and forth. And so the pyramid rises.

Elliott Jaques argues that all organisations are pyramids, and have been so for three thousand years.[310] This is necessarily true if we see a pyramid construction as soon as one person in an organisation takes on more than one other person. The football example illustrates that this is so often the case in an organisation. Based on his faith in the natural pyramid, Jaques pulls apart swathes of management theory without direct references or clear proof. His book *Requisite Organization* might well have offered a refreshing insight had he not so obstinately referred to his own books, his own videos and other products as presenting the correct doctrine. Instead, it is just one in a long line of wearisome management books in which theory is equal to what the author happens to think about the matter. We do not believe him – but we agree that complete flatness is unreasonable as an organisational structure.

Geographers have naturally given greater thought to what is really flat in a world that consists of podzol soil, basalt and granite. A place where all the mountains have collapsed and where the forces of erosion have levelled out every little hill, so that the incline is less than half a percent, is called a peneplain. Rainwater cannot carry material through this landscape when it runs off it. It can take sixty to a hundred million years for a new mountain chain to be eroded and turn into a peneplain.[311] In the same way, pyramids too are eroded over time to result in an extreme degree of flatness.

The organisational peneplain would be an organisation which has become so flat that no fine-tuning or fresh rationalisation would chip away at its height anymore. We believe that the current rage for standardising organisations in different ways has the effect of eroding the organisational pyramid so that it becomes ever flatter. When the water running off this terrain is unable to transport any material, the landscape does not become flatter: it is now a peneplain. In contrast, when total quality management (TQM) and benchmarking can no longer reduce the ratio between managers and subordinates, we still do not have an organisational peneplain.

If an organisational pyramid erodes to become a peneplain anyway, the question remains whether we have an entirely flat pyramid or just something entirely flat, and whether we still actually have an organisation. We are dubious about both the entirely flat pyramid and the entirely flat organisation. Somewhere along the way towards the forming of the peneplain, the argument for organisation loses its relevance. No object can exist in the categories of both organisation and peneplain. The end point is an absurd one. But not so any changes made in its direction.

With increased flattening come the advantages and disadvantages of flatness. We have shown that there is the risk that the conditions necessary for, say, long-term development and cost-effectiveness, dialogue and communication and wellbeing will suffer in the event of flattening.[312]

Let us take an example. Oliver Williamson presents an interesting discussion on the effect of the extremely flat hierarchies that were common in parts of American industry during the period between the American Civil War and the First World War.[313] The case he addresses is the market-like structure involving a number of contracted small businesses on the shop floor at the Winchester Repeating Arms Company. Williamson refers in turn to a study made by John Buttrick. The firearms were manufactured by assembling parts bought in from a large number of legally independent small businesses which, in practice, were subordinate departments. All components were strictly standardised. The system worked as long as it stuck to old tried and tested models, but developing new models was almost impossible. The explanation for this was a lack of incentive among the subordinate component suppliers. However, any excessively zealous product development on the part of one of these suppliers would also have resulted in it no longer being possible put together a gun using the parts. These weaknesses contributed towards the structure subsequently being changed. The disadvantages of flatness are thus neither new nor unknown, even if they have been kept off the agenda for a while.

One type of flat organisation is the assembly line. This can save money, and requires almost no superstructure if there is little need for development. Vertical dialogue is impossible, and is also unnecessary. What would be the benefit to a few managers of being able to talk to so many people, and what opportunity would they have to do so in all seriousness? It doesn't seem particularly attractive at all.

Organisations that only allow themselves the absolute essentials can make short-term gains such as becoming superior in terms of cost-effectiveness and enjoying a high degree of legitimacy, at least as long as slim legs and a washboard stomach are the norm. The question is what happens when operations no longer keep themselves in good shape. Are there then contingencies and scope for changing and developing operations? A theatre that does away with its director, stage manager and set designer may benefit from this as long as the audience buys tickets for the performance billed, but what happens when the audience wants to see a new play? Or if they want to see the work of the set designer?

The tallest of pyramids: the column

Nor can the tallest imaginable hierarchical organisational structure be likened to a pyramid. The flattest possible organisation is one where everyone stands next to each other in a row while none of them has a coordinating role or stands out from the crowd. The least flat organisation should within reason involve rotating this flat row of members through ninety degrees, so that instead of their standing alongside each other they stand on top of each other in a vertical row. Such a row must surely be more ordered than the row where they all stand on flat ground. Circus artists who stand four tall or more on each other's shoulders do not look like an unorganised rabble. Nevertheless, it is doubtful that the vertical row of people represents an organisational structure any more than does the horizontal. It is more likely an end point at which the hierarchy is no longer a pyramid, and where coordination and dialogue are largely lacking.

The column would be formed as an unlikely result of common-sense considerations as to how best to relate the various areas of responsibility and authority to each other. The hens in a chicken run appear – so we have heard – to form an unambiguous pecking order. Agnes pecks Beatrice. Beatrice in turn pecks Cecilia. Cecilia pecks Désirée. Beatrice will not allow herself to be pecked by anyone other than Agnes. And so on. Similar status chains could probably be found throughout our social life, albeit with more refined pecking behaviour than in the chicken run. Many people take a childish delight in drawing up lists in order of rank. Their interest is not limited to which individual – or group – is at the top of the list; when the tabloid press publish a list of the country's richest people, number 47 is also interesting, and it's important that he comes above number 48.

Many of the examples to be found of column-like hierarchies seem to be special cases of so-called informal organisation. Formal organisations set up by an individual in order to serve some desirable purpose and take on a column-like form are hard to find. One conclusion from this is that the informal power structure is more hierarchical than the formal power structure. This leads to two points of view.

The first is that the column as an organisational form is not suitable for any other purpose than ranking its members. This ranking of its own members is, however, an unusual main purpose for companies and public administrations to have. Elements of such formal ranking are possibly seen in flat contexts such as professional ice hockey teams, which rank their players according to the principle that one particular individual is the most valuable player, after which come the second best and third best, right the way down to the player or players who shouldn't really be on the team at all. In order to maintain the credibility of the ranking order, these players are then paid in relation to their place on the list, with a ridiculously high sum going to player number one.

The ranking order of ice hockey players can, however, only be regarded as a secondary activity. The main aim is for them to play ice hockey in front of a paying audience and to win plenty of matches – although not every match, otherwise the audience would lose interest. This type of ranking order does not feature in all relationships that arise. Out on the ice rink, a cheap defence player with a good overall view can, no doubt, act in certain situations as a controlling coordinator in relation to the more expensive forward. However, this is the same as with any formal organisation: it only works to a certain extent and at certain times. A single ranking cannot take an unlimited number of dimensions into account.

The second point of view is that if informal organisation is consistently more column-like than formal organisation, all formal organisations potentially serve to tear down the pyramids – or the columns. In this case, formal pyramids are flatter than informal pyramids, and formal organisational structure can provide a defence against unrestrained hierarchisation and the aspiration to achieve a concentration of power at the top which characterises the spontaneous, informal structure.

This line of reasoning has its catches. The difference between formal and informal organisation has not been sufficiently investigated. Informal organisation may not feature the stability that should be expected in order to apply the term 'structure'. The columns that served as an example seem hopelessly precarious. Even a beautifully formed Greek marble column would seem to be easier to knock over than an Egyptian pyramid. However, pecking orders and various ranking orders hardly bring to mind the idea of such stable and weighty constructions. Rather, they should be compared to rotten fence posts or the towers made up of building bricks that toddlers assemble purely for the pleasure of knocking them down again.

Column-like organisations may be rare or only possible in theory, but there are organisations that have column-like structures near the top. This does not mean that one manager stands directly above another. At any rate, not at many levels. But the Austrian Armed Forces for example, which we know well from the world of light opera, and the Catholic Church, which we have encountered in countless Italian films, certainly do have very few members in the upper hierarchical levels. These are examples of strict chains of command, and as such do not differ from pecking orders.

The Austrian Armed Forces on display before us feature a fanciful variety of rank insignia and wide strips of gold braid to specify the position occupied by each and every one of the commanders assigned superior functions and districts within the internal pecking order. It is almost like a column in which the formality serves mostly as ritual window-dressing. The organisational description does not give those looking for information any clear details of who does what.[314] If this once mighty army were to take up arms again, the division of labour would also be different to what a naïve observer of formalities might assume. A strictly formalised pecking order serves best as guidance for the correct seating positions at banquets. This is not inconsequential to an event organiser, but is

still problematic when trying to describe a column-like organisation which is more than just a ranking list.

To find examples of tall and narrow organisational structures
that meet some purpose other than the ranking of their members,
we can perhaps turn our thoughts from the column and start looking instead for an obelisk. The base must be wider than the top, but
not by much. A person in a superior position can have more than
one subordinate, but not so many as the seven which characterise
the divine hierarchy. In those organisations that are expected to
function well with narrow spans of control, there is a need to meet
only in small groups. Subordinates can be expected to consult with
their managers individually and for long, intensive periods.

In order for the obelisk to be a reliable metaphor, there must be
something more to it than just the intensity of the relationships
within. One explanation could be that those organisations dealing
with information of a secret nature have an obelisk-like structure.
When the left hand is forbidden to know what the right hand is
doing, it can be hard to keep track of more than two hands. For a
long time, we entertained hopes that organised crime might be one
such activity. One might expect that such organisations would feature a high degree of secretiveness and would be profitable enough
to afford ineffective organisational structures. However, closer
studies show that the American version of the Mafia, at least, is not
particularly clandestine at all. Donald Cressey describes the Mafia
as a confederation into which it does not appear to be difficult to
obtain a degree of insight.[315] Certain things must, of course, be
kept secret, but this seems to apply more to individual operations
than to the structure of the organisation. There is no clear evidence
that the Mafia is structured like an obelisk. On the other hand,
the Mafia's organisational chart is not as public as that of the civil
service, so there is still a possibility that Mafia obelisks exist.

The next attempt at the obelisk hypothesis is to consider spy
organisations. Although these form part of what is otherwise a public civil service, the national security service and espionage organisations evade our scrutiny. They should be secret – that's the whole
point. Here we are forced to take a break to consider an empirical
paradox. The only secret organisations on which we can obtain
reliable information are those which have been subject to investi-
gations that bring their secretive status to an end. This includes a

number of religious sects that may have become more open because the secrets they protected for centuries are deemed to be no longer worth protecting. The information revealed in budget paperbacks and videos is about as unsecret as can be. The organisations that have succeeded in maintaining their secretiveness are the ones that have not been studied. We can therefore stick to the theory, for the time being, that secretive organisations are structured like obelisks, although it is a little disturbing that the theory is hard to test.

The fact that the column is unusual or possibly doesn't even exist does not mean that pyramid-building is impossible. However, just like with flattening, there are disadvantages associated with any movement against this end point of the scale. There are well-documented studies of how attempts to create rationally effective formal hierarchies have been completely overturned. One of our favourites, the French organisational sociologist Michel Crozier, used his classic studies of the French postal bank and the tobacco monopoly to depict formal bureaucracy as hell on earth.[316] Here, we find a well-founded criticism of bureaucracy as an organisational form.

Those who have influenced us on the question of bureaucracy primarily associate bureaucratic regulations with the flat organisational structure. Henry Mintzberg, Jay Galbraith and Joan Woodward point towards an increasing amount of work done by subordinates as having to be controlled by rules rather than by direct supervision or direct interaction when there are many subordinates per manager.[317] Rules are one way of economising on managers. It therefore appears to be paradoxical and to make poor economic sense to provide organisational obelisks which have extensive bureaucratic regulations. The impression that obelisks are more regulated than other structures need not, however, be a paradox at all.

Even if the obelisk features fewer rules than those organisations which are more like the peneplain, those rules that exist may be seen as unnecessary. It is not a particularly audacious hypothesis to state that people react more negatively towards unnecessary rules than they do towards a large number of rules. One type of rule that is certainly more common in the obelisk than in the near-peneplain is that relating to the ranking order. When the rules about who can decide on what and who gets to wear gold stars on their collar become numerous and hard to apply, frustration can arise in a way that does not occur when rules are hard to apply in the near-pene-plain. There is a greater tolerance for unnecessary rules regarding operational work, even if in this case too incomprehensible rules generate a degree of adrenaline. This hypothesis appears to corre-spond well with Crozier's studies of the malignant bureaucracy.[318]

Despite all this, one can imagine a column structure in an organ-isation with only a few employees. There will only be a few levels in it: one manager above a middle manager, both of whom are above the person with a task to perform. Tom Cruise in the *Mission Impossible* films springs to mind.[319] It sounds possible, but not sensible. However, when the organisation grows and we have ten, a hundred or a hundred thousand levels, such a structure becomes absurd. Just think of the overheads. Many of those contributing towards the cost involved in having a tall column also risk being underemployed. The lack of anything to do justifies the existence of a whole host of bureaucratic procedures in tall pyramids. In the tall column, the decision paths are made longer and are further extended by complications.

When we look at production, the disadvantages of hierarchisa-tion are again obvious. At the bottom of the column is a single refrigerator assembler, or the assistant refrigerator assembler's deputy assistant. No matter how big the organisation becomes, production will be limited in relation to a flatter pyramid. Production capacity in the column will be an extremely narrow bottleneck in a very narrow bottle. The effect is the same if we place customer-focused sales or complaints, for example, at the bottom of the column.

There are examples of those individuals on the second or third rungs of a hierarchy also focusing mainly on operations rather than the management functions one would normally associate with a higher position. The traditional Swedish glassworks had different teams with one master craftsman in each team. He was the one who carried out the final stage of producing, say, a glass, and affixing the foot. The other team members' work tasks were arranged in a descending scale according to rank. The second member of the team carried out the penultimate stage, and consequently the youngest apprentice gathered up the glass.[320] This hierarchisation follows a kind of collegial logic to which no one seems to have any objections.

Collegial logic is like the agenda at an academic seminar. Typically, a young doctoral student submits a report or a draft for an article. The next step involves a couple of career-hungry young PhDs pulling the doctoral student's text to pieces. Towards the end of the seminar – ideally just before the doctoral student gives up hope completely – some professor from his chair gives a constructive suggestion. Then everyone has coffee.

Locked between metaphors

By this stage, it should be obvious that organisational pyramids are torn down and raised up between two extreme end points. When the pyramid is torn down completely we reach the peneplain, and when it is built up as far as possible we have the column. This type of structural change is bound between these two extremes.

For a long time, organisational pyramids have been torn down in industry and the public sector under the impression that this is beneficial. At least, the flattening ideologists maintain that this is so.[321] Studies of how many companies have actually reduced their number of hierarchical levels show that flattening is relatively common, and also that companies which grow also grow in height.[322] Those that have been reorganised under the label of flattening may certainly have achieved completely different results. They will have been able to take advantage of the legitimacy of flatness without necessarily being troubled by its disadvantages according to known institutional patterns.[323] However, the weak connection between rites that create legitimacy and operational realities can hardly work in the face of obvious hypocrisy. The argument that flattening will reduce costs, increase democracy and job satisfaction, and achieve desired consumer orientation does not stand up to any critical review.[324] Movement towards the peneplain brings with it the disadvantages of flatness to which insufficient attention is paid. However, a movement towards column-like organisations leads to height-related disadvantages.

Neither of the extreme end points offers a sensible organisational structure. This in itself is not an astonishing conclusion. We can refer here to the classic studies made by Tom Burns and George Stalker – among many others – in which they demonstrate that the organisation as an organism and the organisation as a machine are both absurd constructs in their own right but are able to contribute towards our understanding if they are combined.[325] We will round off our thesis here by noting that while benefits are often to be had through change in either direction, there are also increasing disadvantages whatever the direction. By giving the end points names and substance, we have tried to emphasise this argument.

We have also drawn attention to the question of whether or not the lack of metaphor for the end points of the scale provides a partial explanation for the unilateral movement. If we have a scale with a load of useless and outmoded things placed at one end and everything that is modern and good at the other, it will be far too easy to choose which direction to take.

Buridan's ass

As you will no doubt recall, Buridan's ass starved to death while standing between two equally large and equally good bales of hay. Jean Buridan was a French scholastic philosopher who lived in the 14th century.[326] Hungry but without free will, his ass was drawn just as strongly in each direction. Poor beast.

As has been shown in this chapter, neither the column nor the peneplain is like a good bale of hay. Those who carry out organisational change cannot simply be compared to asses, tempting though it may be at times. Moreover, Buridan never wrote anything about the starved ass. In this respect, we have to rely on Peter King who wrote the introduction to *Jean Buridan's Logic* by Jean Buridan, *Philosophielexikon* by Poul Lübcke[327], and a collection of familiar Swedish quotations by Pelle Holm and Sven Ekbo.[328]

And that's not all. From a theoretical point of view, the story about the ass is wrong. The ass standing between the bales of hay is an example of a system in unstable equilibrium. Good old systems theory[329] can be used to describe the ass thus. It stands exactly midway between two equally attractive alternatives. As soon as it moves even slightly away from its state of equilibrium, it comes closer to one alternative than the other, and the force of attraction of the nearest alternative grows stronger. The ass then seeks out this alternative and munches on the hay. Try placing a small nail between two fixed magnets, and you'll see. If it (the ass) stands instead between two repellent alternatives – for example, the organisational column and peneplain – every little movement would mean that the alternative which then comes closer would have a stronger repellent effect, resulting in the ass being returned to the original position. This is called a stable equilibrium.

If the column and the peneplain had any real force of attraction, virtually all organisations would be either one or the other. But they are not good bales of hay. The pyramid appears to be a good compromise, and the similarity between our dilemma and that of the ass is called into question. Even if the two metaphors at the end points of the scale have turned out not to be attractive ones, when taken together they have taught us a great deal about what takes place between them – the raising and tearing down of pyramids.

7. Compare the Metaphor with Reality

Metaphors are a way of describing the world around us so that it becomes tangible. Most people understand that when Mark Turner argues, as we have already mentioned, that 'the sun is a jewel'[330], this does not mean that the sun actually is a jewel. Those who use this metaphor are seeking to clarify what the sun looks like or what, perhaps, is its importance. Children may believe that the moon is made of cheese if we say it is yellow like a cheese. But those of us who are older tend to know that we can't use the moon as a sandwich filling. Likewise when we talk of the dean who is said to be as round as a wheel of cheese – and when he is also as learned as the Devil himself, things get really confusing.[331]

Metaphors are such a common part of our speech that most of us believe we have mastered both their use and their interpretation. But we deceive ourselves all too often. One complication is that metaphors can clarify reality, but also unreality. 'The moon is a star' is one such example. It is not clear here whether the expression is a metaphor which provides an image of something here and now, or whether the metaphor is an image of a fantasy or a misunderstanding. In many different respects, the moon is not a star.

The uncertainty about whether a metaphor provides an image of reality or is a metaphor for a desirable circumstance may be, for example, an element of a conscious argumentation technique or may be due to linguistic clumsiness. In the case of the moon being made of cheese, it would be a matter of making a mistake that can be easily refuted by looking it up in an encyclopaedia. And having a dean made of cheese is an outdated notion. The moon as a star is trickier. Whether the metaphor clarifies or confuses the situation is due to the interpretation of both its originator and recipient.

In this chapter, we will use an example to show that the shift from one metaphor to another makes reality harder to understand. The example accompanying us throughout this chapter is that of 'the market as a pay setter'. The notion of rewarding effort is terribly old-fashioned. If we want to appear at all up-to-date, we should rather be talking about market-rate pay, or even the market setting pay. This expression could be a metaphor, but the source of the metaphor is unclear and so is its meaning – if indeed it means anything. It is used as a description of actual processes, and is assumed to provide an accurate picture of how pay is set. We will nevertheless try – at least occasionally – to disregard the fact that the market is so much more than just a price-setting mechanism in theory, in conception and in practice.

Images of markets

We tend to talk about 'the market' these days. Often in the singular. The market is everywhere, and affects everything we do. It governs our lives, so we need to stay on good terms with it. We have an unpleasant feeling of having heard something similar in some other context. Auguste Comte believed that abandoning the polytheistic religions in favour of consistent monotheism marked a great leap forward in the development of civilisation.[332] Without this shift, no scientific revolution would have taken place. The question is whether this lesson can be applied to the market. When we no longer have one market in one town and another in the next town but just one market which we call 'the Market', this is indeed related to a number of advances having been made, but it is hardly progress in itself.

Once upon a time, the market was a place where we bought and sold things. So when we talk about the market, this is by way of metaphorical reference to the institutions for carrying out trade in times gone by. Although the marketplaces of old had no mysterious properties, things could be extremely troublesome.

We know about these markets of old from reading fiction. Carl 'Snobak'[333] Snoilsky wrote a poem about Värnamo market, in

southern Sweden, set in the spring of 1719.[334] The betrothed couple
Per and Kersti meet there after six long years of saving up to buy a
cow and set up home together. It turns out that their savings consist of token coins issued to finance the Great Northern War and
which have just become worthless. Kersti sheds a few tears, and Per
suggests that they go their separate ways back home to save up for
another six years to buy their cow.

> He spoke many other words
> Of strength and steadfast hope,
> And Kersti, between her tears,
> Looked up from her apron
> And asked, her eyes shining bright
> With love and trust:
> "So shall we meet six years hence
> Once more in Värnamo?"[335]

Sadly, we never learn how things turned out in 1725. We only wish
to point out that the difference in meaning between the example
above and that into which it has been translated – in other words,
between Värnamo market and what scholars in management, economics and business journalists now call 'the market' – is hard to
assess. But it would appear to be considerable.

We have previously studied the image of the market in the public
sector.[336] An in-depth study showed that, by and large, politicians
and officials in the public sector had unrealistic ideas about the
market. For example, managers at various levels thought of consumers as well-informed, strong-willed, calculating, mobile benefit
maximisers. When economists talk about markets, they have an
ideal as to how these markets should work. A market with perfect
competition creates true rationality – or vice-versa perhaps. Four
criteria for perfect competition that are usually cited are many
participants, product uniformity, free entry and exit, and perfect
information.[337]

This idealised image of the market appears to stem from analogies referring to old-fashioned markets or more modern market
stalls selling vegetables. A number of very similar stalls stand close
to each other in the market square. The traders cannot manipulate
the products, and are forced to sell the same goods that all the other

traders are able to offer. The consumer can easily move from stall to stall, comparing products and relating the quality of the product to the price. The mobile and increasingly well-informed consumer can maximise his benefits. He has no ties to any of the stalls, while the stallholders have equal opportunities for marketing their products. One working day is spent choosing cucumbers, and the next getting to grips with tomatoes. Isn't this exactly how we imagine Per and Kersti operating?

Consumers at markets are rarely well-informed, strong-willed, calculating, mobile benefit maximisers. They do not have these characteristics and opportunities. Instead, consumers can often be described as ill-informed and incapable of becoming better informed. One reason is that it is often hard – or at least too expensive – to compare products and get an idea of their quality. Even prices can be hard to compare.

In this context, it is interesting to note that consumers often exhibit an unwillingness to become better informed. Typically, consumers dislike uncertainty and having to make choices. The consumer's method for avoiding making constant choices is to let habit decide.[338] What can prompt a consumer to change supplier or point of purchase is when he or she believes performance to be significantly poorer than that delivered elsewhere. 'Believe' and 'significantly' are two important words here.

Another example of a misconception is that the consumer demands facts – even objective facts. Consumers normally distrust facts, and instead want to know how good a product actually is. People are suspicious towards impartial surveys. Rumour is deemed to be more reliable than fact. If the consumer chooses to make a choice, this will be affected by marketing, the image of the product and irrelevant minor details. Rational choices based on objective facts are the exception rather than the rule.

The idea of the well-informed, fact-seeking consumer is closely related to the expectation that the fittest will survive. This is based on the conviction that the consumer chooses the best producers or services, which quite reasonably excludes the worst. The argument contains an annoying circularity. If the chosen product is the best by definition, the market will always be right. If this is modified to assume that the consumer chooses what he believes to be best, it becomes evident that the best may very well be excluded first.

Generally, one also tends to think that competition leads to lower prices.[339] Who exactly 'one' might be is another matter entirely. The writers of economics textbooks might perhaps be forced to pretend that they believe the message. Competition will result in a downward spiral of prices, in which products and services will become ever cheaper. Instead, the typical market situation is such that similar goods are sold at similar prices. But the goods are also differentiated on a superficial basis by way of, say, branding, making price comparisons more difficult. Great efforts are made to ensure that laundry detergent and toothpaste, for example, appear to be more different than chemical analyses would suggest. The only measurable difference between two refrigerators may be the manufacturer's logo.

We can continue in this vein. There are plenty of misapprehensions about what markets are and how they work in reality. Our impression is that these misapprehensions are widespread throughout all sectors of society. The unrealistic ideas about the market cannot within reason be based on any reality. These types of misapprehension about how markets work are based on neither study nor personal experience. It would seem more plausible that we have conceived these ideas by reading economic theory or studying the plethora of newspaper articles in which such theories are dealt with as if they were a universal reality. We would, however, like to point out that we are not particularly scrupulous about what counts as reality. On the whole, reality is a social construct and elusive by nature. Like Master Örtstedt (Urtstedt), we would return in terror 'Das Ding an sich'[340] to its sender were we to receive such a package.

Urtstedt reads Kant one winter eve and is
intrigued by certain principles of his.

But heavy flows the German of the sage,
and soon our prof is nodding o'er his page.

In dreams the seed of waking thought grows tall.
Kant isn't hard to understand at all.

A bright-wrapped package (here's the metaphor)
Arrives from Königsberg at Urtstedt's door.

'Fragile – Don't Drop!' in spidery letters, drawn
rococo-curlicued, appears thereon.

The sender, and the present's fabricant,
is no one lesser than Professor Kant.

He checks the label at his window-niche.
For 'Contents' Kant put down DAS DING AN SICH.

Around this Thing the world we touch and see
is but a seeming, colored splendidly.

Who'd dare to rip the giftwrap and the strings
off pure Reality, the Thing of things?

Professor Urtstedt backs away unnerved
from what no hand has touched nor eye observed.

Think if his clumsy fingers let it crack!
With many thanks he mails the parcel back.[341]

Reality may be ever so problematic. A theory such as market theory must be about something other than itself. And we would go along with the suggestion that what market theory is really about can be called reality.

We won't waste much space here by levelling criticism at the weak grasp that market theory has on reality. However, well-founded criticism such as the argument that the scientific perspective behind the ideas 'reflects a distinctly androcentric and Western perspective on personality and individual action'[342], and that 'economics has become ideology'[343], has not diminished the metaphorical power of market theory. In this context, it should be noted that economists themselves disparagingly call their very strongest intellectual concept 'the simplest economics textbook model'[344] and criticise it vigorously.[345] And yet the discipline continues to present 'empirical evidence' for its model.[346]

The image of the market as a pay setter

Just as there are images of what the market is and how it works, so too are there images of what market-rate pay is. When it comes to pay, these images fall into two groups. One is the everyday image which is documented in the media. This comes close to the image of the market as the popular version provided by the market theory of economics. In the everyday image, pay reflects the relationship between supply and demand.[347]

Authorities, trade unions and employers with their organisations are responsible for the other image of market-rate pay. The image depicted by Claes Liljedahl of the Swedish Association of Graduates in Business Administration and Economics in extracts taken from a online interview with him is a typical one.[348] According to him, market rate pay is what should be the outcome of pay negotiations. In the same interview he says that this is also the pay one would want to receive, although this hardly follows.

Since the Swedish Tax Agency uses the phrase 'market-rate pay' in various contexts, it is forced to say something in its instructions about what this is. Here, too, the quotation below relates to a kind of standard pay. Note in particular that remuneration agreed on in collective agreements is deemed to be in line with the market rate.

> Market-rate pay should be regarded as that normally paid for the corresponding work performance in that location. In most cases, remuneration can be calculated on the basis of collective agreements. When assessing whether remuneration is in line with the market rate, factors such as training, industry experience, etc. should be taken into consideration.[349]

Jusek, the Swedish association for lawyers, MBA's, systems scientists, personnel managers and social scientists, notes in its pay policy programme that typical pay according to salary statistics should not be standardised.[350] However, when assessing how high or low market-rate pay is, there appears to be a need for better pay statistics. The Trade Union Foundation for Economic Research noted the following in a report issued a couple of years ago:

> Equal pay for equal work and small differences in pay are the aims of traditional solidaristic pay policy. Equal pay for equal

work and small differences in pay are also what the free market will tend to give, at least in the slightly longer term.[351]

The Foundation's representatives imagine a market which achieves equality and desired fairness. The idea that market-rate pay is fair crops up frequently in organisational Sweden. This line of thought is based on equality or differences within reason being fair and the market achieving equality. The fact that employees ask for fair pay comes up in many studies.[352] The commercial market pay database maintained by Löneanalyser AB puts its faith in statistical data.[353] In their case, the aim seems to be to achieve a fair spread of pay.

> Major changes also affect pay setting to a large degree. Central and collective pay setting are a thing of the past – individual pay setting is what applies now. Every individual's pay must be carefully balanced with regard to work tasks and, in particular, what the individual is capable of achieving and is expected to achieve in his or her work. The fact that every work task requires specialist expertise, experience, etc. to a greater extent than before is of great significance in terms of setting pay if companies are to be able to recruit and retain the necessary workforce. This means that companies also need information about workforce prices in the same way that they need information about competitors' prices of various products and services, etc.[354]

In Sweden we first came across the market as a pay setter in official rhetoric in the mid-1990s. The Swedish Equal Opportunities Ombudsman took Örebro County Council to court for not giving women and men equal pay for equal work. It was – and is – the case that pay differences are allowed to be of any size in Sweden as long as they can be explained by gender-neutral arguments. If not, the pay difference constitutes gender-based pay discrimination. This is illegal, just like murder and dismemberment.

In the Örebro case, midwives were compared with medical technology engineers. The work carried out by midwives was more demanding and required higher qualifications, regardless of how the comparison was carried out. The Swedish Labour Court ruled that the pay differential was explained by 'the market serving as the factual grounds for setting pay', and that this was not therefore a matter of pay discrimination.[355]

Enough about the official attitude towards the market as a pay setter. In the media, market-rate pay is used as an explanation for very high salaries being paid to certain male sportsmen. Our Swedish football star Zlatan Ibrahimovic was owned for a time by AFC Ajax where, according to his autobiography, he was duped AFC being paid a far too low salary.[356] His levels of pay thereafter reflected the market rate. However, the question is what one can say about the unbelievably high annual salary of EUR 14 million that he is being paid in Paris Saint-Germain (2013). The Swedish media, at least, feel at times that his salary is now so high that it is preventing Zlatan from changing clubs (but we'll see) – PSG would in that case have offered him one which was not set at the market rate for any other club in the market.

Seen from an international point of view, the pay Swedish managers receive is not remarkably high – but it is high. And the high salaries that individuals such as heads of companies receive are normally seen by the media as being reflecting the market rate. Journalists do indeed bemoan at regular intervals the amount particular bosses get paid, but they always return to the same conclusion that that's how the market works. Any justification as to why bosses earn far, far more than, say, professors is not forthcoming. Market-rate pay is, quite simply, the pay you can get.

His Imperial Majesty Shahinshah arrived unexpectedly at the teahouse where mulla Nasrudin had been left in charge.

The Emperor called for an omelette.

"We shall now continue with the hunt," he told the Mulla. "So tell me what I owe you."

"For you and your five companions, Sire, the omelettes will be a thousand gold peaces."

The Emperor raised his eyebrows.

"Eggs must be very costly here. Are they as scarce as that?"

"It is not the eggs which are scarce here, Majesty – it is the visits of kings."[357]

The salaries managers receive are sometimes so closely aligned to the market rate that they need to be kept secret for as long as possible. One can imagine that they must therefore be even more embarrassingly high. When journalists wonder what a particular manager gets paid, the answer they get is that it reflects the market rate and (in the best case) will be reviewed at a later date.

However, the term 'market-rate pay' as a euphemism for an exceedingly high salary is used by the media. It is sometimes said that a salary is high and should then mean that it deviates from the market rate, but that in all normality it results in lower prices.

'Won't customers have to pay a lot for peppers if the top brass receive enormous salaries?'

'No. The important thing is that we are competitive. Profitability is not our goal, but a means of being able to reduce prices for customers.'[358]

But it's not only industry that conceals its salaries behind the concept of the market rate. When Kjell Ahlberg was interviewed in his capacity as new Finance Manager of the Swedish Trade Union Confederation, he was asked about his salary. 'My pay is in line with the market rate. It doesn't really matter how much I earn.'[359]

To make the rich work harder
you pay them more.
To make the poor work harder
you pay them less.[360]

What rates of pay would the market set?

Let us first assume that the market really does set pay. Let us also assume that this works largely in the way that people believe and economists maintain. We will come to the matter of the reasonableness of these assumptions shortly. What would pay determination look like if it were controlled and set entirely by market forces?

It is quite possible for markets to determine the price of anything whatsoever. Including work. The price is set by matching supply and demand. What is needed in order for the market to be able to determine price is a supply which varies with remuneration. If the employer increases the pay, we will be prepared to work that little bit more, and someone who is not currently in the job market may be attracted to do it. If pay is lowered, the opposite happens. We become less inclined to sell our manpower at the lower price, and some people will leave the industry or the job market. By entering the number of working hours offered on the vertical axis and entering pay on the horizontal axis, we get a supply curve. Nothing unusual about that.

As well as supply, the demand for manpower must also vary with price. When manpower costs less, employers can consider employing more people, while more expensive manpower reduces the scope and results in fewer employees or shorter working hours. If we plot both these curves without investigating in any greater depth what the various relationships are between price and quantity, we see that pay at any given moment in time is the intersection between the two curves. At this precise point, supply and demand in terms of manpower are matched at a certain level called 'market equilibrium wage'.

The nitpicking audience will immediately notice a special case. One of the curves may be vertical, which means that supply or demand can be a fixed volume. However, both curves cannot be vertical since they would then never intersect. Such demand or supply would appear to be far-fetched, but we will come back to this later on. Horizontal curves are even more unlikely, and are therefore discounted.

If pay is set by the market in matching supply and demand, this would result in a number of highly visible effects. Let us then discuss a few examples.

Low management pay

In our culture, pay is not the only reason why senior positions are sought after. We also want power. The fact that we strive for power may be for reasons of status so that other people are not in positions of power over us, or because we want – to some extent, at least – to reshape society. There are many reasons for being interested in having a managerial position. The notion of 'compensatory pay differences'[361] is an attempt to rescue a market model which lacks an empirical foundation. The downside is being subordinate to a manager and not to manage others. Correspondingly, we have rescue attempts which are far-fetched and based on little empirical evidence when there are a number of factors which point to the market not setting pay.

Generous management pay is, from a market-rate pay perspective, a remarkable phenomenon. Particularly in the corporate world, there is a great deal of talk about the market. However, management pay is definitely not market-rate pay. The data does not indicate that we choose the cheapest qualified applicant for a managerial position; rather, it appears to be the case that applicants who demand far too much or are satisfied with far too little are eliminated. An organisation that is – or that wants to be – successful seems, purely for reasons of legitimacy, to require well-paid managers. How else would anyone know that there is a focus on cutting-edge expertise? However, those applicants who are unreasonably miserly do not make suitable managers.

If we were to allow the pay demands of those with sufficient expertise to be the primary factor for recruitment, managerial positions would presumably no longer command higher salaries. Since organisations are normally in the shape of a pyramid, the pool of potential candidates for managerial positions is always relatively large. Of course, some people lack the necessary ability for promotion while others lack the desire to progress. But it still seems unlikely that there would be no applicants for managerial jobs without pay incentives. A reverse action could simply be expected to lead to the most interested applicant accepting a pay cut in order to become a manager.

The idea of someone accepting a managerial position which pays less is not as improbable as it might sound. When choosing between employers, jobs and industries, people often do not choose the option which offers the highest pay. People are prepared to accept a pay cut to get a job that they want for other reasons. This is true of positions both higher up in the hierarchy, such as presidents and prime ministers, and lower down, such as professors and football players.

No unemployment

If the market were to set pay, there would be no unemployment other than that resulting from mobility in the job market. For sufficiently low pay, there would always be a job to be done. It's possible to sell anything if the marketing is crafty enough or if the price is low enough. In this case, the pay would simply drop until the benefit derived from the last employee corresponded to a very small need indeed. Of course, we can derive benefit from a teacher for three euros an hour, a fireman for just two euros, and any old academic for a single euro.

If the job market had no limits, there would be full employment worldwide if the market set pay. However, the free mobility of manpower that this would require is a long way off. As was shown by the discussion surrounding the conflict between the Latvian construction company Laval un Partneri and the Swedish Building Workers' Union in connection with the construction of a school in Vaxholm in 2004/05, most Swedes see Sweden as a limited job market, even within the EU. Overwhelming resistance was mobilised against the use of a workforce which was willing to work in Sweden on another country's terms. Latvian unemployment wasn't Sweden's problem. And this has not changed.

Very low pay in certain industries and certain locations

Even with market-rate pay, the supply of manpower will continue to be 'too high' in certain industries and certain locations. This is a particular problem in those industries which are not so easy to leave because the training and experience gained in these do not make people generally employable. As a consequence of supply being great in relation to demand, pay will be very low here. The same is true of locations which people do not wish to – or cannot – leave.

In order for pay to drop significantly, there must be no alternative remuneration systems. Unemployment benefits – or what is sometimes described in the debate related to this as 'self-selected sick leave' – should not pay more than the lowest wages. There should probably also be an obligation to work, so that even those who earn so little that they do not want to work for the pay offered are still forced to take such jobs.

Pay cuts in connection with students leaving education

If the market were to set pay, this would vary in exactly the same way that, say, the price of crude oil currently does. We would see pay cuts as soon as supply rose. With a new wave of MBA's graduating, salaries for MBA's would drop. With the last of these graduates entering employment, pay would stabilise temporarily at a lower level before slowly increasing (if demand were to continue to grow) until the next cohort arrived.

Professions become exclusive

If the market were to set pay, those in the job market would try to exclude those outside it. High pay requires a limited supply of manpower. One method a profession could use to reduce the supply of manpower would be to ensure that employers require qualifications and certifications for the carrying out of certain work tasks. This, when seen in connection with the desire for high barriers in order to reduce competition, reminds us of the guild mentality.[362] More recent parallels include the US trade unions' restrictions on membership numbers through closed shop policies.[363] Once entry requirements exist, these can be gradually supplemented with others so that it becomes increasingly difficult to join that guild or profession and do the job. Even today, such tendencies are widespread. One clear example is the Swedish teaching profession, in which the ability to assist with student learning has taken a back seat at the expense of ever tougher formal competence requirements.

One alternative to raising the level of requirements in order to protect the interests of wage earners is to work to reduce the number of training places if the market sets pay. It is in the interests of those who are already qualified that as few as possible with the equivalent education credentials should follow them. We can also expect immigrant workers to be seen as a threat. If the market sets pay, an increase in supply will result in lower pay, no matter how this increase comes about. Professions will mobilise and resist. It is quite simply true that the exclusivity of a profession is essential to its existence.[364]

Equal pay for equal work

'The market is colour blind.'[365] If the market were to set pay, it would never discriminate. The market that sets the market equilibrium wage is a machine, and has no prejudices. Anyone who has sufficient expertise and demands the lowest pay gets the job. Full stop.

In Sweden, studies tend to show that the pay difference between men and women that cannot be explained in terms of age, education, profession, etc. is just under ten percent.[366] In an interesting article, William Bridges and Robert Nelson seek out explanations for pay differences between men and women in organisations.[367] They reach the conclusion that these cannot be explained by market patterns. This does not surprise us. How could the market bring about unequal pay when it is not the market that sets pay?

Market control and pay determination?

In point after point, what we know about pay determination differs in reality from a situation in which the market sets pay. Why is this so? What prevents the market from controlling pay determination? And why is the job market not a market?[368]

The explanation for why pay set by the market does not exist is that the requirements for the market to set the price of work have not been met. We will discuss the four main requirements below: the existence of supply that varies with price (a supply curve); the existence of demand that varies with price (a demand curve); the market is consulted about the price; and we do not care about the market's answer.

1. There is no supply curve

In order for the market to be able to set the price of manpower, a supply curve is required. This means that employees are willing to work less at low prices or pay, and to work more or to a greater extent if pay rises. The special cases that we promised to return to above immediately prove unrealistic. In order for there to be a supply curve of manpower (which is inclined), the following must apply:

– Pay is the most important factor in the choice of work – we will return to this.
– Employees must be flexible and mobile.
– There is free competition between employees, who underbid each other.
– There is free access to the job market, so that the quantity offered can vary.
– There is a good degree of knowledge about the demand for manpower on the part of all employees, so that they actually choose the work that offers the highest pay.

If employees only offer manpower at a single fixed price, they will have set this price without consulting the market. In that case we cannot call this market-rate pay. However, the market can set the price if a fixed quantity is offered. A situation in which the supply is one hundred percent fixed, entirely regardless of pay, could probably never arise. At a certain pay level, there will be someone considering working an extra hour.

2. *There is no demand curve*

In order for the market to be able to set the price of manpower, a demand curve is required. The employers' need for manpower must vary with the price.

In order for there to be a demand curve (which is inclined), the following must apply:

– Pay is the most important factor in the choice of manpower.
– Pay must be set freely, which means that it must be possible to raise and reduce pay.
– There is a good degree of knowledge about the supply of manpower on the part of all employers, so that they actually choose the manpower that requires the lowest pay.

If employers are only willing to employ manpower at a single fixed price, they will have set this price without consulting the market. However, the market can set the price if a fixed quantity is demanded. It seems unlikely that this would happen entirely independently of pay demands.

3. *The market is not consulted*

The market can only determine pay if it is consulted. Pay is then determined by the point of intersection between the curves representing the supply and demand of manpower. If the market is not consulted, another party will have set the price.

Consulting the market involves the employer having to gather information and regularly test the market. This takes place through staff turnover and employing new employees at the lowest price. If this is not done, the market cannot respond to the question of price. For employees, consulting the market involves their being mobile and hunting out information and higher pay.

The aim of a lot of labour legislation and agreements between social partners is to prevent the market from setting pay. We have jointly taken steps to guarantee a certain level of basic social security and a certain degree of stability. Other legislation and regulations do their part to prevent the market from setting pay. Examples of this include tax legislation and regulations within the social sphere.

4. *No one cares about the market's answer*

The market can virtually never set pay. Nor are we normally able to allow it to try. But to top it all, nor do we want the market to set pay – we don't want to know the answer! We don't want to know because it might well result in us having our pay cut, and many of us would be unable to live on market-rate pay. And employers don't want to know because it would lead to low pay for easy jobs and constant pay variations to complicate all the planning.

What is the significance of pay?

We promised to come back to the fact that the significance of pay is important in terms of the degree of incline of the supply curve. Many people have asked themselves how significant pay is as an individual factor in the choice of profession or employment. And quite often, we have then asked students, employees and others the same question. As if they would know the answer!

We can note that price is the most important factor in only a few choices of products or services. Even when choosing between similar products such as different types of jeans or very similar products such as different brands of petrol, other factors are involved. The fact that surveys suggesting otherwise may regularly be referred to in the media is due to these studies featuring obvious systematic errors. The same is true when 57.2 percent say they have handed in their resignation due to poor pay.

When researchers of different kinds ask consumers what is the most important factor for them in choosing food in their local store, we are given the answer: 'Price.' However, behaviour shows that other factors are just as important. High-end retailers would have long since gone out of business if price were the only important factor. No supermarket could survive on the handful of customers who, according to the surveys, choose their groceries according to price. Plenty of people still buy their milk and bread from 7-Eleven. Answering surveys has its own logic. Buying bread has a completely different logic.

There are, of course, exceptions. Some customers hunt out the cheapest price as if it were a sport. This reminds us of our friend Sune, who conducts a market analysis before every major purchase. He also notes where the best bargains are to be had in general. If we want to buy a new dishwasher, we consult Sune. He can then tell us which brand gives us the most bang for our buck, and where we can find this brand at the best price. It's mostly Sune's friends who benefit from his research rather than Sune himself. He spends hours keeping tabs on prices and quality, but doesn't buy a dishwasher any more often than the rest of us. His market research should therefore be regarded as a cross between voluntary work and a hobby. And it's probably just as interesting as stamp collecting.

And then there are those who could never imagine going for the cheapest option. The price is important to them, but certainly not in the same way as for us bulk buyers. For those who believe that high prices are positive, the things that cost less are always worse in some respect. They're right insofar that the cheaper items cost less. When there are very large differences in price between relatively similar goods, this leads to the market being divided up. Those of us who want really expensive bicycles don't buy them at the supermarket.

In the same way that price has a certain significance but often comes in second or third place, so too can we expect things to be with pay. Factors other than pay are most important when it comes to the vast majority of choices we make. Pay doesn't govern our choice of education or workplace. The pay offered is a factor among a wealth of other factors, all of which play a certain role in our decision.

The notion that the market sets pay is incorrect. '[When seen] in detail, the standard theory is obviously false.'[369] The fact that it lives on in our world view is not only due to rigorous marketing. After all, employers prefer competent workers who cost less. Employees prefer workplaces where they receive relatively more pay for equally interesting work tasks. Untruths made up of truths have a tendency to be more credible than downright lies. No one will believe you if you offer the Eiffel Tower at a bargain price. Well, almost no one. But plenty of people buy problem-free, great value cars every couple of years.

What does 'market-rate pay' mean, then?

If the market doesn't set pay, how does it work? Which other principles or forces control pay determination instead? The answer isn't all that far away. There are three ways of determining prices, and thus also pay.

1. The market sets pay

The market has the ability to set pay. But as shown above, we do not allow it to. However, the myth is a strong one, and those who look for examples will no doubt find some. In occupations with a shortage of suitable employees, pay is sometimes driven up by market-like bidding. In the longer term, the employee responds with measures such as rationalisation and pay adjustment, putting the market back out of play.

2. Pay is set via an unassailable principle

We can imagine pay being set by legislation. It might sound tricky, but it seems to be possible to give equal pay to everyone or pay according to need. This is certainly not an entirely unassailable principle, but it is a principle that has been established high up in the system and could therefore be an acceptable one.

We can also imagine pay being set on the basis of opinions or habits that are taken for granted. We might then have to think about principles set by forces far removed from us rather than high up. If everyone is on board, such a principle can be entirely voluntary and yet entirely totalitarian. Those of us in the education system normally maintain that education must bring reward. If everyone took this view, it could be taken to an extreme whereby every university credit gave a specific and perpetually fixed additional sum in one's pay packet.

Statistics can be used to show that every year of additional education gives a four percent increase in pay.[370] But that doesn't impress anyone. Nor does anyone bat an eyelid when the calculation of lifetime income for a carpenter works out as being much better than that for a university lecturer. Two things are worth mentioning. Firstly, it is hard to measure the financial value of higher education in a way that everyone agrees upon.[371] And secondly, only an economist would come up with the idea that financial value should be most important factor.[372]

Just like with length of education, job evaluation could also be developed to form an unassailable principle. One formula for job evaluation could be established to control the wages paid by every payroll office. Any payment of wages above those specified in the objective job evaluation could quite simply be penalised. This would be no more absurd than numbering all the cows in Europe. Off to jail with those who steal from our joint pay pool!

These days, when gambling competes with alcohol as the Swedish state's main source of funding for numbing the masses, a pay lottery presents itself as a possibility. This would have to be directed from the top, and would not be as unrealistic as it might sound. Pay already feels like the luck of the draw at times when we tear open our monthly payslips. We need not imagine a tombola or a fairground wheel of fortune. The drawing of lots can just as easily be metaphorical. We receive the pay we happen to get without getting any sensible answer if we ask: 'What have I done to earn so much?' Or if we demand: 'Why the hell don't I earn more?'

3. Pay is set through collective bargaining

> New models of labor markets should surely center on bargaining among existing workers, potential workers, workers' organizations, managers, and government officials with respect to all aspects of jobs: definition, ranking, sorting, and the linkage to other jobs.[373]

Collective bargaining is the usual method for setting pay in Sweden. Collective bargaining can simply be said to be rational in that it involves decisions being made after the arguments on all sides have been aired. It is also a system with a high degree of legitimacy, not least by virtue of being the standard one. However, this requires the parties to it being fairly equal in strength.[374] It can be noted that even those who want market-rate pay call the process 'salary negotiations'.

The rules that set the constraints for these negotiations can be found in agreements and shared ideals. The results of earlier negotiations and previous agreements at other levels in the form of binding collective agreements are important. Nils-Eric Sandberg (Swedish liberal debater) would no doubt agree, but would call this a 'cartelised planned economy'.[375] In any case, a combination of negotiated practice and convention governs the course of events, as in so many other contexts. The role of collective agreements means that we can talk about collective negotiations for many employees.

> Only in exceptional cases, for example, highly coveted manpower with specialist training and expertise, have pay conditions and working conditions been negotiable and open to influence for individual employees ...[376]

Although the historical description by Christer Lundh as quoted above has a political leaning typical of publications by the Centre for Business and Policy Studies, it is obvious that pay determination has been decentralised, the degree of union organisation reduced, and the coverage of collective agreements has shrunk.[377] He believes that 'the scope of the change processes should not be overstated, and their rate should not be overestimated'.[378] No chance – we tend to do the opposite.

Let us step to one side and use Aaron Wildavsky's budget theory as an example.[379] According to this, the budget is determined in negotiation between advocates, who require resources for their operations, and guardians, who sit on the coffers, look at the bigger picture and try to resist. His budget theory includes a number of factors which explain why the advocates sometimes succeed in obtaining lots of money, while at other times the guardians succeed in resisting demands. This is a theory that enables us to understand the budgeting game and explain the outcome of negotiations.

Pay negotiations do not differ from collective bargaining in general. This is an effective method for finding a price, providing that both parties play their roles. A number of handbooks on negotiation which are full of tips and tricks are available. Successful practice that is the message that is conveyed above all else. For example, this could involve more general negotiation techniques[380], business negotiation[381] and job market negotiations[382]. Just like with budget strategies, we can turn to the negotiators for advice and see them as explaining the degree of success of negotiation. If we assume that the writers do not lie and instead recount in all truth their best experiences, we can derive some theoretical value from the joyous acclamations. Are you with us? If we take the advice as advice it is often trite, and if we try it out we still do not become star negotiators. But if we want to understand why things turned out as they did, good normative management literature can often provide suggestions and sometimes even answers.

The outcome of pay negotiations depends on the strength of the parties involved and the nature of the rules, but it depends perhaps most of all on the outcome of previous negotiations. There is a wealth of negotiation theory that we won't be going into here in any depth. There is a good deal of support for the idea that the most accurate prediction of the outcome of negotiations is normally being the same as for past negotiations.[383] Whether or not the differences between these occasions can then be seen as incremental and actually taking place in small stages is open to discussion.[384]

If the market does not set pay now, the question of how pay was determined in the beginning is an interesting one. This is the basis on which negotiation results have been built up over the years. As scholars in management, we do not have any answers. What we can say is that it appears unlikely that the market functioned in the beginning and set the first wages. We have searched without success for information about this in the American comic strip B.C.[385]

Price negotiation is a battle in which strategies and arguments come into conflict with each other. The market may emerge again here, but this time as an argument for a certain level of pay and not as a mechanism that de facto sets market equilibrium wages. Market forces are normally an employee argument. When the matter has arisen in the Swedish Labour Court, the market argument is the employer's explanation. And then the circularity of the market theory comes in handy.

We heard one example of a market argument from a TV1 journalist many years ago. He has subsequently acted in such a way that it is uncertain whether or not he should be trusted. But the story need not be true in order to illustrate the significance of the market argument for setting pay. According to the story told by the journalist, when TV4 was launched, some employees working for TV1 transferred to the new station. These were people who were needed, who fitted in, or who – it was thought – would work well on TV4. These new recruits received pay rises. A certain increase in pay is not unusual when changing jobs, and is certainly not the only driving force. But some of those who remained at TV1 cited the higher salaries, and pointed out that they weren't necessarily there for life. According to our source, these demands pushed up the salaries of the entire collective at TV1. A number of TV1 employees therefore received higher salaries without having demanded these, and never once considered changing employers. The higher salaries at TV1 were cited as having been adapted in line with the market.

See the metaphor

The aim of the discussion about market-rate pay has been to point out how problematic it is when a metaphor is mistaken for reality. Many aspects of the real phenomenon become harder to understand and require detailed explanation. A whole catalogue of excuses appear, making it increasingly hard for us to understand what is happening.

'Market' is a word which now gives rise to two associations: the market in Värnamo and the abstract idea offered for sale by economists. Note that this is a question of selling, and that what is sold is a kind of intellectual concept that it is hard to challenge. The question is simply whether we haven't been any more duped than Per and Kersti were by the worthless copper coins issued by Georg Heinrich von Görtz between 1715 and 1719. Because if we ask for market-rate pay at our next pay negotiations, we're likely to be disappointed. Like Per, we'll have to spend another six years working as the priest's farmhand.

Still, we have also shown how easy it is to get out of this dilemma. Distinguish between the metaphor and that which it represents. The metaphor is an image, and can simply be compared to a map. If we find our way home using the map, that's all well and good. But if we use market theory with a capital 'M', we're bound to lose our way.

When the metaphor clouds our view

The map does not lead us the right way. That's one side of the problem. A second side of the problem is that it leads us astray. But there's also a third side worth mentioning. If we go there with our defective map, it will be easy for us to disagree about things that are of no importance.

During a tour one summer, we were on the road between Olskroken in Gothenburg and Kattunga Skogsbo in Björketorp. We did actually have accurate maps, but the map reader was holding one of the map sheets upside-down. When he said: 'We're now crossing a stream', we actually crossed a railway which, according to the map, should still have been a few minutes away. A discussion ensued about why no one in the car had noticed the stream or mentioned it. We didn't fall out over it, and indeed we had a good laugh when the map was turned back up the right way, but the point has been illustrated. The market metaphor makes it harder to understand the unequal rates of pay and to do anything about it. However, the discussion between employers and the representatives of the employed will also be to some extent about the things that are wrong. The map generates a meaningless conflict.

In another situation, we were studying the merger of Sahlgrenska Hospital, Mölndal Hospital and Östra Hospital in the West Sweden region of Gothenburg.[386] The creation of a single hospital with joint management and finances was the culmination of three years of inquiries and argumentation. A merger – or, in our case, a new and stronger coordinated set-up – was already one of the possibilities mentioned in the terms of reference for the inquiry.

In this context, we may find these continuous mergers surprising. Like the fictional detective Tam Sventon's arch-rival,[387] they force their way into the organisation dressed in their neatly-pressed trousers and their pointy, well-polished shoes. One overriding experience (collective sigh …) in studies of mergers is that the benefits of large-scale production and coordination on which the decision has been based are hard to achieve once the actual merger has been carried out.[388] If they are to prove financially beneficial, this will take time.[389] At today's pace of restructuring, it is doubtful whether anyone can wait for effects that will materialise in ten to fifteen years' time. In the age of shareholder value maximization, mergers should therefore be rare. But that's not the case.

There are also those who try to demonstrate that mergers can be successful.[390] Naturally, success depends on what the starting point was and what it was hoped would be achieved. For example, some suggest that mergers afford a better market position or market power,[391] but the question is what a hospital, say, would want with that. Consultants try to explain successful mergers by saying that their concepts were used to build bridges between different corporate cultures.[392]

Overly sweeping generalisations about how mergers work miss the point that mergers are different. One impression of them is, however, a common feature: just like other reforms, merger decisions are notorious for lacking of a sense of history, in that the merging parties dispense with any reflection on the experiences of others.[393] Indeed, the documentation drawn up in advance of the merger of Sahlgrenska Hospital, Mölndal Hospital and Östra Hospital did not include any consideration of what difficulties might be encountered in its carrying out.[394]

At the risk of making too grand a generalisation, one can say that mergers are always innocent. In retrospect, it can be hard to obtain reliable details about how conscious or unconscious of future problems the investigators and decision-makers were at the time of making the decision. One interpretation may be that this innocence is genuine. No one wants to think about problems before such major changes take place. Another interpretation is that the investigators and decision-makers conspired to hide or minimise the problems. The 'lowball' metaphor crops up again. After the merger has taken place, it is not hard to find people who maintain that they knew all along which problems would arise. If there are documented comments or objections, this sort of hindsight can affect the apportioning of responsibility but not the course of events.

The reason for the merger in question was no doubt that hospital care in Gothenburg would improve. But let us formulate the obvious: the merger between Sahlgrenska Hospital, Mölndal Hospital and Östra Hospital did not involve moving Östra Hospital or Mölndal Hospital to the site of Sahlgrenska Hospital or its immediate vicinity in Änggårdsbergen. And nor did it consist of emptying Östra Hospital of all its equipment and patients and then moving these to Sahlgrenska Hospital. The merger was not an amalgamation, and was never intended to be. The intention is best described as an attempt to bring the hospitals under joint management. However, both the reformers and their opposition drew their arguments from the merger metaphor.

The argument in favour of merging was based on the viewpoint of cure. Operating on a larger scale would provide scope for more specialist and intervention-based treatment. Improved efficiency would do away with queues and duplicated tasks. Everything would be organised individually and streamlined for enhanced efficiency. The argument against, however, was usually based on the perspective of care. Accessibility was one typical argument. Another argument was that the duties of a hospital relate to caring for the 'whole person'. The arguments against also included an expectation that the number of beds would be reduced in the event of a merger.

In view of the fact that no physical merger was intended, this labelling led to a great deal of meaningless discussion. Several years of public debate between politicians, healthcare workers and others who thought they had something to say ended up dealing with the wrong issues. Those taking part in the debate were holding the map upside down, as it were. The difficulties in reaching a decision would just as surely also have been significantly reduced on implementation if a different metaphor had been used. The same reform content under another name would have aroused less – but possibly more valuable – resistance. It is also possible that the opponents would have won the debate had it been about something other than a merger. 'An interesting case, on the whole.'[395]

People can, of course, use whichever words they wish when describing what happens or what they themselves do. We can't stop them. The extensive use of metaphors provides a great deal of freedom. But it can still be practical to use terms and concepts which have a reasonable connection to what is happening. Words cannot be used in just any way if we want to avoid complete disarray. No reasonable interpretation of the word 'market' leads to the conclusion that the market sets pay. And as long as the hospitals remain where they are, the word 'merger' is confusing.

8. Using Metaphors to Transfer Knowledge

Many people are well versed in a great many things that they do not believe have a bearing on everyday life within an organisation. These could be experiences gained through leisure activities, or further reading alongside professional training. It can be nice to think about other things during one's free time than those to which one devotes oneself at work. Others may see it as a privilege to be able to use the full extent of their knowledge at work. In this chapter, we show how such practical experience or the insight gained from books can be transferred to the organisation we want to understand better.

We all know something about the way people speak different languages. We intend to use the concept of language in a transferred, metaphorical sense. German and French are two languages. Someone who speaks them both is bilingual. We have an everyday knowledge of bilingualism. Bilingualism has also been studied in depth. If the word 'language' is used as a metaphor in our example, 'bilingualism' naturally also becomes a metaphor.

We have taken our example from the world of the school. We try to see how the actual transfer of knowledge takes place in terms of the school's management organisation being a bilingual environment in which a language of management and a language of education are both spoken. We attempt here to transfer our knowledge of bilingualism to that of organisational control.

The actual phenomenon of bilingualism can be problematised. Power has one language, and love has another. We could say: 'Your words are fair, but your actions speak another language.' Someone once said that men and women speak different languages. In this particular case, we doubt that can be true. If that were the case, bilingualism would need to do away with the biological gender boundaries. We are not against this, but let us now move on to the world of the school.

The school's two languages

The example we will be using in this chapter is one of the successfully revamped schools in central Gothenburg. Our focus is on the teachers, the head teachers and the head teachers' manager, and on the fact that the way in which they express themselves helps differentiate between them so clearly. They do not actually speak two languages, but what happens if we apply something of what we know about bilingualism to understand what we see within the organisation?

We will call one of the languages Management-Speak.[396] It is spoken by the operational manager who manages the head teachers, among others, and it is also spoken by the head teachers themselves. The operational managers speak Management-Speak to each other and to the head teachers. The head teachers speak Management-Speak to the operational manager and, in certain situations, to the teachers.

Management-Speak is taught at schools of management and economics and other institutions where these subjects are studied.[397] Those who are fluent in the language are often MBA's. They can quite easily tell the difference between revenue and income. Terms such as 'standard ancillary expenses' and 'incentive structure' just trip off their tongues. As well as those terms that may have a precise meaning, Management-Speak also includes a significant number of words and phrases that hardly have any precise meaning but act instead as padding. They are nevertheless extremely important to those who speak Management-Speak. Without terms such as 'competitive strategy', 'cutting-edge expertise' or 'quality assurance', this language could only be used in extremely limited contexts. These examples may have been given a strict definition in a particular book or article, but are used quite freely these days. 'Incentive structure' has now ended up in this category.

Many people who speak Management-Speak know full well that some of the terms in this language are rather woolly, and they use them in an innocuous sense. For example, 'quality assurance' often means: 'I'd like to say something clever, if only I could.' When used in certain contexts or certain ways, Management-Speak comes under the heading of 'corporate bullshit'.[398] It's an attitude that gets you nowhere. It's like giving French, for example, a derogatory epithet when you don't like what's being said. Shoot the messenger instead.

One problem with Management-Speak is its popularity. It is used by many more people than just those who have studied management or economics. Many have learnt Management-Speak as a foreign language. Some become very good at it and can converse fluently in this foreign language, while just as many try to get by with halting articulation, a limited vocabulary or simply a tourist phrase book. This is all due to the fact that Management-Speak has become the language of power.

We will call the second language Pedagogy-Speak. Now things become difficult, because in the interests of consistency we have to call Pedagogy-Speak the schools' national language. Pedagogy-Speak is just as abstract as Management-Speak, but the terminology is different. Those who speak Pedagogy-Speak talk of knowledge and learning. This knowledge may be constructed, in which case they talk about how pupils construct their knowledge. That said, everyday exchanges are also conducted in Pedagogy-Speak, and in the world of the school these relate to matters such as chalk and grades.

The teachers at the school we studied, just like those we encountered in an earlier project,[399] strictly (or, at least, relatively strictly) stick to Pedagogy-Speak. They listen to – and claim to understand – the Management-Speak that is spoken, although they actually speak Management-Speak only reluctantly and rarely. The teachers interviewed say that they never speak Management-Speak when speaking to each other. The reason given is that 'there's nothing that relates to managerial questions to talk about'. One of the teachers interviewed believed that more autonomous working teams who are in charge of finances would be more interested in management issues. The lack of influence makes discussion about the school's finances uninteresting. In addition, the teachers virtually never use Management-Speak in their contact with pupils and their parents. If Management-Speak really were the language of power, one might expect to find loan words from Management-Speak in Pedagogy-Speak, but we have found no evidence of this. Instead, there is a more general tendency for Management-Speak to borrow words from other technical languages to reinforce its rhetorical power.

Head teachers, too, usually speak Pedagogy-Speak in their contact with teachers, other school staff, pupils and parents. The impression given that Management-Speak is rarely spoken with parents is reinforced by letters to parents and similar texts that are often written by head teachers.

The existence of considerable factual interest in educational issues shone through in our interviews with head teachers and the documents issued for use at the school. However, it was also impossible not to notice a very strong interest in sticking to budgets. This was seen as being part of the head teachers' duties. Failure was penalised by the operational manager when the resources for the following year were allocated, but it also made it hard to continue working as a head teacher in the long term.

The operational manager does not want to 'get involved in the inner workings of the schools', and therefore avoids Pedagogy-Speak. He can speak the language, which is also confirmed by the head teachers interviewed. The operational manager here described his not speaking Pedagogy-Speak as a matter of free choice.

A short detour

Before we go any further, a few words are needed on the empirical field. Education up to and including upper secondary level is one of the key responsibilities of the municipal administration which involves significant elements of state control. Production is in part contracted out to 'independent schools', which is another way of saying that there are organisations and companies which offer both pupil places and teaching hours, normally on a non-profit or small-profit basis. The school is controlled – or receives control impulses – not only from above but also to an increasing degree from pupils and their parents.

This study was carried out at a school with just over 400 pupils from preschool to year nine. The school has two head teachers: one for preschool to year three and after-school activities, and one for years four to nine.

The City of Gothenburg is divided up into districts in which certain decisions are made by district councils appointed by the City Council, which means that election results are seen throughout the municipality. When it comes to schools, the district councils deal with those tasks which 'in accordance with the Swedish Education Act and other statutes are included in the remit of the local education authority and which relate to preschool classes and primary and lower secondary schools, and which have not been assigned to any other body', according to the Children's and Young People's Plan 2002–2004. Following pressure from the Swedish National Agency for Education, the City Council drew up a school plan several years ago. The budget had previously been used as the basis for the school plan. The control documents attributed great importance to the balanced scorecard and in particular a 'consumer satisfaction index' and an 'employee satisfaction index', as well as generally observed targets.

On the civil service side of things, operations are led by a district manager. Beneath him, activities are divided up into a number of operational areas, each with its own operational manager. The head teachers' manager is one of these operational managers. Within the district studied, the operational manager had around six hundred subordinates.

Interviews were carried out with the two head teachers, the operational manager and two teachers who are also working team representatives. We are well aware that there are many members of staff at the school other than teachers, such as child minders, teaching assistants, recreational leaders, preschool teachers, school meals staff, school nurses, special needs teachers, cleaners, caretakers and possibly psychologists and counsellors. The data collected does not provide a basis for drawing far-reaching conclusions. The study should be regarded instead as a preliminary study which provides inspiration and goes beyond the constraints within which we normally regard schools.

Three types of bilingualism

There are three types of bilingualism at the bilingual schools. Operational managers, head teachers and teachers can all speak both Management-Speak and Pedagogy-Speak. However, it is usually only the head teachers who actively use two languages. A simple, albeit broad, definition is that someone who 'uses more than one language' is bilingual.[400] We would like to regard those who – without further learning – would comfortably be able to speak two languages as being bilingual. One test would be to try, in more than one language, to describe a film as being 'super cool but indie', or to explain what old-style porter tastes like. If one cannot talk about film or beer in any language, it's simply a case of trying to describe something else that is not that easy.

The operational managers and the teachers know two languages, but have refrained from or actively repressed one of these languages. However, they can still be said to be bilingual. The operational manager explicitly says that he doesn't want to interfere with operations, and avoids speaking Pedagogy-Speak for this reason. The actual reason may be something else, such as delegated decision making, convenience or a lack of time. The result will still be that the operational manager avoids speaking Pedagogy-Speak.

The teachers interviewed expressed uncertainty about the encroachment of Management-Speak in schools. They explained that they themselves have a certain understanding of the use of Management-Speak, but that they have closer contact with the head teacher than teachers in general do. Other teachers were far more negative. Part of the explanation may also lie in how familiar teachers are with Management-Speak. A social scientist will often have been unable to avoid having a certain degree of formal knowledge in management and economics. The point is that not only are languages chosen – and also rejected – as appropriate, but also that this is done in accordance with convictions that accompany the role in question.

The second type of bilingualism we see involves the school's administrative domain being a place where two languages are spoken. There are parallels with countries where multiple languages are used, such as Belgium, Finland, Switzerland and South Africa. But the difference is obvious insofar as the languages there are not primarily used to talk about different things. In the world of the school, people do not talk about pupil development, problems or performance, for example, in Management-Speak.

In Finland, as in other places, no doubt, where bilingualism must be validated by law and then interpreted, people talk about another kind of bilingualism. They differentiate between 'bilingual services' (such as medical care, where both Finnish and Swedish are spoken) and 'monolingual services'.[401] Explanations of the Management-Speak situation are, to a certain degree, a monolingual service since they are provided in Management-Speak. Resource accounts provided in the local context can, however, be said to come under bilingual services because they are provided in both Management-Speak and Pedagogy-Speak.

We will continue by dealing with bilingual individuals, bilingual environments and bilingual services. No one would be more surprised than us if the defining boundaries between them turned out to be clear ones.

Concealed disadvantages

There is plenty of literature about bilingualism. For example, Miguel Benito and Andreas Kaiser's annotated 1998 select biography *Tvåspråkighet* ('Bilingualism') lists six other biographies in the same field. There are rich pickings here for those wishing to lay bare an organisational image.

Much of the literature about bilingualism deals with how children become bilingual;[402] for example, it looks at how conditions may vary, and discusses the effects of bilingualism on other types of learning. Any problems that have to be dealt with in a bilingual family occur during the learning phase.[403] The same is true of any problems with the child's language development on the way towards achieving bilingualism.[404]

Once it has been acquired, bilingualism is not thought to bring any disadvantages for people who know two languages. However, a negative attitude and suspicion towards bilingualism is not uncommon among those who make up the monolingual majority.[405] The aversion of teachers towards open bilingualism at the school studied here is partly to do with strict monolingualism being 'more refined' if the one language is Pedagogy-Speak. Any disapproval of bilingualism comes from other teachers who are also partly bilingual.

The idea that more and even more of the same thing will bring only happiness is fascinating. Towards the end of a summer's evening, it can in fact be the case that instead of improving one's sense of wellbeing, one more beer ruins both the rest of that evening and the next day. No one has captured this dilemma better than Douglas Adams, when he talks about the Babel fish in *The Hitchhiker's Guide to the Galaxy*. When the Babel fish is placed in one's ear, 'you can instantly understand anything said to you in any form of language'.[406] This sounds great, but 'the poor Babel fish, by effectively removing all barriers to communication between different races and cultures, has caused more and bloodier wars than anything else in the history of creation'.[407] In other words, it is not obvious that the many languages of the world really were a punishment for building the Tower of Babel all the way up to heaven – they may have been a reward.

Power and distance

We have shown in other contexts the disadvantages of coming too close to issues if one wishes to be able to influence the outcome.[408] In *Går det att spara?* ('Can Savings Be Made?') by Nils Brunsson and Björn Rombach, the issue concerned the power distribution between politicians and civil servants, particularly in the budgeting process.[409] A dramatic imbalance of power was normally seen – and is still seen – there in favour of the civil servant. The strategies used by civil servants included attempts to add to the detailed knowledge that politicians had. The politicians then found themselves on an impossible middle ground where they were dragged into the task of reviewing details yet could not influence which details were to be emphasised and how they were to be described. 'It becomes an in-depth examination on the terms of the civil servants – an insight that offers slim opportunities for influence.'[410]

One way of keeping oneself at a distance for those who want to control or avoid being controlled is not to accept the language of one's opponent. Medical care is an example of a political field in which those involved in its operations resisted and refused for a long time to engage in discussion on scope and priorities while communicating in Management-Speak. Proximity and knowledge may not require a shared language, but it does make things easier. If nothing else, we can draw this conclusion from studies of the connection between language and culture.[411]

Management-Speak is a language and a culture in the same way that other languages are. The question is whether the language of management is so important that we cannot imagine economism – the culture of management – without it. We do not need to go any deeper in order to note that a lack of linguistic community makes the cultural – and thus the knowledge-related – community less likely to occur.

Like many others, Magdalena Jaakkola notes that 'social interaction requires a common language'.[412] But the connection between language and culture is about more than just communication. Language also has 'monological functions'.[413] It matters whether one thinks in Management-Speak or Pedagogy-Speak, regardless of which language one speaks.

Duration

Clearly bilingualism does not last forever. When a language is no longer used, we talk about 'language death'.[414] This is normally due to a language shift process. In the case studied here, Pedagogy-Speak is not threatened but has been pushed a way off.

Bilingualism can also cease to exist at the individual level.[415] Diseases which cause the loss of language (such as Alzheimer's) are not relevant here. However, it is interesting that languages which are not used lose their power and are even lost.[416] The Swedish term *förbleknande* (literally, 'fading') is Åke Viberg's graphic translation of the English word 'attrition'.[417]

In the long run, the operational manager who has chosen not to use Pedagogy-Speak will at the very least find he has a poorer command of the language. This poorer command may not affect all elements of the linguistic ability equally. In *Language Attrition from the Psycholinguistic Perspective*, Emiko Yukawa differentiates between 'speaking, listening, reading, writing and metalinguistic judgement'.[418] The ability to understand Pedagogy-Speak probably remains at a satisfactory level, even if one does not speak the language particularly often. That said, while new words and intellectual concepts are incorporated into the language, those who do not speak it regularly will find that their understanding get poorer.

Unlearning in connection with learning is also an interesting line of thought. The question is what happens when we learn Management-Speak well – the language and thus also the way of thinking. Can we really disconnect ourselves from this and think in 'pure' Pedagogy-Speak again? Isn't it the same as with ideas? Once we've met the idea, it's impossible to get rid of it.[419]

And when it comes to a certain type of question in a bilingual environment the choice of language is not always a foregone conclusion either. We talk about loss of domains of usage when a language is no longer used in a context where it was once natural.[420] The question is whether we can talk about a loss of domains of usage when it comes to Pedagogy-Speak at school, or whether the discussion simply relates to new issues. If we look at it over a longer period of time, a school cannot be described as rich. Despite the fact that this is hardly ever done today, it should be possible to talk about economising with meagre resources, even in Pedagogy-Speak.

Teachers like their head teacher to have been a teacher, and head teachers in turn like their administrative manager to have been a teacher. It was once a requirement in many industries that managers had worked their way up and knew the trade. We have heard, for example, that right up until the 1980s it was impossible to become CEO at KF – The Swedish Cooperative Union[421] unless one had the trademark blue hands that resulted from years of working with chilled goods. These days, we see leaders who are managers by profession in many places. The fact that teachers still resist this trend may be because they see Pedagogy-Speak as being so weak when it comes face to face with languages such as Management-Speak in the context of argument. This sub-theme can also be seen in Rickard Wahlberg's account of resistance to Management-Speak in the world of highbrow culture.[422]

Semilingualism?

According to the reasoning in *The Rise of Management-Speak*, the strength of Management-Speak should lie in the fact that it is now understood by most people.[423] Not completely understood, but certainly enough. And the trend appears to be continuing. Major languages are becoming bigger and bigger; 'global languages are gaining ground'.[424] Nowhere at the school was a more sophisticated form of Management-Speak used. It was more like the case of Swedes meeting each other abroad, mistaking each other for German and speaking schoolboy German with each other. The idea of 'semilingualism' springs readily to mind, even though linguists would no doubt defend themselves against such free use of the concept.

Semilingualism, in the sense here of not being able to speak any language properly, is a problem which is dealt with early on in the bilingualism literature of Nils Erik Hansegård, for example.[425] This means that one or more languages have not been acquired sufficiently well. The linguistic status of those who are semilingual has been compared to mild forms of aphasia 'in which language can be used in a concrete sense, but not in an abstract sense'.[426] However, when it comes to abstract technical language, it is more reasonable to see semilingualism as 'not having the language entirely at one's disposal'.[427] Based on this definition, it would be strange to assert, as Gisela Håkansson does, that 'no scientific proof was found that semilingualism actually exists'. [428]

At the school in question here, poor knowledge of Management-Speak does not necessarily mean that one has learnt Pedagogy-Speak. If we regard Management-Speak as the second language and Pedagogy-Speak as the native language, it is an 'enduring myth [...] that the native language should have a negative impact on the second-language learning of the minority-language pupils'.[429] The generally poorer performance of bilingual pupils at school is thought to be due to a covariance between bilingualism and a number of other factors which explain how well one does in the classroom.[430]

It is not fair to talk about the school environment here as being semilingual when it comes to Management-Speak, for the simple reason that the linguistic deficiencies are not that great. The operational manager, like the head teachers, speaks simple Management-

Speak. But the operational manager could definitely prove himself to be better versed in Management-Speak. His failure to do so is thought to be because he is afraid of causing offence. He speaks it as he does so that he is understood, but also – more importantly – so that he is accepted.

Linguistic adaptability

We often adapt our way of speaking according to the context. For example, we can choose not to use swearwords and dialectal expressions just as easily as we can technical terms and flowery language. The explanation is not only that one or the other may be more socially accepted, but also that we want that which we say to achieve something. Fredrik Lindström[431], who has enjoyed a great deal of influence thanks to his presence on TV and his books about the Swedish language, makes the whole matter very simple in encouraging people to accept and like the way they happen to talk. An objection is that the listener should be included in the assessment, and there should be an understanding that the way we 'talk' is because we intend something entirely other than wishing to be natural or understood, such as our wanting to oppress others or signify group affiliation. We often – perhaps most often – talk the way we do not just to make ourselves understood by others or because it comes naturally to us. For example, a simple country dialect consisting of few words may not be a wise choice to use should we want to progress in trade and industry or lose our critics at an academic seminar.

Because bilingualism is often a choice made on behalf of immigrant children, the literature often deals with bilingualism in their situation. It can be noted that more than 140 different languages are used by children in Sweden.[432] Simultaneous bilingualism involves learning two languages at the same time as a child.[433] The question is what to call the ability to speak two languages just as well as the way monolingual people speak their one language? Or is the question simply wrongly phrased and too narrow? 'Double monolingualism' would appear to be a possible name, since a double monolingualism norm is described in the literature as being very common.[434] However, double monolingualism is not only hard to achieve; as a norm, it has also been called into question. In particular, criticism has been directed at the fact that, according to this norm, the languages must be kept separate.[435] We imagine that bilingual people should be monolingual, in two languages. Just like in the question above. But bilingualism can be more than that.

A double bilingual person who uses two languages by keeping them completely separate from each other does not use his linguistic ability to the full, according to Inger Lindberg,[436] among others. If the two languages are kept apart, they do not have any opportunity to complement each other. Normann Jørgensen and Anne Holmen go as far as to raise the question of whether the ability to use two languages simultaneously in practice should be taught.[437]

Perhaps 'perfect bilingualism' could be used to denote being truly bilingual and 'making full use of one's linguistic potential and one's entire linguistic register'[438]. Of course such perfect bilingualism does exist, but reason suggests that it must be common for one of the languages to be weaker and to become even weaker over the years, or for the norm of double bilingualism to be restricted in terms of language use. The weakening of linguistic ability has, however, proven to be hard to measure.[439]

Self-estimation of linguistic proficiency among bilingual pupils shows that languages can have different degrees of strength.[440] Someone who is bilingual without being perfectly bilingual (in the sense that one language is weaker) is, in all contexts where this weaker language is used, an oddity – and perhaps one could also say an immigrant. The head teacher who has nevertheless learnt relatively good Management-Speak may, for example, feel like an immigrant when meeting MBA's who work in a municipal administration. Johan Berglund shows that the same thing can also happen outside the school environment.[441]

It is also possible for the languages to become combined, so that Management-Speak and Pedagogy-Speak become Managogy-Speak. There are parallels here with Stockholm's Rinkeby Swedish (or Gothenburg's Gårdsten Swedish), which includes words from many other languages as well as Swedish. Those who speak Managogy-Speak should be able to speak pure Management-Speak or Pedagogy-Speak to varying degrees. Many myths have sprung up around mixed languages such as Rinkeby Swedish. In the journal *Socialpolitik*, Ulla-Britt Kotsinas recounts the following story:

When Radio Sweden planned to record Rinkeby Swedish, the reporter heard about three young people who, it was claimed, spoke this type of Stockholm Swedish. However, once they were in front of the microphone, these young people used the completely normal language of Stockholm youth.

After all, this was radio, where people speak standard Swedish and not Rinkeby Swedish. Quite a lot of young people who had grown up in areas with large immigrant populations probably have this ability to switch – more or less obviously – between the language they spoke with their friends and more 'ordinary' language. The same is also true of young people with Swedish parents. Some of them speak 'Swedish' at home but Rinkeby Swedish with their friends. ('Although not as perfectly as we do,' as one immigrant lad put it.)[442]

Managogy-Speak could be thought of as a low-status language, yet one which should also be able to confer local status and even become the norm. A teacher could end up completely isolated at the school were she not able to speak the 'language spoken among friends'[443] with other teachers – Managogy-Speak. It is also possible to imagine a spreading of mixed language. If Rinkeby Swedish could become trendy in the affluent Stockholm district of Östermalm, Managogy-Speak could certainly become popular on the conference circuit, for example.

If we pursue the idea of native languages and foreign languages, it could be that teachers do understand Management-Speak – but not completely. For example, 'extensive customer contact' sounds simple when the operational manager says it, but there is no guarantee that all of the deeper significance included in the customer concept as used by an MBA will be fully understood by teachers if it reaches their ears. A discussion about square meter per pupil may have absolutely no effect on learning in Management-Speak, but it certainly does if expressed in Pedagogy-Speak in terms of, say, a room for group activities. And in Management-Speak, the issue of profiling is part of the work involved in 'retaining funding' and 'integrating' a saving. In Pedagogy-Speak, 'music classes' and 'integrated special needs education' are not without their operational significance.

Moreover, it is not particularly strange that teachers could speak Pedagogy-Speak better than Management-Speak. Their training often includes little or no management or economics. And their everyday conversations are held in Pedagogy-Speak. Their knowledge of Management-Speak is of the everyday type – as is the same for other professions which come across Management-Speak when out and about in society and at general meetings within their organisation.

One conclusion might be that if the head teachers really want to get the teachers on board, they should translate their arguments from Management-Speak into Pedagogy-Speak. And the same applies if they want to initiate a dialogue and come up with better solutions. However, they should stick to Management-Speak if they want to improve their chances of getting their wishes through intact.

The basis for choice of language

Those who are bilingual know two languages, and must therefore choose which language to speak in any given situation. If one is addressed in one language, it makes sense to respond in that same language. But in bilingual environments, the choice is far from obvious. If the person to whom one is speaking understands both languages, one's own preferences or other circumstances may dictate the choice of language. If someone who is not bilingual is present, it is often this fact which determines the language used by the bilingual people when choosing to include or exclude the monolingual person. Also, it is not unusual for there to be an official language which is used by, say, authoritative bodies and controls the choice of language in contexts where contact is made with these authorities. In the same way, we adapt our language according to the authority we are in touch with in a monolingual environment.[444]

One particularly interesting group in this context is that of the bilingual head teachers. The head teachers speak Management-Speak. They do so when speaking individually with their manager and at the weekly meeting with the management team for the classes which he heads. They also do so among themselves sometimes, and to pupils and parents when required to do so by the agenda. They speak Management-Speak to their manager, but only do so at the school when they deem this to be necessary. The head teachers normally speak Pedagogy-Speak at the school. Pedagogy-Speak is thought to be the language with which they are most comfortable. The issue at hand may, however, guide their choice of language towards Management-Speak.

A parallel can be drawn with the Torne Valley on the border of Sweden and Finland, 'where both Swedish and Finnish are used by individuals alternately in different functional areas'.[445] Diglossia is the name of the situation whereby languages or language variants are used in different areas of life and 'live side-by-side in a single society'.[446] It is not only in the school context that both bilingualism and diglossia arise. We can imagine bilingualism without diglossia; in other words without the languages being used in different functional areas. However, we can also imagine diglossia without bilingualism at individual level, with someone actually being able to communicate using one language in the different functional areas.[447]

The head teachers are bilingual in the same way that many children are. They speak Pedagogy-Speak at home (i.e. at the school) and Management-Speak with their manager at work. Sometimes they also speak Management-Speak at home. This is because they are unable to express themselves in their native language, which could be interpreted as a degree of semilingualism if the matter can even be expressed in Pedagogy-Speak. That said, the reason for their failure to use their native language might also be that they can ride roughshod over 'their family' by using their work language in a way that they cannot use their native language. And all too often, they win the argument. Even a monolingual person can use language to their advantage in these situations, but not by changing languages.

The head teachers differ from the operational manager and the teachers in two significant respects. The head teachers live their daily lives in a bilingual environment. They encounter and use both Management-Speak and Pedagogy-Speak. The operational manager's and teacher's environments are normally monolingual. In addition, the head teachers in our study do not appear to be particularly weighed down by principles. They choose the language which best serves their purposes in any given situation.

The teachers have made an active choice to stick to Pedagogy-Speak, or they have possibly chosen not to speak Management-Speak. They are probably not afraid of the language, but they want to demonstrate their dissociation from the problems that are often presented in Management-Speak and economism itself – the culture of management. Pedagogy-Speak is their language, and it suits their professional world view.

The operational manager has in the past battled for the school's resource allocation in relation to other lines of business. Now that this battle has been won, he sees getting the school to stick to its budget as his main task. He does not see issues that relate more specifically to individual operations as being his business. The operational manager is responsible for a children's and young people's plan which includes general and publicly known operational guidelines.

The operational manager has also made an active choice of language. The principle is not to encroach on the head teachers' domain of controlling operational content. This linguistic restriction is chosen by the operational manager interviewed despite having worked as a head teacher himself. During the interview, we spent a long time on the subject of premises. This was discussed as if it didn't actually have anything to do with operations but was a financial matter. The cost of premises that are too large affects other areas of operations. The fact that the premises here were too large was due to external circumstances in the form of lower childbirth rates. These lower childbirth rates and the possibility of facing growing competition from other schools represented a significant threat to operations. Threats of future streamlining are a very common concept in management rhetoric, and are also known as crying wolf.

And what good did the transfer of knowledge do?

By seeing the organisation as though it were bilingual, we have been able to use what we know about bilingualism to discuss issues that we would not have identified otherwise. The school studied was a credible example of a bilingual environment. It is not unlikely that this would also be true of other schools. We are convinced that corresponding analyses would be beneficial in all larger organisations. If nothing else, they could serve to provide an explanation that is presently excluded because the metaphor appears unreasonable: can this organisation really be seen as bilingual?

The organisation has changed, and we have been given a number of suggestions for further consideration, such as the idea that bilingualism is common in large organisations and that this can be both good and bad. At the individual level, less attention is paid to the disadvantages of bilingualism while the advantages are often assumed to exist without need for further discussion. In those environments addressed by bilingualism literature, bilingualism is regarded as a given at the macro level, whereas it can be used as a tool of influence in the immediate environment. The family can choose whether or not to be bilingual, whereas society is hard to influence. An exit in the spirit of Albert Hirschman is a possibility here.[448] But even if there are countries or areas which suit the individual better in linguistic terms, the opportunity to move is often not practically possible.

We do not know any more about whether or not influence can be brought to bear on the bilingualism we discussed at an organisational level than we did when our study began. If the disadvantages are obvious, they can be compared with the costs in any attempt to achieve a monolingual environment. Significant potential cost savings could justify attempts to bring about monolingual organisations. The spread of Management-Speak in the public sector, for example, could be seen as an effort to create a common language for multiple professions. It would be interesting to find out the cost of changing languages.

Another line of thinking that we can follow for a while deals with the ever elusive concept of power. As always, we refer those who believe that power is a simple concept to Claes Gustafsson's *Om utsagor om makt* ('Statements Made About Power').[449] One interesting question regarding the bilingual organisation is whether those who refuse to become bilingual in a partly bilingual organisation deprive themselves of power. It seems obvious that the choice of monolingualism at the individual level makes the person weaker in certain arenas. The monolingual person is excluded from debates taking place in the wrong language. He may not even be invited to join in certain debates.

However, the opposite can just as often be true. Those who do not accept one of the spoken languages can adhere strictly to the language of their own profession. They speak this language better than many others. What goes against this strategy of monolingualism in seeking to obtain power is that, at the very least, the immediate manager in charge of production often comes from the same profession as his subordinates. This should mean that he speaks the same language well. This group may be harder to control by sticking rigidly to the language of the operation since certain things will be impossible to say in that language. Cut-backs, for example, may be unpleasantly resolute.

If nothing else, linguistic differences can lead to problems for middle managers who act as a buffer between different choices of language. The middle manager feels pressure from above in one language, yet cannot exert pressure further downwards in order to pass on responsibility in the same terms. Instead, he must take a fresh approach and translate these demands into the language of his subordinates. If we are to look at this in a positive light, the effect is that one cannot routinely manage others as one is managed oneself, something which should have revitalising consequences for management.

There is a link here to the effects we have seen in other studies where market thinking has been introduced in the public sector.[450] Turning citizens – such as pupils – into customers was more than just a play on words or a change of languages. The relationship between the customer and the seller became different to what it had been between the public-sector producer and the pupil or patient, for example. The conclusion was that the change of language and the resulting change in approach had led to a fundamental change in the municipality's identity.

In this context, the school's identity can be described as stable. This chapter has dealt with the discussion conducted within schools and by those in management immediately above about day-to-day operations and their control. The school has never been textual. It is an organisation where one speaks, rather than writes. The teachers certainly read a great deal, but can almost be described as reluctant to write. The head teachers and their manager definitely write more than do the teachers, but still devote most of their time to talking. We do not know how good people at the school are at listening. It is rare for individuals to possess both the ability to talk and the ability to listen.

The school's product is speech and dialogue in the form of teaching, or else it is something formed with the help of speech if we (like scholars in management) dare to see the pupils as products in progress. The speech that constitutes the product or else forms it can from a purely practical point of view be referred to as talk within or on behalf of the operation. The talk about the operation relates to how the operation should be run and, subsequently, how it has worked. It relates to control and monitoring, and the latter is also a type of control.[451]

A little unfortunately, formative speech between employees about operations, operational goals and the effects within the organisation has been labelled as 'small talk' by the likes of Gunnar Ekman.[452] This suggests a qualitative difference between speech that controls and is thought to come from above and that which is horizontal speech or informal dialogue. The latter types of speech are largely based on interpreting the talk that constitutes control impulses.

In the case of the school, just as with the police force studied by Gunnar Ekman, for example, text must be translated into action. It is not obvious how the wording of legislation and various types of instructions are converted into correct action by the police in each individual case. And there is certainly something to be said for highlighting the significance of collegial dialogue as Ekman does in his thesis *Från text till batong* ('From Text to Truncheon').[453] But when managers are given the good advice that they 'must take part in small talk and thereby win the confidence of employees',[454] this assumes a rather manipulative sense. Ekman also misses the fact that hierarchy cannot be ignored in a patrol car, and he makes things much too easy for himself when he simply looks at how text intended for interpretation or translation that focuses on the local context is formulated.[455] The small talk that Ekman has listened to is largely intended to achieve control.

Another line of thought relates to the contact that management has with reality, users and the base level of the organisation. In the longer term, language diversity between operational levels may lead to these levels losing contact with each other. If people speak different languages, it is likely that they think differently. In recent years, the isolation of senior management has become apparent.

This has happened as a result of the rewards that senior management enjoy and deem to be reasonable having been noticed by those of us who see them as being ludicrously high.

Management-Speak is also historically associated with the exercise of power in a way that makes it the language of power. In the past (in the 18th century), French was spoken at many European royal courts, whatever the nation's own language. In Sweden, King Gustav III was so determined to use French that when Johan Jacob Anckarström shot him at a masked ball in 1792 he cried: '*Ah! Je suis blessé, tirez-moi d'ici et arrêtez-le*'.[456] The King did not die immediately, succumbing instead to an abscess and a high fever. 'He endured his suffering for thirteen days, and played the self-assumed role of hero brilliantly.'[457] French was thus the King's first language of choice, even when he was agitated and downright bewildered. But for every royal who spoke French almost as though it were his native language, there appears to have been a whole crowd of people who tried to muddle along with modest knowledge in order to share thereby in the language of power.[458] Many of the Swedish middle class peppered their language with words borrowed from French, with varying degrees of success. They declared themselves to be '*effauchéed*' or '*changéed*', or perhaps '*amuséed*'.[459] But as J.A.G. Acke and his companions point out:

I Paris schangtila salar
värsta buse franska talar[460]

This little nursery rhyme was difficult to translate. The message itself borders to banality. It says that in Paris even those without education and manners speak French. The people that helped us with translating this text were unable to give justice to the richness of associations and witty, understated irony of the original. Pyttan was a young lady of about four years of age who had the privilege of knowing quite a substantial part of the Swedish cultural elite at the turn of the century 1900. Those 'uncles' decided to present her a book with rhymes and illustrations – one rhyme for each letter in the alphabet. The result is hilarious, but you have to know Swedish. This underlines our point that having a native tongue, a first language, gives an ability to express and understand advanced messages that a second language hardly allows for.

The same can also be said of Management-Speak. Many people try to learn the language, only to find that they speak with an accent that makes them hard to understand. There are also people who speak it fluently without it giving them any power.

When Gustav III wanted to speak to the peasants, he had to climb down from his French high horse and speak Swedish. That was fine, as it was his native language after all. Things were harder for the next king of Sweden, King Karl XIV Johan. (There were actually two chaps in between King Gustav III and King Karl XIV Johan, but King Gustav IV and King Karl XIII weren't proper kings – more like historical padding.) King Karl XIV Johan was a Frenchman, and was already 47 years old when he was elected Crown Prince of Sweden in 1810. Despite his remaining alive until 1844, he never learnt to speak Swedish. He gradually learnt the names of various Swedish official positions and a few other Swedish chancellery terms, but that was all. When he once tried to speak to the Swedish Parliament using a phonetic manuscript, the Members of Parliament laughed so much at his unintelligible gibberish that he never tried again.[461] French retained its position as the language of power. For a while, at least.

In the long term, it can be imagined that a language within an organisation will take over and be used universally, or that everyone in the organisation will become more or less perfectly bilingual. It is even more likely that each group will lose a language it rarely uses. There would be a particular risk of this in the case of management that speaks Management-Speak which is afforded higher status than that of the operational language. It is also not infrequent for Management-Speak to be seen as a more general and neutral language. The motivation to maintain a second language then declines. If we compare this with real languages, French has played out its part as the language of power in Sweden. Instead, we now have English. English is spoken at the head offices of large Swedish companies, but it still does not seem to be the language of power. Rather, we speak broken English with people from other countries because it is convenient and practical. However, at home and in our everyday life we still speak our native language. The same can be said of Management-Speak. We speak broken Management-Speak to outsiders and have our own native language, such as Pedagogy-Speak, that we speak to our colleagues and peers.

One complication that occurs when lots of people try to communicate in a language they have not mastered is the use of pidgin language. If many people are forced to speak in broken Management-Speak, a simplified pidgin language will develop that is only any good for very simple communication and unnuanced information. There is now a special 'lite' version of Management-Speak for so-called regular folk, which can be found in places such as the financial pages of the tabloid newspapers.[462] This is like the Latin spoken at academic ceremonies. It may sound grand, but it is too lacking in content and communication potential for our taste.

When most people at a conference we attend speak a form of English that is closer to our own than to the English spoken at Oxford, the opportunities for expression are limited. It is certainly true that a scientific conference can be extremely dry. It doesn't matter that Shakespeare's plays and Hemingway's novels make full use of the richness of the English language. Pidgin speakers experience poverty rather than richness. The literature on Russenorsk[463] is likely to remain limited, particularly as Russenorsk is now as dead as Latin and Sanskrit.

One scenario is that management finds itself out of touch with operations where a language other than Management-Speak is spoken. This in turn can be imagined to have completely different consequences. The communication problems experienced by the operational levels can mean fewer opportunities for control in certain areas. By using Management-Speak either alone or in the main, management is able to control finances – heavy-handedly if necessary. However, it will be hard for management to achieve controlled operational development. If language is essential to our understanding, how can we control what we do not comprehend?

The advantages of loose connections between management and operations as a result of this confusion of languages include a greater degree of freedom to build facades. It is mainly the way in which those who represent the organisation express themselves and the image that the organisation's members give of the organisation that control the way others in the organisation's immediate environment act towards it. If such a thing as 'the organisation in itself' exists, it cannot provoke reaction when this 'reality' is hidden behind the image. Creating the facade that constitutes the image of an organisation is usually seen as management's primary task.

Of the instruments at management's disposal for creating the image of an organisation, talk is the most important.[464] Decisions must in turn be conveyed, and the actual implementation is often more expensive than the talk. The lack of knowledge about operational details that comes about as a result of the monolingualism of management makes this talk all the freer. In the same way, the choice of another language does not give operations any particularly good opportunities for reinterpreting management talk. Everything has to be translated into another language. This may certainly lead to inaccurate translations – although maybe also accurate and interesting translations.

9. Thinking Freely or Thinking for Oneself ...

Mankind's most characteristic feature is that we live our entire lives in organisations. These organisations leave their mark on us and take up most of our time. We may be able to forget these organisations temporarily, but we can never leave them. Despite this – or perhaps for this very reason – it is amazing how hard we find it to understand organisations and how little attention this problem attracts. Organisations can be influenced, our lives can be better or worse within them, and they can be used for various purposes. All this is easier to manage for those who have a better understanding of what happens within organisations.

Our ambition with this book has been to provide a set of tools for gaining a better understanding of the process of organising. We are not tempted to repeat here the content of the previous chapters. If you have come straight here from Chapter One without going via Chapters Two to Eight, you are kindly requested to go back. We don't believe in instant replays. Nevertheless, it is appropriate to say something about what we have stated so far. The earlier chapters all focus on the same theme, but are otherwise separate entities. It is therefore tempting to say something about what comes next after having now set everything out. Before doing that, however, we thought we might revisit the discussion on the phenomenon of metaphors as mentioned in Chapter One. It was made clear there that there are many depictions. If you want to stand out from the crowd, there's no point hiding your light under a bushel. The question here is what we have contributed to this argument.

Different ways of understanding organisations

Now that we've reached Chapter Nine, we can allow ourselves to look back. Following on from an introduction and a foothold in the literature of metaphor, we devoted Chapter Two to saying the opposite. The aim was to obtain a counterimage. If we see no further than a method for reaching a decision, providing a solution to a problem or changing direction, it is hard to take a critical approach to a situation. What lies on the table in front of us appears to be reasonable and well thought out.

We showed that a counterimage appears when we maintain the opposite. Things can always be turned the other way around. The counterimage that appears when we say the opposite is not obviously any better than the image that existed before. This is not a problem, however. The counterimage is not primarily – or indeed, not at all – an alternative course of action. Its function is to facilitate a critical review of the main alternative. The counterimage allows for free thinking.

One alternative to maintaining the opposite is to fully accept the problem description or solution offered. In Chapter Three, we showed the benefit of continuing to follow the route already taken by the organisation right to the end. Full acceptance of solutions has the same effect as enlarging them. Problems become more visible when they are enlarged. This method does not result in finding new solutions either. However, by pushing the problem descriptions or solutions further in the recommended direction, we can more easily take a critical attitude towards them.

In Chapter Four, we proposed another simple model. It often lends itself to construction, and it turns out that it facilitates the problematisation of ideas that are taken for granted. We used the most common model in social science, the two-by-two matrix, to problematise a common conception. This model can also be used to question ideas that we believe to be a matter of fact.

In Chapter Five, we were assisted by a few historical thinkers in the form of invigorating criticism and creating alternative images. As we demonstrated, three comic strip characters would have worked just as well. By borrowing thinkers with radically different perspectives, we can allow these comic strip characters to make interpretations in our place. The image before us is called into question, and counterimages are created from the comfort of our armchair.

Many changes can be described in terms of more or less of a certain thing. Perhaps we can even go so far as to say that the image of any change is always an increase or a reduction in some respect. In Chapter Six, we identified and then named the end points on the scale along which change occurs. What does it look like at the end where it is at its smallest, and at the opposite end where it is as big as possible?

Once the end points of the scale have been identified, it is possible to talk about the advantages and disadvantages of moving in either direction. This is because it is unlikely that there will only be good at one extreme and bad at the other. This approach makes it easier to see the pros and cons of changes. There is also another alternative, other than not doing anything: to strive for change in the opposite direction.

The example in Chapter Seven showed how hard it is to find our way with a map that describes a completely different landscape to the one we are wandering around. This is particularly true if we do not realise that we have the wrong map, and do not have a compass or any other tools. The chapter illustrates the way in which critical questioning enables us to see relatively easily that the map differs so dramatically from the landscape that it does more harm than good.

The choice of map also concerns labelling, and this is what guided us through the discussion. The map that leads us the wrong way thereby hides or shifts the cause of the problems. If we change maps, it may well be that problems which had previously seemed almost never-ending can now be easily resolved.

In Chapter Eight, we showed how the information provided by a chosen designation can be used to gain a better understanding of an organisation. Knowledge can be transferred between very different areas using labels. That which we want to understand better in an organisation is given a name which belongs to an area where we have access to knowledge. We tried to view the organisation as a bilingual environment.

As we discussed in the introductory chapter, usable knowledge doesn't just come under any old labels. What we should add here is that whatever it is that works partly depends on the person already having some knowledge of whatever he is seeking to understand. If this happens to be boxing, for example, it may be worth seeing the organisation as a boxing ring.

Back to the metaphors

We have summarised above the journey we have just made without using the word 'metaphor'. This can be done because we do not often see metaphors. We know that the moon is not made of cheese, but we believe we know that the manager leads or should lead others. But it also turns out that, if anything, our contribution to the literature of metaphor is to broaden the perspective.

Some readers may have expected a collection of delightful metaphors in the style of Gareth Morgan. Those who have followed popular science metaphor literature will be familiar with Morgan's 1986 book *Images of Organization*. No other book on this theme has had such a wide reach. Morgan launched a variety of metaphors for describing organisations: machines, organisms, brains, cultures, political systems, psychic prisons, flux and transformation, and instruments of domination. At the time, this made for exciting reading. Different images of what organisations are led to new analysis opportunities and insights into how we can look at the organisation in different ways.

Metaphors control our thinking in all life's changes, and having important images analysed is entertaining. This is what Helge Svare does in his book *Livet er en reise* ('Life is a Journey').[465] Despite all the limitations that metaphors involve, they also offer the opportunity to feel a sense of community. When we hear your metaphors, it enables us to think along similar paths to you. We can continue to build on what the metaphor has conveyed, rather than just accepting or rejecting it. This creates a relationship between us that is one of neither uncontact (excuse the neologism) nor submission but is of, well, community.

We could have put forward the argument that the organisation can be seen as a bag, as a rubbish dump or as a fox hunt if these metaphors were available. The bag has already been used by Pastor Jansson who claimed in Hasse Alfredson's famous monologue from 1962 that 'Life is like a bag'.[466] Hasse Alfredson is a comedian, actor and author who is well known to those Swedes who are not quite so young any more. However, sooner or later our children will be older than we are now, and Hasse Alfredson is on the point of becoming better known as the father of the two film directors Tomas and Daniel Alfredson. Many other metaphors are used as well: the goldfish bowl and the sardine tin, for example.[467] It would have been tempting to continue along this line. The question is simply what to do with the insight that enables us to see the organisation as a fox hunt. Does it really help us when we try to make our own workplace work better?

Entertainment of the variety created by Morgan could be found in the management consultants' repertoire in the 1980s and in the academic lectures of the time. Since his message is hard to apply for practical purposes, it has fallen out of fashion. The audience is not satisfied simply with theatre (even if repetition creates a feeling of security and homeliness); it also wants help with more practical matters. The fact that organisations are hard to understand is not much help when this is both the starting point and the conclusion.

Organisational theory is often about putting a phenomenon into its context. We are part of a sorting science. This is where metaphors of the type offered by Morgan have a place. Labelling gives us a certain overview. Metaphors are 'thought organisers'[468] for better or worse. On the whole we are in favour, even though the high level of abstraction sometimes leaves the air too rarefied to breathe. What we criticise and try to ensure we avoid are unawareness and bewilderment when dealing with metaphors.

There is plenty of management literature that takes us in the opposite direction. Instead of abstraction, this literature provides us with the likes of quality control or employee discussion complete with recommendations. These are certainly concrete enough ideas to be usable, but the reward for this concretion is mole-like tunnel vision. In principle we are against this sort of thing, but at the same time we are forced to admit that for want of better alternatives we sometimes use these concrete recommendations ourselves and forward them on to others.

We may take pride in our clear-sightedness when we note with a wry smile that the latest documentation procedure is an example of the fox hunt metaphor approach. However, this insight is unusable in practice. We might as well swear. The hard task is to find a way of taking an analytical and critical approach to that which is of practical everyday use.

In this book, we have tried to strike a balance between the extremes of the abstract and comprehensive views which much of contemporary organisational theory provides and the practical but rather meagre recommendations normally offered by management literature. We haven't come up with a good name for this balance yet, but we're working on it. Using metaphors, objecting to metaphors and occasionally inventing metaphors adds a functional touch to the understanding that we hope to have contributed here. When used in this way, the metaphor becomes a tool, like a garden hoe or a spreadsheet program, which you can try to use yourself.

The references show that we are not alone. But we've said it before: anyone who thinks they are researching alone in an unexplored region has the bigger problems.

Think for yourself!

Now we have reached the concluding section, we can ask whether metaphors really do lend themselves to all this. The answer is that it appears so. But neither we nor anyone else can offer a handbook that can be used to deal with all kinds of problems. We have contributed a set of tools to make it easier to reveal problems, and also to provide a better foundation on which to build those reasons to be in favour. Not everyone can be against if we're ever going to get this boat launched and the sail hoisted.

It's easy to be in favour of everything that's good and that leads to success, but it's hard to know what exactly is good. What's more, even if we do know, it's hard to get there. Many of us certainly dream about the natural and authentic contribution that leads to what is good without too many flourishes. In the world of fiction, happy endings abound and the journey is pleasingly imaginary.

One favourite in the world of fiction is Mma Ramotswe, who runs *The No. 1 Ladies' Detective Agency*.[469] The lack of evil means that the novels are feel-good books rather than actual detective stories. The writer, Alexander McCall Smith, has himself said that 'the world needs more novels about cakes and drinking tea'.[470] In the first book of the series, when Happy Bapetsi wants to find out whether the old man who sponges off her really is her long-lost father, Mma Ramotswe is able to solve the case with ease. The truth is the undisputed good aim. Mma Ramotswe tricks the supposed father into believing that the daughter needs a blood transfusion. A lot of blood is needed, and it has to be the father's. Since it sounds risky, the imposter immediately reveals his true identity.

When we try to expose bad theories about how organisations work, things are never as easy. One problem is finding the very worst theories. If the half-bad theories are exposed with great fanfare, there is a greater risk that the really bad theories will be used. Another problem is the difficulty in obtaining a straightforward acknowledgement. In the best case, we can get the guilty party to admit to the shortcomings of the theory.

It would be tempting to round off with a case in which someone applied critical methods and used various approaches by way of metaphor to resolve their practical problems. Of course, such cases that could be used do exist. Almost everything we can think of already exists. Earlier in the book we stated that progress is a reasonable interpretation of what happens in our current age – although the stories about how well everything turns out belong to another genre: the literature of simple solutions. All the tales we can think of are full of objections and questions.

The books about Mma Ramotswe offer a pleasant diversion, and we would like to lose ourselves in the dream for a moment. We wish we could also find clever tricks that immediately reveal the good truths. But in the end, it is hard to explain away every complication. Lies are Mma Ramotswe's route to the truth in *The No. 1 Ladies' Detective Agency*, and McCall Smith simply leaves it at that. This insight could mean that even the false father was on his way to the truth via a lie. This is what our world looks like. Narratives are about people who work to find their way in a world of contradictions. They take the wrong turning and have to make a detour. Then things work out sufficiently well again for a while. It is in this sort of world that we believe our texts can be of use. If we didn't have such great problems with the word 'reality', we would say it was the real world.

Now we have made it through our book, a little humility is appropriate. We can admit that we have not completely succeeded in differentiating between organisations and what is said about organisations. The idea behind the metaphor is that it is an image of something. The image of the organisation and that which it depicts sometimes merge together in our eyes. That makes the idea of depiction problematic. The question is what causes this merging together. One obvious explanation is that it is not a question of two different things but one and the same thing. Behind the image lies another image.

Organisations do not exist in any more reliable a manner. And nor does that which goes on within organisations exist in any way other than as images. For some people, this is a problem. For others, it is a matter of fact. Although we belong to the latter group, the text slips up at times. The reality that then seems to come into our view is, quite simply, a more fruitful image. The moon is 'the Earth's only natural satellite, and by far the nearest celestial body of planetary size', according to the Swedish National Encyclopaedia. So ...

Chapter by chapter, one technique after another has been presented to suggest how we escape from the tyranny of metaphor. Yet it is still completely obvious that a great many difficult matters remain whereby none of these techniques offers any help. What should we do then? Our advice is this: think for yourself. And contact Osten.Ohlsson@spa.gu.se or Bjorn.Rombach@spa.gu.se if you come up with anything we should know about.

A research programme

The subjects that we have touched upon are, as the reader will understand, not an overview of the entire organisational field; rather, they are just a few examples. Some of them are central concepts in the literature of organisational theory, while others have been included simply to reflect our own particular experiences and interests.

There are yet more subjects and themes to address using the methods we have used. Others are welcome to join in too. We will certainly pick up on some of these threads in the future. We have devoted a great deal of time trying to understand the present time. In doing so, we have often looked backwards. We are now drawn towards the future. After all, everyone else looks forward. Forecasts, visions and strategies could be an exciting theme for our next book. We could add to the assertion that we live our lives in organisations the fact that we largely live in the future – living it here, and being seen as immature and bestial. In a student's essay that we graded, one of the municipality's leading representatives says:

We can now see the light at the end of the pipeline, but it's angled upwards[471]

What does this quotation actually say about the future? Is light really what we want to see in the pipeline? Is it a good sign if it has started to incline upwards? Shouldn't oil – or half-finished projects, for that matter – flow forwards without any gradient? And what does this say about the organisation? If we create our own future, what we say about it would seem to be important.

Another way of understanding research in this field is by looking in further depth at the themes we have dealt with. Each chapter in this book could be a book in itself. For example, continuing on the lines of what we have said about the market and change is an attractive thought. Chapter Eight, which looks at how knowledge can be transferred with the aid of metaphor, could also serve as an introduction or perhaps a synopsis for a more in-depth book. Not that there is any lack of publications on these themes, but we have noticed a need for completely different books.

We began this book by writing that the time had come to throw out much of what has been written about organisation and the process of organising. The reason for this is that the field has become bogged down with a great many theories and models which have lost any explanatory capacity they may have once had. And this is where we stand. It's time to clear out old theories and for taking consumers' complaints seriously. Theories and models that do not explain or help us in our efforts to understand should be flushed out. This will clear some space on the shelves for new research findings.

The meagre allocation of research funding to social science over a number of years is largely due to our inability to clear out the old. Why should we stock up on more theory if the shelves are already full to overflowing? Consumers working both in practice and in academia who have tested a number of lousy theories will change to another supplier. This provides scope for all manner of management gurus who offer fresh and delicious brews produced by using their own recipes. If theories do not provide knowledge and lead us in the wrong direction, we may as well use fantasies.

What we have written about and what you have read here can be seen as an overview description for a research programme. The sequel is yet to come. We hope you will join us in our next book.

References

Books and journals

Abrahamsson, Carina (1994) *För ändring – En studie i teorier för organisatorisk förändring.* Gothenburg: BAS.

Acke, Johan Adolf Gustaf; Albert Engström; Verner von Heidenstam; Gustaf Fröding & Birger Mörner (1925/1896) *Pyttans A-B och C-D-Lära.* Stockholm: Bonniers.

Adams, Douglas (1988/1979) *The Hitchhiker's Guide to the Galaxy.* London: Picador.

Adams, Scott (2000/1996) *The Dilbert Principle.* London: Boxtree.

Ahrne, Göran & Apostolis Papakostas (2002) *Organisationer, samhälle och globalisering.* Lund: Studentlitteratur.

Almqvist, Bertil (2012/1948) *Barna Hedenhös. Bilder från stenåldern.* Stockholm: Bonnier Carlsen.

Almqvist, Carl Jonas Love (1979/1826) *Ormus och Ariman.* The Department of Literature, Uppsala University.

Alvesson, Mats (1996/1991) *Communication, Power and Organization.* Berlin: Gruyter.

— (2006) *Tomhetens triumf.* Stockholm: Atlas in collaboration with Liber.

Alvesson, Mats & Yvonne Due Billing (2009/1997) *Understanding Gender and Organizations.* London: Sage.

Alvesson, Mats & Dan Kärreman (2003) 'Att konstruera ledarskap. 'Ledarskap' i praktiken'. *Nordiske Organisasjonsstudier*, vol. 5, pp 36–60.

Andersson-Felé, Lena (2008) *Leda lagom många.* The School of Public Administration, University of Gothenburg.

Angelöw, Bosse (1991) *Det goda förändringsarbetet.* Lund: Studentlitteratur.

Anker, Herman, ed. (1991/1988) *När doktorn blir sjuk. Nio läkare berättar.* Stockholm: Natur och kultur.

Apel, Karl-Otto (1973) 'Das Apriori der Kommunikationsgemeinschaft und die Grundlagen der Ethik'. In: *Transformation der Philosophie.* Band 2, Karl-Otto Apel, pp 358–435. Frankfurt a.M.: Suhrkamp.

Arbetsmiljöverket (2003) Mobbning och trakasserier. *Korta sifferfakta* Nr 1. 2003. Solna: The Statistics Division.

Arjouni, Jakob (2003) *Idioten. Fünf Märchen*. Zürich: Diogenes.

Aspelin, Gunnar (1977a/1958) *Tankens vägar. En översikt av filosofiens utveckling*. Del I. Lund: Doxa.

— (1977b/1958) *Tankens vägar. En översikt av filosofiens utveckling*. Del II. Lund: Doxa.

Barker, Richard (1997) 'How can we train leaders if we do not know what leadership is?' *Human Relations*, vol. 30, issue 4, pp 343–362.

Barry, Dan (1994/1951–1956) *Blixt Gordon. Dan Barrys klassiska äventyr 1951–1956*. Solna: Semic press.

Barry, Dan & Harvey Kurzman (1988, 1951–1953) *Flash Gordon: The Complete Daily Strips, November 1951–April 1953*. Princeton, WI: Kitchen Sink Press.

Baudrillard, Jean (1988) *Selected Writings*. Cambridge: Polity Press.

Baumann, Gerlinde (2003) *Love and Violence. Marriage as Metaphor for the Relationship between Yhwh and Israel in the Prophetic Books*. Collegeville, Minnesota: Liturgical Press.

Baumol, William & Alan Blinder (1979) *Economics – Principles and Policy* (fourth edition). San Diego: Harcourt Brace Jovanovich.

Beck, Ulrich (2013/1986) *Risk Society: Towards a New Modernity*. London: Sage.

Bengtsson, Frans Gunnar (1960/1935). *The Life of Charles XII, King of Sweden 1697–1718*. London: Macmillan.

— (1993/1935). *Karl XII:s levnad (tredje boken). Från Altranstädt till Fredrikshall*. Stockholm: Månpocket.

Benito, Miguel & Andreas Kaiser (1998) *Tvåspråkighet: En kommenterad urvalsbiografi*. Borås: Invandrarförlaget.

Berglund, Johan (2010/2005) 'Management-Speak in the Professional Struggle for Power'. In: *The Rise of the Management-Speak*, eds. Björn Rombach & Patrik Zapata, pp 53–66. Stockholm: Santérus Academic Press.

Bergstrand, Bengt Olof & Jan Åke Hermansson (1999) *Att bygga ett kvalitetssystem*. Höganäs: Bokförlaget Kommunlitteratur.

Bergström, Ingmar & Wilhelm Forsling (1995/1992) *I Demokritos fotspår. En vandring genom urämnesbegreppets historia från antiken till Nobelpriset*. Stockholm: Natur och kultur.

Berlin, Eva & Jan Enqvist (2002) *Mobbningsboken*. Stockholm: Arbetsmiljöforum.

Berle, Adolph & Gardiner Means (1932) *The Modern Corporation and Private Property*. New York: Macmillan.

Bertalanffy, Ludwig von (1971/1968) *General Systems Theory*. Harmondsworth: Penguin Books.

The Bible, King James Version.

Bies, Robert & Thomas Tripp (1998) 'Two faces of the powerless. Coping with tyranny in organizations'. In: *Power and Influence in Organizations*, eds. Roderick Kramer & Margaret Neal, pp 2003–219. London: Sage.

Björk, Gunilla (1999) *Mobbning – en fråga om makt.* Lund: Studentlitteratur.

Björkegren, Dag (1986) *Företags-ledarutbildning – en fallstudie* (with an English summary). The Economic Research Institute, Stockholm School of Economics.

Björklund, Anders (1999) 'Utbildningspolitik och utbildningens lönsamhet'. In: *Tillväxt och ekonomisk politik*, eds. Lars Calmfors & Mats Persson, pp 135–174. Lund: Studentlitteratur.

Björklund, Anders; Per-Anders Edin; Bertil Holmlund & Eskil Wadensjö (2000/1996) *Arbetsmarknaden* (2 ed). Stockholm: SNS.

Björkman, Gunnar (1925) *Metaforernas bleknande.* Uddevalla: Bohuslänningen.

Black, Max (1996/1993) 'More about Metaphor'. In: *Metaphor and Thought* (2 ed.), Andrew Ortony ed, pp 19–41. Cambridge University Press.

Blake, Robert & Jane Mouton (1964) *The Managerial Grid.* Houston: Gulf Publishing.

Blauner, Robert (1964) *Alienation and Freedom: The Factory Worker and his Industry.* University of Chicago Press.

Blomberg, Jesper (1998) *Myter om projekt.* Stockholm: Nerenius & Santérus.

Blundell, Richard; Lorraine Dearden & Barbara Sianesi (2005) 'Measuring the returns to education'. In: *What's the Good of Education?*, Stephen Machin & Anna Vignoles, pp 117–145. Princeton University Press.

Boje, David (1991) 'The story-telling organization. A study of story performance in an office-supply firm'. *Administrative Science Quarterly*, vol. 36, issue 1, pp 106–126.

Borgert, Leif (1992) *Organisation som mode* (with an English summary). Stockholm University.

Bowles, Martin (1997) 'The Myth of Management: Direction and Failure in Contemporary Organizations'. *Human Relations*, vol. 50, issue 7, pp 779–803.

Bridges, William & Robert Nelson (2001) 'Economic and sociological approaches to gender inequality in pay'. In: *The Sociology of Economic Life* (second edition), eds. Mark Granovetter & Richard Svedberg, pp 163–190. Cambridge, MA: Westview Press.

Brouthers, Keith; Paul van Hastenburg & Joran van den Ven (1998) 'If most mergers fail why are they so popular?' *Long Range Planning*, vol. 31, issue 3, pp 347–353.

Brunsson, Nils (1989) *The Organization of Hypocrisy. Talk, Decisions and Actions in Organizations.* Chichester: John Wiley & Sons.

Brunsson, Nils & Bengt Jacobsson, eds. (1998) *Standardisering.* Stockholm: Nerenius & Santérus.
— (2000) *A World of Standards.* Oxford University Press.

Brunsson, Nils & Johan Olsen, eds. (1993) *The Reforming*

Organization. London:
Routledge.

Brunsson, Nils & Björn Rombach
(1982) *Går det att spara?* Lund:
Doxa/Studentlitteratur.

Buchanan, David & Andrzej
Huczynski (2004) *Organizational
Behaviour – An Introductory Text*
(fifth edition). Harlow, England:
Prentice Hall.

Buridan, Jean (1985/ca 1330) *Jean
Buridan's Logic.* Dordrecht: D.
Reidel.

Burke, Peter (1964) *The Fabrication
of Louis XIV.* Yale: Yale University
Press.

Burman, Carina (1993) *Min salig
bror Jean Hendrich.* Stockholm:
Bonniers.

Burns, Tom & George Stalker
(1994/1961) *The Management of
Innovation.* Oxford University
Press.

Bäckström, Henrik (1999) *Den krat-
tade manegen. Svensk arbetsorgani-
satorisk utveckling under tre decen-
nier.* The Department of Business
Studies, Uppsala University.

Bärtås, Magnus & Fredrik Ekman
(2000) *Orienterarsjukan och
andra berättelser.* Stockholm:
Bokförlaget DN.

Cacciari, Christina (1998) 'Why do
we speak metaphorically?' In:
Figurative Language and Thought,
Albert Katz, Cristina Cacciari,
Raymond Gibbs & Mark Turner,
pp 119–157. Oxford University
Press.

Calmfors, Lars & Katarina
Richardson (2004) *Marknads-
krafterna och lönebildningen
i landsting och regioner.* The
Institute for Labour Market
Policy Evaluation, Uppsala
(IFAU) report 2004:9.

Capp, Al (2008/1949–1950) *Al Capp
Complete Shmoo.* Milwaukie, OR:
Dark Horse Comics.

Capp, Al (2012/1949–1952) *Li'l
Abner.* Volume 4. San Diego, CA:
IDW Publishing.

Capp, Al (1976/1951–1952) *Special-
Comics 9. Knallhatten.* Stockholm:
Carlsen.

Carlqvist, Knut (1996) *Kung Erik av
folket.* Stockholm: Timbro.

Carlson, Sune (1991/1951) *Executive
Behaviour.* Reprinted with contri-
butions by Henry Mintzberg and
Rosemay Stewart. Uppsala: Acta
Universitatis Upsaliensis.

Carlzon, Jan (1989/1985) *Moments
of Truth.* New York: Perennial
Library.

Charteris-Black, Jonathan (2005)
*Politicians and Rhetoric. The
Persuasive Power of Metaphor.*
Basingstoke, Hampshire:
Palgrave Macmillan.

Cherry, Daniel & Jeff Spiegel (2006)
*Leadership, Myth, & Metaphor.
Finding Common Ground to Guide
Effective School Change.* Thousand
Oaks, California: Corwin Press.

Collberg, Dan & Haukur Viggósson (2004) 'Detta är ett noll-
summespel'. Rektor som lönesät-
tare'. In: *Nära gränsen? Perspektiv
på skolans arbetsliv,* The Swedish
Institute for Working Life
(NIWL), pp 115–151. Katrineholm:
Arbetslivsinstitutets förlag.

*Collins COBUILD, English Language
Dictionary* (1987). London:
Williams Collins Sons.

Comte, Auguste (2009/1865/1848)
A General View of Positivism.
Cambridge University Press.

Cressey, Donald (1971) *Criminal Organization: Its Elementary Forms*. London: Heinemann Educational Books.

Crozier, Michel (1964/1958) *The Bureaucratic Phenomenon*. Chicago, Illinois: University of Chicago Press.

Crumb, Robert (1984/1968–1984) *Fritz the Cat*. Stockholm: Medusa.

Czarniawska-Joerges, Barbara (1988a) *Ideological Control in Nonideological Organizations*. New York: Praeger.

— (1988b) *To Coin a Phrase: On Organizational Talk, Organizational Control and Management Consulting*. The Economic Research Institute, Stockholm School of Economics.

— (1997) *Narrating the Organization: Dramas of Institutional Identity*. University of Chicago Press.

— (2004) *Narratives in Social Science Research*. London: Sage.

Czarniawska-Joerges, Barbara & Guje Sevón, eds. (1996) *Translating Organizational Change*. Berlin: Walter de Gruyter.

Dahlstrand, Ulf & Anders Biel (1995) *Pro-environmental Habits. Propensity Levels in Behavioural Change*. The Department of Psychology, University of Gothenburg, stencil.

Danielsson, Tage (1964) *Sagor för barn över 18 år*. Stockholm: Wahlström & Widstrand.

Davidson, Donald (1984) *Inquiries into Truth and Interpretation*. Oxford University Press.

Davis, Lee (1997) *Quality Assurance. ISO 9000 as a Management Tool*. Copenhagen: Handelshøjskolens Forlag.

Dawkins, Richard (2006) *The God Delusion*. Boston: Houghton Mifflin.

De Crescenzo, Luciano (1989/1977) *Thus Spake Bellavista. Naples, Love and Liberty*. New York: Grove Press.

DiMaggio, Paul & Walter Powell (1983) 'The iron cage revisited'. *American Sociological Review*, vol. 48, pp 147–160.

Dobers, Peter & Stefan Tengblad (2002) 'Metaforer som verktyg för ideologisk styrning. Fågel, fisk eller mittemellan?' *Nordiska Organisasjonsstudier*, vol. 4, issue 1, pp 60–83.

Eberstein, Gösta; Stig Humlin & Jonas Milton (2003) *Förhandlarboken* (fourth edition). Stockholm: Norstedts juridik.

Edsö, Ingvar (1999) *Kvalitetssäkra nu!* Stockholm: Svensk Byggtjänst.

Egidius, Henry (1983) *Tankelinjer i europeisk filosofi*. Stockholm: Natur och kultur.

Ekman, Gunnar (1999) *Från text till batong*. The Economic Research Institute, Stockholm School of Economics.

— (2003) *Från prat till resultat*. Stockholm: Liber.

Ekstrand, Lasse (1993) *Eolus & Herakleitos*. Gothenburg: Korpen.

Englisch, Johannes (2010) *Das Verhältnis von Pidginsprachen zu ihren Super- und Subbstratsprach am Beispiel des Yokohama-Pidgin-Japanischen, der Eskimo-Pidgin und Russenorsk*. Munich: GRIN.

Engwall, Lars & Sven Jungerhem (2010/2005) 'Management-Speak in the Academic Field'. In: *The Rise of Management-Speak*, eds. Björn Rombach & Patrik Zapata, pp 85–107. Stockholm: Santérus Academic Press.

Eriksson, Björn (2001) 'Mobbning: en sociologisk diskussion'. *Sociologisk forskning*, issue 2, pp 8–42.

Eriksson-Zetterquist, Ulla; Henrik Hansson, Mikael Löfström, Östen Ohlsson & Martin Selander (2006) *Ett möte med förhinder. Om IT-satsningar i skolan*. Gothenburg: BAS.

Falkinger, Ann (2001) *Förhandla kvinna!* Bromma: Annfa utbildning.

Fayol, Henri (1949/1916) *General and Industrial Administration*. London: Sir Isaac Pitman and Sons.

Feyerabend, Paul (1975) *Against Method*. London: NLB.

Fombrun, Charles (1986) 'Structural Dynamics within and between Organizations'. *Administrative Science Quarterly*, vol. 31, issue 3, pp 403–421.

Foster, Hal (Harold) (2009–2012/1937–1948) *Prince Valiant*, Vol 1–6. Seattle, WA: Fantagraphics Books.

French, Wendell & Cecil Bell (1984) *Organization Development* (third edition). Englewood Cliffs: Prentice-Hall.

Frid, Bisse (1997) *TQM – en introduktion*. Malmö: Liber.

Fröberg, Peter (2006) *Pol Pots leende*. Stockholm: Atlas/Arena.

Fröding, Gustaf (1997/1893/1891) *Guitar and Concertina*: Poems. Wintringham: Oak Tree Press.

Fukuyama, Francis (1993) *The End of History and the Last Man*. New York: Avon Books.

Furberg, Mats (1969) *Vision och skepsis. Från Thales till skeptikerna*. Stockholm: Bonniers.

— (1975) *Allting en trasa? En bok om livets mening*. Lund: Doxa.

Furusten, Staffan (2003) *God managementkonsultation – reglerad expertis eller improviserat artisteri*. Lund: Studentlitteratur.

Galbraith, Jay (1977) *Organization Design*. Reading, Massachusetts: Addison-Wesley.

Geertz, Clifford (1967/1964) 'Ideology as a cultural system'. In: *Ideology and Discontent*, ed. David Apter, pp 47–76. New York: Free Press.

George, Jennifer & Gareth Jones (2005) *Understanding and Managing Organizational Behavior*. Upper Saddle River, NJ: Pearson Prentice Hall.

Gibbs, Raymond (1998) 'The fight over metaphor in thought and language'. In: *Figurative Language and Thought*, Albert Katz, Cristina Cacciari, Raymond Gibbs & Mark Turner, pp 88–118. Oxford University Press.

Gillispie, Charles Coulston; Robert Fox & Ivor Grattan-Guinness (2000/1997) *Pierre-Simon Laplace 1749–1827. A Life in Exact Science*. Princeton University Press.

Goatly, Andrew (1998/1997) *The Language of Metaphors*. London: Routledge.

Goodman, Benny & Irving Kolodin (1939) *The Kingdom of Swing*. New York: Stackpole.

Goodman, Nelson (1984) *Of Mind and Other Matters*. Harvard University Press.

Gordon, Judith (2002) *Organizational Behavior – A Diagnostic Approach* (seventh edition). Upper Saddle River, NJ: Prentice Hall.

Grant, David & Cliff Oswick (1996b) 'Introduction: Getting the measure of metaphors'. In: *Metaphor and Organizations*, eds. David Grant & Cliff Oswick, pp 1–20. London: Sage.

Gröndahl, Britta (1988/1959) *Pierre-Joseph Proudhon: socialist anarkist federalist.* Stockholm: Federativa klassiker 10.

Gullberg, Hjalmar (1979/1937) *Gentleman, Single, Refined and Selected Poems, 1937–1959.* Stockholm: Norstedts.

Gustafsson, Claes (1979) *Om utsagor om makt.* Turku: Åbo Academy Foundation.

— (2011/1994) *The Production of Seriousness: The Metaphysics of Economic Reason.* Basingstoke: Palgrave Macmillan.

— (1995) *Bellmankulturen och andra betraktelser.* Turku: Åbo Academy.

Hacking, Ian (1999) *The Social Construction of What?* Harvard University Press.

Hallberg, Lillemor & Margaretha Strandmark (2004) *Vuxenmobbning i människovårdande yrken.* Lund: Studentlitteratur.

Hallsten, Lennart; Katalin Bellaagh & Klas Gustafsson (2002) 'Utbränning i Sverige – en populationsstudie'. *Arbete och hälsa* 2002:6. The National Institute for Working Life.

Hallström, Per (1933) *Carl Snoilsky – en levnadsteckning.* Stockholm: Bonniers.

Hamilton, Carl (2004) *Det infantila samhället. Barndomens slut.* Stockholm: Norstedts.

Hammarén, Maria (2006) *Skriva hop sig. Om att uppfinna sig själv.* Stockholm: Santérus.

Hansegård, Nils Erik (1974/1968) *Tvåspråkighet eller halvspråkighet?* Stockholm: Bonniers.

Hansson, Henrik & Östen Ohlsson (1997) *The Consultant as a Carrier of Reform.* Paper prepared for the 13th EGOS Colloquium, July 3–5, 1997.

Harding-Esch, Edith & Philip Riley (2012/2003/1986) *The Bilingual Family.* Cambridge University Press.

Hedberg, Bo & Anders Ericson (1979) 'Insiktströghet och manövertröghet i organisationers omorientering'. In: *Från företagskriser till industripolitik*, eds. Bo Hedberg & Sven-Erik Sjöstrand, pp 54–70. Stockholm: Liber.

Hedberg, Bo; Paul Nystrom & William Starbuck (1976) 'Camping on seesaws: Prescriptions for a self-designing organization'. *Administrative Science Quarterly*, vol. 21, issue 1, pp 41–65.

Heilbroner, Robert (1999) *The Worldly Philosophers. The Lives, Times and Ideas of the Great Economic Thinkers.* London: Penguin.

Hellberg, Inga (1991) *Professionalisering och modernisering. En studie av nordiska akademiker i offentlig tjänst.* Stockholm: The Swedish Centre for Working Life.

Hene, Birgitta (1987) *De utländska adoptivbarnen och deras språkutveckling.* The Department of Philosophy, Linguistics and

Theory of Science, University of Gothenburg.

Hersey, Paul & Kenneth Blanchard (1969) *Management of Organizational Behavior: Utilizing Human Resources*. Englewood Cliffs: Prentice-Hall.

Hicks, John (1964/1963) *The Theory of Wages* (second edition). London: Macmillan.

Hirschman, Albert (1991) *The Rhetoric of Reaction*. Cambridge, Mass: Belknap Press.

Hofstede, Geert (1994) *Cultures and Organizations*. London: Harper Collins.

Holm, Pelle, revised by Sven Ekbo (1995/1989) *Pelle Holms Bevingade ord*. Stockholm: Bonniers.

Holmberg, Åke (1955/1948) *Tam Sventon, Private Detective*. London: Methuen.

— (1966/1949) *Tam Sventon, Desert Detective*. London: Methuen.

— (1950) *Ture Sventon i London*. Stockholm: Rabén & Sjögren.

— (1968/1954) *Tam Sventon and the Silver-Plate Gang*. London: Methuen.

— (1955) *Ture Sventon och Isabella*. Stockholm: Rabén & Sjögren.

Holmberg, Åke & Sven Hemmel (1973) *Ture Sventon i stora världen*. Stockholm: Rabén & Sjögren.

— (1974) *Ett intressant fall sa Ture Sventon*. Stockholm: Rabén & Sjögren.

Horgan, John (1996) *The End of Science*. London: Little, Brown and Company.

Hugemark, Agneta (1994) *Den fängslande marknaden. Ekonomiska experter om välfärdsstaten* (with an English summary). Lund: Arkiv.

Huss, Leena Marjatta (1991) *Simultan tvåspråkighet i svensk-finsk kontext* (with an English summary). Uppsala University, Studia Uralica Upsaliensia 21.

Hutt, William Harold (1964) *The Economics of the Colour Bar*. London: Institute of Economic Affairs.

Hyltenstam, Kenneth & Christopher Stroud (1991) *Språkbyte och språkbevarande*. Lund: Studentlitteratur.

Hyltenstam, Kenneth & Loraine Obler, eds. (1989) *Bilingualism Across the Lifespan: Aspects of Acquisition, Maturity, and Loss*. Cambridge University Press.

Håkansson, Gisela (2003) *Tvåspråkighet hos barn i Sverige*. Lund: Studentlitteratur.

Jaakkola, Magdalena (1973) *Språkgränsen: En studie i tvåspråkighetens sociologi*. Stockholm: Aldus/Bonniers.

Jackson, Norman & Pippa Carter (2007/2000) *Rethinking Organisational Behaviour*. Harlow, England: Pearson Prentice Hall.

Jaques, Elliott (1996/1988) *Requisite Organization* (second edition). Arlington, Virginia: Cason Hall

Jay, Antony (1967) *Management and Machiavelli*. London: Hodder and Stoughton.

Jensen, Christian (2002) *Maktens språk och språkets makt. Om hur Västra Götalandsregionen blev till* (with an English summary). Gothenburg: BAS.

Jerome, Jerome K. (1889) *Three Men in a Boat*. Bristol: Arrowsmith.

– (2009/1900) *Three Men on Bummel*. New York: Digireads Book.

Jimenez, Jacques & Timothy Johnson (1998) *Metaphors at Work. The Unseen Influencers*. Rowayton, Connecticut: Helix Press.

Johannisson, Karin (1990) *Medicinens öga*. Stockholm: Norstedts.

Johansson, Patrik (2004) *I skandalers spår. Minskad legitimitet i svensk offentlig sektor*. The School of Public Administration, University of Gothenburg.

Johansson, Staffan; Mikael Löfström & Östen Ohlsson (2007) 'Separation or Integration? A dilemma when Organizing Development Projects' *International Journal of Project Management,* vol 25, issue 5, pp 457–464.

Jönsson, Sten, & Rolf Lundin (1977) 'Myths and wishful thinking as management tools'. In: *Prescriptive Models of Organizations*, eds. Paul Nystrom & William Starbuck, pp 157–170. Amsterdam: North Holland.

Jørgensen, Normann & Anne Holmen, eds. (1997) *The Development of Successive Bilingualism in School-Age Children*. Copenhagen Studies in Bilingualism, vol. 27. Copenhagen: The Royal Danish School of Educational Studies.

Karlsson, Klas-Göran (2003) *Terror och tystnad*. Stockholm: Atlantis.

Katz, Albert (1998) 'Figurative language and figurative thought'. In: *Figurative Language and Thought*, Albert Katz, Cristina Cacciari, Raymond Gibbs &

Mark Turner, pp 3–43. Oxford University Press.

Keiser, Alfred (1997) 'Rhetoric and Myth in Management Fashion'. *Organization,* vol. 4, issue 1, pp 49–74.

Klang, Eva (2003) *System, sympati och arbetsdelning. En studie av Adam Smiths teorier om människan och samhället*. Lund Papers in Economic History, issue 92.

Klintberg, Bengt af (2005) *Glitterspray och 99 andra klintbergare*. Stockholm: Atlantis.

Knorz, Carmen & Dieter Zapf (1996) 'Mobbing – eine extreme Form sozialer Stressoren am Arbeitsplatz'. *Zeitschrift für Arbeits- und Organisationspsychologie,* vol. 40, issue 11, pp 12–21.

Koller, Veronika (2004) *Metaphor and Gender in Business Media Discourse*. Basingstoke, Hampshire: Palgrave Macmillan.

The National Institute of Economic Research (NIER) (2002) *Egnahemsposten i konsumentprisindex – En granskning av KPI-utredningens förslag*. Special study issue 2, May 2002. Stockholm: The National Institute of Economic Research (NIER).

Kotsinas, Ulla-Britt (1996a) 'Kravet på en 'god' svenska'. *Social politik,* issues 1–2, reference from website: Socialpolitik.

– (1996b) 'Rinkebysvenska – ett ungdomsspråk'. In: *Alla vi svenskar*, eds. Åke Daun & Barbro Klein, pp 29–45. Fataburen 1996, Nordiska museets och Skansens årsbok.

Kuhn, Thomas (1970/1962) *The Structure of Scientific Revolutions* (second edition). University of Chicago Press.

Källström, Anders (1995) *I spetsen för sin flock: normer för svenskt management*. The School of Business, Economics and Law, University of Gothenburg.

Kövecses, Zoltán (2005) *Metaphor in Culture. Universality and Variation*. Cambridge University Press.

Lagercrantz, David & Zlatan Ibrahimovic, 2013 (2011). *I am Zlatan Ibrahimovic*. London: Penguin.

Lagerqvist, Lars (2005) *Karl XIV Johan. En fransman i Norden*. Stockholm: Prisma.

Lakoff, George & Mark Johnson (1981/1980) *Metaphors We Live By*. University of Chicago Press.

Leijon, Svante & Östen Ohlsson (1994) *Utvärdering av Belastningsskadeprogrammet. Från Åtgärder mot belastningsskador till Jobb i förändring*. Stockholm: The Swedish Work Environment Fund.

Lewin, Kurt (1947) 'Frontiers in group dynamics'. *Human Relations*, vol. 1, issue 1, pp 2–38.

Leymann, Heinz (1986) *Vuxenmobbning. Om psykiskt våld i arbetslivet*. Lund: Studentlitteratur.

Liefooghe, Andreas & Kate Mackenzie Davey (2001) 'Accounts of workplace bullying: The role of the organization'. *European Journal of Work and Organizational Psychology*, vol. 10, issue 4, pp 375–392.

Lindberg, Folke (1947) *Hantverkarna. Första delen: medeltid och äldre vasatid*. (Den

svenska arbetarklassens historia). Stockholm: Tidens förlag.

– (1949) *Hantverkarna. Andra delen: stormaktstiden, frihetstiden och gustavianska tiden*. (Den svenska arbetarklassens historia). Stockholm: Tidens förlag.

– (1964) *Hantverk och skråväsen under medeltid och äldre vasatid*. Stockholm: Prisma.

Lindberg, Inger (2002) 'Myter om tvåspråkighet'. *Språkvård*, issue 4, pp 22–28.

Lindström, Fredrik (2001/2000) *Världens dåligaste språk*. Stockholm: Bonniers.

Ljungberg, Anders & Everth Larsson (2001) *Processbaserad verksamhetsutveckling*. Lund: Studentlitteratur.

Llosa, Mario Vargas (2004/2003) *A Way to Paradise*. London: Faber and Faber.

Lukkarinen, Margita (2001) *Vård på eget språk*. Helsinki: Ministry of Social Affairs and Health.

Lundh, Christer (2002) *Spelets regler. Institutioner och lönebildning på den svenska arbetsmarknaden 1850–2000*. Stockholm: SNS.

Lübcke, Poul, ed. (1988/1983) *Filosofilexikonet*. Stockholm: Forum.

Lyotard, Jean-François (1997/1979) *The Postmodern Condition. A Report on Knowledge*. Manchester University Press.

– (1997/1993) *Postmodern Fables*. University of Minnesota Press.

Lönnquist, Jenny (1999) *Processutveckling: inspiration och metod*. (Separate working papers containing documentation forms are available). Vänersborg: Region Västra Götaland.

Machiavelli, Niccolò (1999/1513) *The Prince*. London: Penguin Books.

Malmström, Ida (1941) *Hushållets rationalisering*. Malmö: Förlagshuset Norden.

Marc-Wogau, Konrad, ed. (2005/1991) *Filosofin genom tiderna*. Stockholm: Thales.

Marcuse, Herbert (1991/1964) *One-dimensional Man: Studies in the Ideology of Advanced Industrial Society*. London: Routledge & Kegan Paul.

Martinson, Harry (1936/1935) *Flowering Nettles*. London: Cresset Press.
— (1963) *Aniara: A Review of Man in Time and Space*. London: Knopf.

Marx, Karl (2012/1847) *The Poverty of Philosophy*. New York: Digireads Book.

McCall Smith, Alexander (1998) *The No. 1 Ladies' Detective Agency*. Edinburgh: Polygon.
— (2000) *Tears of the Giraffe*. Edinburgh: Polygon.

Melin, Lars (2004) *Corporate Bullshit*. Stockholm: Svenska förlaget.

Meyer, John & Brian Rowan (1977) 'Institutionalized organizations: Formal structure as myth and ceremony'. *American Journal of Sociology*, vol. 83, issue 2, pp 340–363.

Miller, Anne (2004) *Metaphorically Selling. How to Use the Magic of Metaphors to Sell, Persuade & Explain Anything to Anyone*. New York: Chiron Associates.

Miller, Donald (1992) *The Reason of Metaphor. A Study in Politics*. London: Sage.

Mintzberg, Henry (1979) *The Structuring of Organizations*. Englewood Cliffs, New Jersey: Prentice-Hall.
— (1983) *Power In and Around Organizations*. Englewood Cliffs, New Jersey: Prentice-Hall.

Mitford, Nancy (2012/1967) *The Sun King, Louis XIV at Versailles*. New York: New York Review of Books.

Morgan, Gareth (1999/1986) *Organisationsmetaforer*. Lund: Studentlitteratur.
— (1986) *Images of Organization*. Newbury Park, California: Sage.

Mullins, Laurie (2002) *Management and Organisational Behaviour* (sixth edition). Harlow, England: Financial Times, Prentice Hall.

Muna, Farid (2003) *Seven Metaphors on Management. Tools for Managers in the Arab World*. Aldershot, Hampshire: Gower.

Mårtens, Ylva, ed. (1999) *Sjömanskostymen*. Stockholm: Raster.

Möller, Bengt (2003) 'Ambassadanställda fruktar lönesänkning'. *Lön&jobb*, issue 11, 2003-12-18, website: Lön&jobb.

Nilsson, Göran (2003) *Processorientering och styrning. Regler, mål eller värderingar* (with an English summary). Stockholm School of Economics.

Nilsson, Ingemar & Hans-Inge Peterson (2000/1998) *Medicinens idéhistoria*. Stockholm: SNS.

Norin, Karolina (2006) *En delad kommun – en studie av kriskommunen Gullspång*. The School of Public Administration, University of Gothenburg, Master's thesis.

The New English Bible. New Testament. (1970) Joint committee on the new translation of the Bible. Oxford University Press.

Obama, Barack (2008) 'Modern Health Care for All Americans'. *New England Journal of Medicine*, vol. 359, issue 15, pp 1537–1541.

Ohlsson, Östen (2001) *Sammanslagna sjukhus? Argument och motargument inför SU-fusionen.* The University of Gothenburg, Evaluation Programme, Region Västra Götaland report 7.

Ohlsson, Östen & Björn Rombach (1998) *Res pyramiderna. Om frihetsskapande hierarkier och tillplattningens slaveri.* Stockholm: Svenska Förlaget.

— (2000a) *Organisationspyramiden och Buridans åsna – en lagom teori.* The School of Public Administration, University of Gothenburg, report issue 27.

— (2000b) 'Den sjuka organisationen'. *Økonomistyring & informatik*, vol. 16, issue 3, pp 245–267.

— (2005) 'Förnöjsamhetens boja – Varför inte tvärtom?' In: *Samtalet fortsätter – Bortom ledarskapets gränser*, eds. Daniel Ericsson & Markus Kallifatides, pp 137–163. Lund: Academia Adacta.

Olsson, Henry (1981/1980) *Carl Snoilsky.* Stockholm: Norstedt & Söner.

Ortony, Andrew (1975) 'Why metaphors are necessary and not just nice'. *Educational Theory*, vol. 25, issue 1, pp 45–53.

— (2002/1993) *Metaphor and Thought* (second edition). Cambridge University Press.

Oxford Dictionary of Foreign Words & Phrases (2010/1992) ed. Andrew Delahunty, first edition by Jennifer Speake. Oxford University Press.

Pappas, Christos (2003) *Metaforer i det politiska språket. En studie av de socialdemokratiska och de konservativ-liberala partiledarnas retorik i Grekland och Sverige vid millennieskiftet.* The Department of French, Italian and Classical Languages, Stockholm University.

Parkinson, Northcote (1957) *Parkinson's Law and Other Studies in Administration.* Boston: Houghton Mifflin.

Pelle Holms Bevingade ord (fifteenth edition) revised by Sven Ekbo (1989) Stockholm: Bonniers.

Pennings, Johannes (1981) 'Strategically interdependent organizations'. In: *Handbook of Organizational Design*, eds. Paul Nystrom & William Starbuck, pp 431–455. Oxford University Press.

Perkin, Harold (1996/1989) *The Rise of Professional Society.* England Since 1880. London: Routledge.

Perrow, Charles (1993/1972) *Complex Organizations.* New York: McGraw-Hill.

Persson, Annika (1991) *Metaforer som tankeorganisatörer.* The Department of Philosophy, University of Gothenburg, Editor's series issue 31.

Popper, Karl (1989/1963) *Conjectures and Refutations. The Growth of Scientific Knowledge.* London: Routledge.

— (2002/2001/1998) *The World of Parmenides.* London: Routledge.

Porter, Michael (1987) 'From competitive advantage to corporate strategy'. *Harvard Business Review*, vol. 65, issue 3, pp 43–59.

Propp, Vladimir (1968/1928) *Morphology of the Folktale.* University of Texas Press.

Proudhon, Pierre-Joseph (1972/1846) *System of Economical Contradictions or, The Philosophy of Misery.* New York: Arno Press.

Ranson, Stewart; Bob Hinings & Royston Greenwood (1980) 'The structuring of organizational structures'. *Administrative Science Quarterly*, vol. 25, issue 1, pp 1–17.

Raymond, Alex (2012/1934–1937) *Flash Gordon. On the planet of Mongo. Sundays 1934–1937.* London: Titan Books.

— (2012/1937–1941) *Flash Gordon. The Tyran of Mongo. Sundays 1937–1941.* London: Titan Books.

— (2013/1941–1944) *Flash Gordon. The fall of Mongo. Sundays 1941–1944.* London: Titan Books.

Rayner, Charlotte; Helge Hoel & Cary Cooper (2002) *Workplace Bullying. What We Know, Who Is To Blame, and What Can We Do?* London: Taylor & Francis.

Rehn, Alf & David Sköld (2010/2005) 'From Wallet Arithmetics to Stock-Market Thriller'. In: *The Rise of Management-Speak*, eds. Björn Rombach & Patrik Zapata, pp 129–144. Stockholm: Santérus Academic Press.

Rentzhog, Olof (1998) *Processorientering. En grund för morgondagens organisationer.* Lund: Studentlitteratur.

Ricoeur, Paul (1977/1975) *The Rules of Metaphor. The Creation of Meaning in Language.* London: Routledge.

Robbins, Stephen (2000) *Essentials of Organizational Behavior* (sixth edition). Upper Saddle River, NJ: Prentice Hall.

Robbins, Stephen (2003) *Organizational Behavior* (tenth edition), Upper Saddle River, NJ: Prentice Hall.

Rockman, Bert (2012) 'The Obama Presidency: Hope, Change and Reality'. *Social Science Quarterly*, vol. 93, issue 5, pp 1065–1080.

Rodgers, Irene; Charles Gancel & Marc Raynaud (2002) *Successful Mergers, Acquisitions, and Strategic Alliance. How to Bridge Corporate Cultures.* New York: McGraw-Hill.

Rollinson, Derek (2005) *Organisational Behaviour and Analysis* (third edition). Harlow, England: Prentice Hall/Financial Times.

Romaine, Suzanne (1989) *Bilingualism.* Oxford: Blackwell.

Rombach, Björn (1986) *Rationalisering eller prat.* Lund: Doxa/Studentlitteratur.

— (1990) *Kvalitet i offentlig sektor.* Stockholm: Norstedts.

— (1991) *Det går inte att styra med mål!* Lund: Studentlitteratur.

— (1997) *Den marknadslika kommunen.* Stockholm: Nerenius & Santérus.

Rombach, Björn & Patrik Zapata, eds. (2010/2005) *The Rise of Management-Speak.* Stockholm: Santérus Academic Press.

Rombach, Björn & Kerstin Sahlin-Andersson, eds. (1995) *Från sanningssökande till styrmedel.*

Stockholm: Nerenius & Santérus.

Rombach, Björn & Rolf Solli (1999) 'Vad vi vet om ledarskap'. *Nordiske Organisasjonsstudier*, vol. 1, issue 2, pp 105–110.

Rorty, Richard (1998/1991) *Objectivity, Relativism, and Truth.* Cambridge University Press.
 — (1999) *Philosophy and Social Hope.* London: Penguin Books.

Rousseau, Jean-Jacques (2007/1762) *Emile or On Education.* Nu Vision Publications.

Rowlinson, Michael (1997) *Organizations and Institutions.* London: Macmillan.

Rudolfsson, Liza (2003) *Guldfisk eller sardin? Hur man ökar omställningsförmågan i företag och organisationer.* Stockholm: Ekerlids.

Ruigrok, Winfried; Andrew Pettigrew; Simon Peck & Richard Wittington (1999) 'Corporate restructuring and new forms of organizing: Evidence from Europe'. *Management International Review*, vol. 39, issue 2, pp 41–64.

Runeberg, Johan Ludvig (1900/1832) *Älgskyttarne.* Stockholm: Beijers.

Russell, Bertrand (1972/1945) *A History of Western Philosophy and Its Connection with Political and Social Circumstances from the Earliest Times to the Present Day.* New York: Simon and Schuster.

Røvik, Kjell Arne (2000/1998) *Moderna organisationer.* Malmö: Liber.

Salin, Denise (2001) 'Prevalence and forms of bullying among business professionals: A comparison of two different strategies for meas-uring bullying'. *European Journal of Work and Organizational Psychology*, vol. 10, issue 4, pp 425–441.

Sandberg, Nils-Eric (1996) 'En marknad för arbete'. In: *Verkstadsindustrin, lönebildningen och framtiden*, ed. Nils-Eric Sandberg, pp 34–56. Stockholm: Industrilitteratur.

Sandholm, Lennart (1997) *Total Quality Management.* Lund: Studentlitteratur.

Sartre, Jean-Paul (2003/1943) *Being and Nothingness.* London: Routledge.

Schermerhorn, John; James Hunt & Richard Osborn (2000) *Organizational Behavior* (seventh edition). New York: John Wiley.

Schön, Donald (1996/1993) 'Generative metaphor: A perspective on problem-setting in social policy'. In: *Metaphor and Thought* (second edition), ed. Andrew Ortony, pp 137–163. Cambridge University Press.

Seldon, Arthur (2004/1990) *The Virtues of Capitalism. The Collected Writings of Arthur Seldon*, Volume 1. Indianapolis: Liberty Fund.

Shah, Idris (1998/no date of earliest publication known) *Den ojämförlige Mulla Nasrudins bedrifter.* Stockholm: Bonniers.
 — (1973) *The Exploits of the Incomparable Mulla Nasrudin.* London: Pan Books LTD – Picador edition.

Shirer, William (1998/1960) *The Rise and Fall of the Third Reich.* London: Arrow Books.

Simon, Herbert (1997/1947) *Administrative Behavior.* New York: Free Press.

Sjölund, Jan-Olov; Leena Hedman & Peter Rosenthal (1996) *Sju steg på vägen till totalkvalitet*. Lund: Studentlitteratur.

Sjöstrand, Sven-Erik (1997) *The Two Faces of Management. The Janus Factor*. London: Thomson Business Press.

Sjöstrand, Sven-Erik & Gunnar Westerlund (1979/1975) *Organizational Myths*. London: Harper and Row.

Skinner, Burrhus Frederic (1976) *Walden Two*. New York: Macmillan.

Slater, Lauren (2005/2004) *Opening Skinner's Box*. London: Bloomsbury.

Slaughter, Frank (1967/1966) *War Surgeon*. London: Hutchinson/ Random House.

Smith, Adam (2009/1784) *The Wealth of Nations* (complete and unabridged). New York: Classic House Books.

Snabbguiden till miljö- och kvalitetscertifikat (1996). Mölndal: Swerea IVF.

Snoilsky, Carl (1904) *Samlade dikter I–V*. Stockholm: Hugo Gebers.

Sontag, Susan (1978/1989) *Illness as Metaphor; and, AIDS and its Metaphors*. New York: Picador/ Farrar, Straus and Giroux.

Spengler, Oswald (1928/1922) *Decline of the West. Vol. 1, Form and Actuality*. New York: Knopf. — (1928) *Decline of the West. Vol. 2, Perspectives of World History*. New York: Knopf.

Starbuck, William (2004) Vita Contemplativa: 'Why I stopped trying to understand the real world'. *Organization Studies*, vol. 25, issue 7, pp 1233–1254.

Sten, Viveca Bergstedt (2003) *Förhandla i affärer*. Stockholm: Svenska förlaget.

Stenius, Erik (1953) *Tankens gryning*. Stockholm: Almqvist & Wiksell.

Stogdill, Ralph (1948) 'Personal factors associated with leadership: A survey of the literature'. *Journal of Psychology*, vol. 25, pp 35–71.

Stowell, Phyllis & Jeanne Foster, eds. (2002) *Appetite: Food as Metaphor. An Anthology of Women Poets*. Rochester, New York: Boa Editions.

Strahler, Alan & Artur Strahler (1992) *Modern Physical Geography*. New York: John Wiley.

Strassmann, Diana (1994) 'Ingen fri marknad. Om nationalekonomins auktoritativa retorik'. *Häften för Kritiska Studier*, vol. 27, issue 1, pp 15–25.

Streeck, Wolfgang (2005) 'The sociology of labor markets and trade unions'. In: *The Handbook of Economic Sociology* (second edition), eds. Neil Smelser & Richard Swedberg, pp 254–283. Princeton University Press.

Striem, Jörgen (1997) *Sjukvårdens huvudprocesser. Budskap och verktyg*. Stockholm: The Swedish Association of Local Authorities and Regions (SALAR).

Strindberg, August (1912/1902) 'The Dream Play'. In: *Plays* (translation: Edwin Björkman). London: Duckworth & Co.

Stålhammar, Mall (1997) *Metaforernas mönster i fackspråk och allmänspråk*. Stockholm: Carlssons.

Sullivan, Robert (2006/2004) *Rats. Observations on the History of the*

City's Most Unwanted Inhabitants.
London: Bloomsbury.

Svanlund, Jan (2001) *Metaforen som konvention: Graden av bildlighet i svenskas vikt och tyngdmetaforer* (with an English summary). Stockholm: Almqvist och Wiksell.

Svare, Helge (2002) *'Livet är en reise.' Metaforer i filosofi, vitenskap og daglig liv.* Oslo: Pax Forlag.

Svedberg, Lars (1997) *Gruppsykologi. Om grupper, organisationer och ledarskap.* Lund: Studentlitteratur.

Svenska akademiens ordbok över svenska språket (1978). Stockholm: Norstedts.

Svensson, Robert (2000) Strategiska brott. Vilka brott förutsäger en fortsatt brottskarriär? *BRÅ-rapport* 2000:3.

Södergren, Birgitta (1992) *Decentralisering: Förändring i företag och arbetsliv* (with an English summary). The Economic Research Institute, Stockholm School of Economics.

Söderstedt, Eva (1995) *Första steget mot kvalitet.* Malmö: Liber Ekonomi.

Taylor, Frederick Winslow (1998/1911) *The Principles of Scientific Management.* New York: Dover Publications.

Tegern, Gunilla (1994) *Frisk och sjuk. Vardagliga föreställningar om hälsan och dess motsatser* (with an English summary). Tema Hälsa och samhälle, Linköping University.

Tegnér, Esaias (1822/1819) *Inträdestal, hållit i Svenska Akademien den 22 juni 1819.* Extract from Svenska Akademiens handlingar från år 1796, vol. 9, pp 47–112.

With Anders af Kullberg's response on pp 113–118(119).

Tehrani, Noreen (2004) 'Bullying: a source of chronic posttraumatic stress?' *British Journal of Guidance & Counselling*, vol. 32, issue 3, pp 357–366.

Themerson, Stefan (1967/1951) *The Adventures of Peddy Bottom.* London: Gaberbocchus Press.

Thompson, James (2003/1967) *Organizations in Action.* New Brunswick, N.J.: Transaction.

Thompson, Kenneth (1980) 'Organizations as constructors of social reality (1)'. In: *Control and Ideology in Organizations*, eds. Graeme Salaman & Kenneth Thompson, pp 216–236. Milton Keynes: Open University Press.

Thomsen, Claus; Klaus Lund & Kim Knudsen (1996) *Total quality management – resultat och visioner.* Lund: Studentlitteratur.

Thor, Lars (1989) 'Glasblåsare'. In: *Hantverk i Sverige*, eds. Bengt Nyström, Arne Biörnstad & Barbro Bursell, pp 148–155. Stockholm: LT:s förlag.

Thorsrud, Einar & Fred Emery (1974/1969) *Form and Content in Democracy: Some Experiences from Norway and other European Countries.* London: Tavistock Publications.

Thunander, Mats (1956) 'Skrå, stat och samhälle'. In: *Sveriges hantverk, första delen*, eds. Nils Niléhn, Wiliam Karsson & Henning Persson, pp 176–210. Malmö: Bernces förlag.

Thylefors, Ingela (1987) *Syndabockar. Om utstötning och mobbning i arbetslivet.* Stockholm: Natur och kultur.

Tillhagen, Carl-Herman (1977/1958) *Folklig läkekonst.* Stockholm: Natur och kultur/ LT:s förlag.

Tilly, Chris & Charles Tilly (1994) 'Capitalist work and labor markets'. In: *The Handbook of Economic Sociology*, eds. Neil Smelser & Richard Swedberg, pp 283–312. New York: Sage.

Toonder, Marten (1980/1979) 'Nivelleringslikaren'. In: *Moderna Fabler 3. Tom Puss*, pp 1–33. Stockholm: Alvglans.

Tunbrå, Lars-Olof (2003) *Psykopater som chefer – lika farliga som charmiga.* Stockholm: Liber.

Tuomela, Veli (2001) *Tvåspråkig utveckling i skolåldern* (with an English summary). The Centre for Research on Bilingualism, Stockholm University.

Turner, Mark (1998) 'Figure'. In: *Figurative Language and Thought*, Albert Katz, Cristina Cacciari, Raymond Gibbs & Mark Turner, pp 44–87. Oxford University Press.

Unt, Iwar (2005) *Förhandla effektivt.* Malmö: Liber.

Wahlberg, Rickard (2010/2005) 'The Status of Management-Speak in the Cultural World', In: *The Rise of Management-Speak*, eds. Björn Rombach & Patrik Zapata, pp 33–52. Stockholm: Santérus Academic Press.

Wallquist, Einar (1948) *Kan doktorn komma? Läkarhistorier från lappmarken.* Stockholm: Bonniers.

Vandekerckhove, Wim & Ronald Commers (2003) 'Downward workplace mobbing: A sign of the times?' *Journal of Business Ethics*, vol. 45, issues 1–2, pp 41–50.

Weber, Max (1978/1922) *Economy and Society: An Outline of Interpretive Sociology.* University of California Press.

Webster, Maud (2003) *Maffians värld. Historien om Cosa Nostra.* Lund: Historiska media.

Wedberg, Anders (1982/1958) *A History of Philosophy. Antiquity and the Middle Ages.* Vol 1. Oxford: Clarendon Press.

Vega, Gina & Debra Comer (2005) 'Bullying and harassment in the workplace'. In: *Managing Organizational Deviance*, eds. Roland Kidwell & Christopher Martin, Chapter 8. London: Sage.

Weick, Karl (1979) *The Social Psychology of Organizing* (second edition). Reading, MA: Addison-Wesley.

— (1995) *Sensemaking in Organizations.* London: Sage.

Wellros, Seija (1998) *Språk, kultur och social identitet.* Lund: Studentlitteratur.

Westrup, Ulrika (2000) *Processorienterad styrning i sociala verksamheter. Styrförutsättningar och processlogiker.* The Swedish National Institute of Economic Research, Lund University.

Viberg, Åke; Veli Tuomela & Pirkko Bergman, eds. (1993) *Tvåspråkighet i skolan.* The Centre for Research on Bilingualism, Stockholm University, BAS report 1.

Wiklund, Ingrid (2002) *Social Networks and Proficiency in Swedish.* The Centre for Research on Bilingualism, Stockholm University.

Wildavsky, Aaron (1979/1964) *The Politics of the Budgetary Process.* Boston: Little, Brown and Co. – (1986/1975) *Budgeting.* New Brunswick: Transaction Books.

Williamson, Oliver (1975) *Markets and Hierarchies.* New York: Free Press.

Wise, Lois & Alf Sjöström (1999) 'Paradigmskifte inom svensk lönebildning'. In: *Lön för mödan. Lönesättning i offentlig sektor,* eds. Maivor Sjölund *et al.,* pp 33–63. Stockholm: Kommentus.

Womack, James; Daniel Jones & Daniel Roos (1990) *The Machine that Changed the World. The Triumph of Lean Production.* New York: Macmillan.

Wonnacott, Thomas & Ronald Wonnacott (1972) *Introductory Statistics.* New York: John Wiley & Sons.

Woodward, Joan (1965) *Industrial Organization: Theory and Practice.* Oxford University Press.

von Wright, Georg Henrik (1987) *Vetenskapen och förnuftet.* Stockholm: Bonniers.

– (1993) *Myten om framsteget.* Stockholm: Bonniers.

Wulff, Henrik; Stig Andur Pedersen & Raben Rosenberg (1992/1986) *Medicinens filosofi.* Gothenburg: Daidalos.

Yukawa, Emiko (1997) *Language Attrition from the Psycholinguistic Perspective: A Literature Review.* The Centre for Research on Bilingualism, Stockholm University.

Zapf, Dieter (1999) 'Mobbing in Organisationen – Überblick zum Stand der Forschung'. *Zeitschrift für Arbeits- u. Organisationspsychologie,* vol. 43, issue 1, pp 1–25.

Zwerin, Mike (2000) *Swing under the Nazis. Jazz as Metaphor for Freedom.* Lanham, Maryland: Cooper Square Press.

Åhnberg, Lars (2005) *Arbetsrätt och förhandling. Förhandlingskunskap för lokala förhandlare.* Uppsala: Lars Åhnberg.

Daily and evening newspapers, and trade press

Aftonbladet 17/11/2004, Johan Hakelius, 'Allt förändras – utom Rod', 59, Herakleitos.

Dagens Nyheter 12/04/2002, Cecilia Jacobsson, 'Fem frågor'.

Dagens Nyheter 14/02/2006, Lotta Olsson, 'Må bra med Mma Ramotswe'.

Dagens Industri 22/03/2003, Henrietta Eriksson, 'Är din chef en psykopat?'

Metro 13/01/2005, Missing.

Svenska Dagbladet 06/06/2003, Maria Wahlberg & Sara Larsson, 'Chefskarusellen dyrbar affär för KF.

Time 02/04/2009, Michael Grunwald, 'How Obama Is Using the Science of Change'.

Films

Animatrix (2003) Peter Chung, Andy Jones, Yoshiaki Kawajiri, Takeshi Koike, Mahiro Maeda, Kouji Morimoto & Shinichirô Watanabe.

Any Given Sunday (1999) Oliver Stone.

Arbetets döttrar (1987) Jean Hermanson.

Beck – mannen med ikonerna (1997) Pelle Seth.

Code 46 (2003) Michael Winterbottom.

Elizabeth – The Virgin Queen (1998) Shekhar Kapur.

Matrix (1999) Andy & Larry Wachowski.

Matrix Reloaded (2003) Andy & Larry Wachowski.

Matrix Revolutions (2004) Andy & Larry Wachowski.

Mission Impossible 1 (1996) Brian de Palma.

Mission Impossible 2 (2000) John Woo.

Mission Impossible 3 (2006) Jeffrey Abrams.

Silence of the Lambs (1991) Jonathan Demme.

Sound recordings

Alfredson, Hasse (1962) *Ringaren*.

Cole, Nat King (1950) *Mona Lisa*, Capitol CL. 13308

Eurythmics (1989) *We Too Are One*.

Simon and Garfunkel (1964) *Last Night I had the Strangest Dream* (by Ed McCurdy, 1950)

Websites

Apoteket (21/08/2013) www.apoteket.se

Arrive Inter Media (22/08/2013) www.aim.se/tjanster/kvalitets-sakring.html

BBC News, Pharaonic tomb find stuns Egypt (21/08/2013) news.bbc.co.uk/2/hi/middle_east/4700032.stm

B.C. by Johnny Hart (22/08/2013) www.creators.com/comics_show.cfm?comicname=bc

Brainy Quote (21/08/2013) www.brainyquote.com/quotes/topics/topic_truth.html#BOVrlTCW, Marcus Aurelius

CRIC Library Collection

(22/08/2013) www.cutr.usf.edu/cric/BookDetail.asp?BookID=8605

Dataföreningen i Sverige (21/08/2013) www.dfs.se/kretsar/sodra/natverken/testochkvalitets-saekring/

Dilbert (5/9/2014) www.dilbert.com

Encyclopaedia Britannica (18/10/2013) www.britannica.com/bps/search?query=metaphor

Etour (This page has been removed) www.etour.se/dialogsamverkan/kvalitetssakring.4.do9ad3f34c5f2 9b97fff3333.html

Fawlty Towers (1/9/2014) www.bbc.co.uk/comedy/fawltytowers

Frihetstiden (22/08/2013) www.
komvux.gotland.se/historia/sve-
rige1700.htm

Gyllene snittet (20/04/2006) www.
ludd.luth.se/~micke/scientium/
sci_5-6_94/gyllene.htm

IRM, Information Research
Management (21/08/2013) www.
irm.se/Default.aspx?id=5

KF – The Swedish Cooperative
Union (14/02/2014) https://
www.coop.se/Globala-sidor/
In-english/

Kvalitet handlar om förväntningar
(This page has been removed)
http://www.hotelsmaland.se/
kvalitet.htm

LetsSingit (15/11/2013) artists.lets-
singit.com/nat-king-cole-lyrics-
mona-lisa-3736lm3

Li'l Abner and Al Capp
(23/08/2013) www.al-capp-lil-
abner.com/

Litteraturberget (22/08/2013)
www.litteraturberget.se/page.
cgi?action=view&ID=1153

Löneanalyser (This page has been
removed) http://www.loneanaly-
ser.se/löneanalyser/

Löneassistans (This page has been
removed) https://www.loneassis-
tans.loneanalyser.se/la2/ld/2101.
html

Metamatrix (14/10/2013) www.
metamatrix.se (www.metama-
trix.se/fmv/kvalitetssakring.asp
[29/05/2006] This page has been
removed)

Modesty Blaise, Umeå University,
Department of Computing
Science (21/08/2013)
www8.cs.umu.se/~kenth/
modesty.html

Nerikes Nerikes Allehanda
(10/05/2006) www.na.se/debatt/
inlaggen.asp?id=125522

Prata inte bara pengar (This page
has been removed) content.
jobline.se/148_sv_pf.asp

Project Runeberg, Anckarström
(22/08/2013) runeberg.org/sbh/
ancstrjj.html

Rock genius (15/11/2013) rock.rapg-
enius.com/Sam-cooke-mona-lisa-
lyrics#lyric

Skatteverkets allmänna råd
(21/08/2013) www.skatteverket.
se/rattsinformation/allmanna-
rad2006/04/skva200423ink.4.18e
1b10334ebe8bc80002620.html

Socialpolitik (22/08/2013) www.
socialpolitik.com

Sommar i P1 (21/08/2013) www.
sr.se/cgi-bin/P1/program/index.
asp?ProgramID=2071

Statistics Sweden (SCB) (15/11/2013)
www.scb.se

Stiftelsen Fackföreningsrörelsens
Institut för Ekonomisk forskning (This page has been
removed) http://www.fief.se/
current_research/archive/2002/
wp172.html

Swedish Bible Society (21/08/2013)
www.bibeln.se

Svenskt kvalitetsindex (SKI) (2013-
08-22) www.kvalitetsindex.se

The Austrian armed forces
(22/08/2013) www.bmlv.gv.at/
facts/bh_2010/archiv/downloads.
shtml

The Stanford Encyclopedia of
Philosophy (18/10/2013) plato.
stanford.edu

The Swedish Association of
Graduate Engineers (15/11/2013)
www.sverigesingenjorer.se

The Swedish Quality Index (SQI)
(22/08/2013) www.kvalitetsin-
dex.se

The Mobbing Encyclopaedia
(22/08/2013) www.leymann.se

The Swedish Consumer Agency
(21/08/2013) www.konsument-
verket.se

The Swedish Medical Association,
ethical rules (21/08/2013) www.
slf.se

The Swedish National Council for
Crime Prevention (21/08/2013)
www.bra.se

The newspaper Lutherhjälpen
(This page no longer exists.
Lutherhjälpen has been merged
with The Church of Sweden
Mission.)

Tidernas mest missuppfattade citat
(This page has been removed)
http://www.mattias.st/listor/lis-
tor.asp?ID=70&av=Mattias

Utopia (22/08/2013) ota.ahds.ac.uk/
texts/2080.html, Thomas More
1518

World of Warcraft (18/10/2013)
eu.battle.net/wow/en/

List of Notes

1. *Cf.* Weick 1995
2. Eriksson-Zetterquist *et al.* 2006
3. Why not learn more on this subject by reading about Peddy Bottom in Themerson 1951
4. See website: CRIC Library Collection
5. Morgan 1986
6. Collins COBUILD English Language Dictionary 1987
7. Svanlund 2001, p 9
8. *Ibid.*, p 99 (our translation)
9. Miller 1992, p 57
10. Ortony 2002, pp 3, 90, 330, 368 and 422 (by various authors in the edited volume)
11. Baumann 2003
12. Ricoeur 1977, p 19 onwards
13. Website: Encyclopaedia Britannica
14. Goodman 1984
15. See Turner 1998, p 62
16. Ortony 1975
17. Katz 1998, p 21. For Ortony 1975, see note above.
18. Goatly 1998, p 14
19. Norstedts uppslagsbok 1973, p 1034
20. Keiser 1997 or Meyer & Rowan 1977
21. *Ibid.*
22. Sjöstrand & Westerlund 1975
23. *Ibid.*
24. Sjöstrand & Westerlund 1979/1975, p 157
25. Jönsson & Lundin 1977
26. Goatly 1998, pp 108–109
27. Svenska akademiens ordbok över svenska språket 1978, p 300
28. Black 1996
29. Svanlund 2001, p 10 (our translation)
30. Morgan 1986
31. See *e.g.* Cacciara 1998
32. See Stålhammar 1997
33. Lakoff & Johnson 1981
34. Goatly 1998
35. See *e.g.* Charteris-Black 2005 and Pappas 2003
36. See Czarniawska-Joerges 1988b
37. See Miller 2004
38. Grant & Oswick 1996b
39. Schön 1996
40. Ahrne & Papakostas 2002
41. Baudrillard 1988
42. Matrix 1999; or any of its sequels
43. Website: World of Warcraft
44. Jimenez & Johnson 1998
45. *Ibid.*, p 19
46. Dobers & Tengblad 2002, p 60 (our translation)
47. Koller 2004, p 172 onwards
48. Muna 2003

49. Goatly 1998, p 168

50. *Cf.* Kövecses 2005

51. Zwerin 2000

52. Stowell & Foster 2002, p 12

53. Goatly 1998, p 6 and chapter 3

54. *Ibid.*, p 83

55. Gibbs 1998, p 88 onwards

56. Katz 1998

57. *Ibid.*, p 6

58. *Cf.* Geertz 1964 and Thompson 1980

59. See Goatly 1998, p 41

60. Gibbs 2001, p 13 and p 25 onwards

61. Hacking 1999, p 35

62. Mårtens 1999, inside cover (our translation)

63. Hedberg *et al.* 1976

64. Czarniawska 1988a, p 50

65. Davidson 1984; see also Svanlund 2001, section 2.2.1

66. Feyerabend 1975

67. Kuhn 1962

68. Rorty 1999

69. Apel 1973

70. We were thinking of *Allt om mat*, but extensive reviews are available on various websites

71. *Cf.* Ohlsson & Rombach 2005

72. *Cf.* Horgan 1996

73. Fukuyama 1993; see also Horgan 1996

74. Strindberg 1902

75. Strindberg 1912/1902, p 75

76. Marcuse 1991/1964

77. Gröndahl 1988, p 28 (our translation)

78. Ohlsson & Rombach 1998

79. Almqvist 1948

80. Bärtås & Ekman 2000, back cover (our translation)

81. *Ibid.*, p 40 (our translation)

82. *Ibid.*, p 41 (our translation)

83. Beck 1986

84. Beck 2013/1986, p 20

85. See website: Fawlty Towers

86. Hamilton 2004, p 122

87. Blauner 1964

88. Ohlsson & Rombach 1998

89. *Cf.* Rombach 1991

90. Rorty 1991, or why not 1999?

91. There is a selection of Max Weber titles to choose between.

92. De Crescenzo 1989/1977

93. If you can read Swedish see *Skriva ihop sig. Om att uppfinna sig själv* by Maria Hammarén 2006

94. Runeberg 1900/1832, pp 1–2 (our non-metric translation)

95. Website: Tidernas mest missuppfattade citat

96. Rousseau 2007/1762, p 11

97. Spengler 1922 and 1928

98. Sullivan 2004 for those who want to know more about the lives of rats

99. Brunsson & Jacobsson 1998, p 17; Brunsson & Jacobsson 2000

100. Website: LetsSingit or Rock genius, se also recording by Nat King Cole (1950)

101. See also Ohlsson & Rombach 2000b

102. See *e.g.* Morgan 1986

103. See *e.g.* Czarniawska 1997

104. *Cf.* Tegern 1994, p 95 onwards

105. *Ibid.*, p 91 (our translation)

106. See Nilsson & Peterson 2000, p 43 onwards

107. Website: The Swedish Medical Association's ethical rules (our translation)

108. Slaughter 1967, from the back cover of the Swedish translation (our translation)

109. Tegern 1994, p 45 (our translation)

110. Sontag 2008/1977, p 5

111. Various euphemisms can also be used

112. Sontag 2008/1977, p 3

113. Anker 1988

114. *Ibid.*, p 63 (our translation)

115. Wulff *et al.* 1992

116. *Ibid.*, p 99 (our translation)

117. *Cf.* Ohlsson & Rombach 1998

118. *Ibid.*

119. *Cf.* Thompson 1967

120. See *e.g.* Rombach & Solli 1999

121. Sjöstrand 1997

122. Hedberg & Ericson 1979

123. See Rombach 1990

124. Website: Kvalitet handlar om förväntningar (our translation)

125. See Klintberg 2005

126. Weber *e.g.* 1922

127. Metro 13/01/2005; see also website: Svenskt kvalitetsindex

128. See *e.g.* Czarniawska-Joerges 1988b and Furusten 2003

129. *Cf.* Anker 1988

130. Tillhagen 1977/1958, p 4 (our translation)

131. Starbuck 2004, pp 1249–1250

132. Edsö 1999, Söderstedt 1995, Bergstrand & Hermansson 1999, Frid 1997, Davis 1997, Snabbguiden till miljö- och kvalitetscertifikat 1996 and Sjölund *et al.* 1996

133. Sandholm 1997 and Thomsen *et al.* 1996

134. Söderstedt 1995, p 16 (our translation)

135. Blomberg 1998, Johansson *et al.* 2007

136. Blomberg 1998, Johansson *et al.* 2000

137. Website: Etour (our translation)

138. Website: Dataföreningen i Sverige (our translation)

139. Website: Metamatrix (our translation)

140. Website: Arrive Inter Media (our translation)

141. Wallquist 1948, p 43 (our translation)

142. Toonder 1980, p 12

143. *Ibid.*, p 33

144. Website: Apoteket

145. Malmström 1941

146. Källström 1995

147. Foster 1937–1948

148. Mark 2:14

149. Dawkins 2006

150. See *e.g.* Cherry & Spiegel 2006

151. *E.g.* Robbins 2000, at only around 250 pages, or the same Robbins in a volume which is three times as thick from 2003, Mullins 2002, George & Jones 2005, Buchanan & Huczynski 2004, Schermerhorn *et al.* 2000, Gordon 2002, Rollinson 2005 etc. ...

152. Blake & Mouton 1964

153. The reference is probably Stogdill 1948, but we have not read this

154. Hersey & Blanchard 1969

155. One favourite is Carlson 1951

156. Oxford Dictionary of Foreign Words & Phrases 2010

157. See *e.g.* Barker 1997

158. *E.g.* Alvesson & Kärreman 2003

159. A genre in which Danielsson 1964 is a Swedish classic, and Arjouni 2003 is a newer addition

160. *Cf.* Gustafsson 2011, p 167 onwards

161. See Propp 1928 and Czarniawska 2004

162. See Sartre 1943

163. *Cf.* Skinner 1976

164. Slater 2004

165. Smith 2009/1784

166. See Klang 2003

167. From Simon 1947 onwards

168. Wonnacott & Wonnacott 1972

169. *Cf.* Ohlsson & Rombach 1998, chapter 4

170. Code 46, 2003

171. The thinker in question is Weick 1979

172. Martinson 1935, p 14

173. Martinson 1936

174. Martinson 1963

175. Almquist 1979/1826, p 45 (our translation); see also Furberg 1975

176. Website: The newspaper Lutherhjälpen (our translation)

177. Website: Litteraturberget (our translation)

178. See website: Modesty Blaise

179. Nobel Laureate in Physics 1903 and in Chemistry 1911

180. Called 'Mahatma', meaning 'great soul'

181. The Madonna we are referring to is Madonna Louise Veronica Ciccone, born 1958

182. See Boje 1991

183. A bookseller can provide you with current sources

184. The Penguin as played by Danny DeVito can be seen in Tim Burton's 1992 film *Batman Returns*

185. *E.g.* Shirer 1991

186. *E.g.* website: Nerikes Allehanda (our translation)

187. See *e.g.* works by James Buchanan and Gordon Tullock

188. See *e.g.* Webster 2003

189. See website: The Swedish National Council for Crime Prevention (BRÅ) and BRÅ-rapport 2000:3 (Svensson 2000). However, the statistics do not show what proportion of the population has fallen foul of the law. A highly uncertain estimate has been obtained based on the statistics of the number suspected with good reason and the number of criminals born in 1960.

190. Alvesson 1991

191. Our own studies include Rombach 1990 and 1997

192. See website: Dilbert

193. Adams 1996

194. Was it Stael von Holstein?

195. *E.g.* Tunbrå 2003

196. See again Tunbrå 2003, or Eriksson on Tunbrå in *Dagens Industri* 22/03/2003

197. Jerome 1889

198. Bengtsson 1960/1935

199. Bengtsson 1993/1935, p 320 (our translation)

200. The Swedish National Encyclopaedia 2000 on CD

201. The Swedish National Encyclopaedia 2000 on CD (our translation)

202. *The Silence of the Lambs* 1991

203. Machiavelli 1999/1513, chapter XVII

204. *Ibid.*, chapter VII

205. Carlqvist 1996

206. Jay 1967

207. *E.g.* Rombach & Solli 2002

208. *Any Given Sunday*, 1999

209. See Rombach & Solli 2002, chapter 2

210. See Johansson 2004

211. *Elizabeth – The Virgin Queen*, 1998

212. See Rombach & Solli 2002, chapter 4

213. *Ibid.*, chapter 5

214. Björkegren 1986

215. Alvesson 2006

216. See Burke 1964

217. See Mitford 2012/1967

218. Burke 1996

219. See Ohlsson & Rombach 1998

220. Fayol 1916

221. *Cf.* Ohlsson & Rombach 1998

222. For definition, see website: The Mobbing Encyclopaedia; see also Leymann 1986 and Thylefors 1987

223. *Cf.* Björk 1999

224. See *e.g.* Knorz & Zapf 1996; Zapf 1999; Hallsten *et al.* 2002

225. *E.g.* the Swedish Work Environment Authority (Arbetsmiljöverket) 2003

226. Berlin & Enqvist 2002, p 10

227. See Vega & Comer 2005

228. Tehrani 2004

229. See Hallberg & Strandmark 2004

230. Eriksson 2001

231. See Bies & Tripp 1998

232. *E.g.* Liefooghe & Mackenzie Davey 2001

233. See also Vandekerckhove & Commers 2003

234. Rayner *et al.* 2002

235. Salin 2001

236. If you can read Swedish see also Gunnar Björkmans Ph.D. thesis about the fading of metaphors 1925

237. Tegnér 1822, p 98 (our translation)

238. Time 02/04/2009, Michael Grunwald

239. Obama 2008

240. Rockman 2012

241. Lewin 1947; French & Bell 1984; Angelöw 1991; et al

242. Matrix, 1999

243. Psalm 23 'A Psalm of David', attributed to King David. The Bible, King James Version

244. Website: IRM (our translation)

245. Rentzhog 1998, Ljungberg & Larsson 2001

246. Nilsson 2003, p 11

247. For astounding information on this from the Federation of Swedish County Councils, see Striem 1997, or for information from Västra Götaland see Lönnquist 1999. See also Westrup 2000

248. Simon and Garfunkel 1964

249. The most recent song we heard is 'We Too Are One', which was released in 1989

250. 'I natt jag drömde', lyrics by Cornelis Vreeswijk and music by Ed McCurdy. Hit version recorded by the Hep Stars; see Landén & Palm 2004, p 223 onwards

251. Website: Utopia, Moore 1518

252. Llosa 2003

253. Why not see Karlsson 2003?

254. Lyotard 1979

255. Lyotard 1993

256. Wright 1993

257. Egidius 1983, p 18 (our translation), with reference to Bertrand Russell

258. Wedberg 1982/1958

259. Popper 1963 and 1998

260. Heilbroner 1999, website: the Stanford Encyclopedia of Philosophy

261. See *e.g.* Meyer & Rowan 1977 or Brunsson 1989

262. See Eriksson-Zetterquist *et al.* 2006

263. Popper 2002 with reference to Aristotle, pp 119–120

264. Website: Li'l Abner and Al Cap

265. See *e.g.* website: Li'l Abner and Al Cap

266. See *e.g.* Barry & Kurzman 1988/1951–1953

267. Raymond 2012/1934–1937, p 198

268. Olle Dahllöf in Barry 1994

269. See Crumb 1984, p 104

270. Ekstrand 1993, p 15 (our translation)

271. See Stenius 1953, p 164 onwards, or Bergström & Forsling 1995, p 73 onwards

272. See Aspelin 1977a, p 69 onwards

273. See *e.g.* the Swedish National Encyclopaedia 2000

274. For an introduction, see Gillispie *et al.* 1997

275. See Aspelin 1977b, p 239

276. Marc-Wogau 2005, p 24

277. Heraclitus, quoted in Furberg 1969, p 19 (our translation)

278. The Swedish National Institute of Economic Research (Konjunkturinstitutet) 2002

279. Aspelin 1977a, p 43 (our translation)

280. Stenius 1953, p 65 (our translation)

281. Furberg 1969, p 21 (our translation)

282. Aftonbladet 17/11/2004, Johan Hakelius – but similar information is available from many other sources

283. Stenius 1953, p 17 (our translation)

284. Leijon & Ohlsson 1994

285. Bäckström 1999

286. Taylor 1911

287. Womack, Jones & Roos 1990

288. Bäckström 1999

289. *E.g.* Thorsrud & Emery 1969

290. Website: Brainy Quote, Marcus Aurelius

291. Ohlsson & Rombach 1998

292. See *e.g.* website: The Swedish Consumer Agency (Konsumentverket KO)

293. Hansson & Ohlsson 1997

294. Ohlsson & Rombach 1998; see also Ohlsson & Rombach 2000a

295. See Fombrun 1986

296. *Cf.* Rayner *et al.* 1980

297. See Ruigrok *et al.* 1999

298. Ohlsson & Rombach 1998

299. Alvesson & Due Billing 2009

300. For an exception, see website: BBC News, Pharaonic tomb find stuns Egypt

301. Rowlinson 1997

302. Galbraith 1977

303. Woodward 1965

304. For a review, see Andersson-Felé 2006, chapter 4

305. Parkinson 1957

306. Svedberg 1997

307. See *e.g.* website: Gyllene snittet

308. Simon 1947

309. Mintzberg 1979, p 232 onwards

310. Jaques 1988

311. Strahler & Strahler 1992

312. Ohlsson & Rombach 1998

313. Williamson 1975, pp 95–98

314. Website: The Austrian Armed Forces

315. Cressey 1971

316. Croziers 1958

317. Mintzberg 1979, Galbraith 1977 and Woodward 1965

318. Croziers 1958

319. *Mission Impossible 1, 2 & 3*

320. Thor 1989 and telephone conversation with the author in 1999

321. Södergren 1992

322. Ruigrok *et al.* 1999

323. Meyer & Rowan 1977

324. Ohlsson & Rombach 1998

325. Burns & Stalker 1961

326. Circa 1295 to after 1358, according to Lübcke 1988, p 83

327. Heilbroner 1999 or website: the Stanford Encyclopedia of Philosophy would do as well

328. Buridan 1985/1330, p 3; Lübcke 1988, p 83 and Holm/Ekbo 1995, p 37

329. See Bertalanffy 1968

330. See Turner 1998, p 62

331. Fröding 1893/1891, poem 'Våran prost'

332. Comte 2009/1865/1848

333. Hallström 1933, p 27; for more about Snoilsky, see Olsson 1980

334. Snoilsky 1904/1886, pp 148–155

335. Snoilsky 1904, p 155 (our non-metric translation)

336. Rombach 1997

337. Baumol & Blinder 1979, p 558

338. Dahlstrand & Biel 1995

339. *E.g.* Baumol & Blinder 1988

340. Immanuel Kant meant that the thing in itself is inaccessible to our observation

341. Gullberg 1979/1937, p 9

342. Strassmann 1994, p 15 (our translation)

343. Göran Greider in *Dagens Nyheter* 01/11/1995 on Agneta Hugemark's book *Den fängslande marknaden* (1994) (our translation)

344. Calmfors & Richardson 2004, p 20 (our translation)

345. For a classic, see Hicks 1963

346. *E.g.* Calmfors & Richardson 2004

347. See *e.g.* Sandberg 1996, p 36

348. Website: Prata inte bara pengar

349. Website: Skatteverkets allmänna råd (our translation)

350. Website: The Swedish Association of Graduate Engineers (Sveriges Ingenjörer)

351. Website: Stiftelsen Fackförenings-rörelsens Institut för Ekonomisk forskning

352. See *e.g.* Wise & Sjöström 1999 or Collberg & Viggósson 2004

353. Website: Löneanalyser

354. Website: Löneassistans (our translation)

355. Swedish Labour Court 1996 ruling no. 41/96, Swedish Labour Court 2001 ruling no. 13/01

356. Lagercrantz & Ibrahimovic 2013

357. Shah 1973 no date for earliest publication known, p 126

358. Nina Jarlbäck as per *Svenska Dagbladet* 06/06/2003, Maria Wahlberg & Sara Larsson (our translation)

359. *Dagens Nyheter* 12/04/2002, Cecilia Jacobsson

360. This quotation can be found in various sources. We have taken it from Jackson & Carter 2000, p 180

361. See *e.g.* Calmfors & Richardson 2004, p 24 (our translation); Björklund *et al.* 2000, p 112 onwards

362. See *e.g.* Lindberg 1947 and 1949 or 1964

363. Thunander 1956, p 180

364. See *e.g.* Perkin 1989 or Hellberg 1991

365. We believe that the original source is Hutt 1964, but the quotation is also used without source reference by well-reputed writers – see *e.g.* Seldon 2004, p 403

366. Website: Statistics Sweden (SCB)

367. Bridges & Nelson 2001

368. Streeck 2005

369. Tilly & Tilly 1994, p 299

370. Björklund 1999

371. See *e.g.* Blundell *et al.* 2005

372. See Rombach 2005

373. Tilly & Tilly 1994, p 307

374. See Wildavsky 1964 and 1975

375. Sandberg 1996, p 40

376. Lundh 2002, p 29 (our translation)

377. See also Tilly & Tilly 1994, p 307

378. Lundh 2002, p 293 (our translation)

379. Wildavsky 1964 and 1975

380. *E.g.* Falkinger 2001 and Unt 2005

381. *E.g.* Sten 2003

382. *E.g.* Eberstein *et al.* 2003 and Åhnberg 2005

383. *Cf.* Wildavsky *e.g.* 1964 and 1975

384. Which we have also done in Rombach 1986

385. See website: B.C. by Johnny Hart

386. Ohlsson 2001

387. See *e.g.* Holmberg 1948, 1949, 1950, 1954, 1955 ...

388. See Porter 1987

389. See Perrow 1993, p 212

390. Brouthers *et al.* 1998

391. See *e.g.* Pennings 1981, p 443

392. See *e.g.* Rodgers *et al.* 2002

393. See Brunsson & Olsen 1993 and DiMaggio & Powell 1983; Borgert 1992

394. See Ohlsson 2001

395. Holmberg & Hemmel 1973 or 1974, the last words in every single one of the cases

396. *Cf.* Rombach

397. See Engwall & Jungerhem 2005

398. By *e.g.* Melin

399. Particularly in Rombach 1997

400. Håkansson 2003, p 13

401. Lukkarinen 2001

402. See also Tuomela 2001

403. *Cf. e.g.* Harding & Riley 2012/2003/1986

404. *E.g.* Hene 1987

405. See *e.g.* Romaine 1989, chapter 7

406. Adams 1988/1979, p 55

407. *Ibid.*, p 56

408. Brunsson & Rombach 1982

409. *Ibid.*

410. *Ibid.*, p 144 (our translation)

411. *C.f.* Wellros 1998

412. Jaakkola 1973, p 13

413. Hansegård 1974, p 44

414. Hyltenstam & Stroud 1991, p 58

415. *C.f.* Hyltenstam & Obler 1989

416. Yukawa 1997

417. In Viberg, Tuomela & Bergman 1993, p 7

418. Yukawa 1997, p 6

419. *Cf.* Gustafsson 1995

420. See Håkansson 2003, p 37 onwards

421. Website: KF – The Swedish Cooperative Union (Kooperativa förbundet)

422. See Wahlberg 2005

423. See Rombach & Zapata 2010

424. Hansegård 1974, p 47 (our translation)

425. Hansegård 1974

426. *Ibid.*, p 43 (our translation)

427. *Ibid.*, p 58 (our translation)

428. Håkansson 2003, p 23 (our translation)

429. Lindberg 2002, p 23 (our translation)

430. See Wiklund 2002

431. Lindström 2000

432. Håkansson 2003

433. *E.g.* Huss 1991

434. *E.g.* Jørgensen & Holmen 1997

435. See Lindberg 2002, pp 26–28

436. Lindberg 2002

437. Jørgensen & Holmen 1997, p 143

438. Lindberg 2002, p 27 (our translation)

439. See Håkansson 2003, p 159

440. Viberg, Tuomela & Bergman 1993

441. Berglund 2005

442. Kotsinas 1996a, quote from website: Socialpolitik (our translation)

443. Kotsinas 1996b, p 39

444. *Cf.* Lindström 2000

445. Jaakkola 1973, back cover (our translation)

446. Håkansson 2003, p 31 (our translation)

447. See Jaakkola 1973, p 19 onwards

448. Hirschman 1991

449. Gustafsson 1979

450. *E.g.* Rombach 1997

451. *Cf.* Rombach & Sahlin-Andersson 1995

452. Ekman 2003

453. Ekman 1999

454. Ekman 2003, p 58 (our translation)

455. Czarniawska-Joerges & Sevón 1996

456. Website: Projekt Runeberg, Anckarström

457. Website: Frihetstiden (our translation)

458. See Jensen 2002

459. Burman (1993) recreates the French usage in his novel about Johan Henrik Kellgren

460. Acke *et al.* 1896

461. Lagerqvist 2005

462. Rehn & Sköld 2005

463. *Cf.* Englisch 2010

464. *Cf.* Rombach 1986

465. Svare 2002

466. In the monologue 'Ringaren' ('The Bell Ringer') from the revue *Gröna hund* ('Green Dog'), 1962

467. Among others by Rudolfsson 2003

468. Persson 1991

469. See *e.g.* McCall Smith 1998 or 2000

470. *Dagens Nyheter* 14/02/2006, Lotta Olsson

471. Norin 2006, p 16 (our translation)

The Authors

ÖSTEN OHLSSON is Professor of Management at the University of Gothenburg, Sweden. His research has largely dealt with how reforms and new management concepts are converted into development activities in large organizations. In the past decade, his interest has shifted towards a general criticism of the management discourse.

BJÖRN ROMBACH is Professor of Public administration at the University of Gothenburg, Sweden. Over the years he has undertaken a number of research projects on financial management, quality enhancement, organization and leadership.

www.ingramcontent.com/pod-product-compliance
Lightning Source LLC
Chambersburg PA
CBHW021554210326
41599CB00010B/443